Emperor in Reverse

Carson Haze

Dedication:

To my baby girls:
I know I always lectured you both on becoming triple
threats, but you made it. I am so proud of you both. I love you
more than words could ever express.

Emperor in Reverse

Paperback ISBN: 979-8-9906685-6-0
E-book ISBN: 979-8-9906685-7-7
First paperback edition Silence of the Seventh November 2022
Published: www.genxpub.com

In Memory of:

Michele C. Sharon C. & Kevin F.
Your lights are truly and deeply missed.

Grammy B and the coffee crew.
Genuine love and much respect.

David B.
Some of us fight battles that no one else can see.
Your light was an incredible gift to the world.
In your loving memory, my contribution to humanity

Acknowledgements

Cindy B. My mother. There are not enough words to allow you to understand the weight of my love, my thanks, and my appreciation.

Richard F. My earthly father. I can't thank you enough, master magician. You flourished through adversity. Hold steady in the silence and dare to dream a little dream. Godspeed. CO4-179.

Anthony J. I want to thank you for lending me your essence. I can only hope it will help others to see.

God and his Universe Thank you for the constant guidance and protection.

To all the people I have met along my way. Thank you.

Table of Contents

Trigger Warning***

This is a fiction work. Any resemblance to characters in real life is coincidental.

Undoubtedly something discussed in this book will offend someone, somewhere. Self-reflect and figure out why.

Undoubtedly something in this book will trigger trauma within someone. Trust me, I know, I went through it too.

This book contains graphic language, sarcasm, drug activity, crimes, and prison references. Personality disorders and mental illness. Emotional, verbal, financial and physical abuse within a domestic partnership.

Alternative perspectives on hot button issues, religion and societal expectations.

To you with love from God & Generation X

Evocation

"Always the last to be seen" my grandfather's voice uttered from atop a mound of tightly compacted snow. His snowshoes aligned the mound to protrude from the edge. You could see the despair in his eyes. He was exhausted. Not only from the elements, but from the repeated search occurrences.

The concern was growing with all the volunteers of this small town, as he glanced across the open field. The snow and below freezing temperatures, however, were fighting quickly for the number one position of everyone's concern. Dusk was descending and everyone was discouraged, knowing that this was their last opportunity of the season.

The descent from the snow pile was a quick one, but one that would haunt my grandfather for the remainder of his life. Surrendering, he leaned his snowshoe against a cluster of rocks that were barely peering from the days of heavy snowfall. They were all friends, the type of community where no one went unnoticed, and everybody knew everyone. The bustle of rumors and gossip filled the vacancy in time until the spring thaw.

It was five long months later, before he learned of his friend's death. Realizing that buried only feet below, on the mound of snow, he had stood for quite some time upon his friend's frozen body. Hearing the echo of my grandfather speaking on this tragedy even now beyond his death and decades later; I could almost peer below the memory of his once weathered face and see the concern of that day. "Always the last to be seen" his voice echoed in my mind as he shook his head in disbelief and a slight bit of disgust.

Not the disgust of the others though and I always had to be thankful for that. He wasn't judging and he wasn't involved. The quietness of this man and his Zen-like quality always warmed my soul. It made me feel thankful and in a strange way, safe. He was hardworking, diligent, and resourceful. Wise and very much loved by all he met, except possibly by my grandmother at times.

"No one ever really knows someone until you have lived with them." I used to giggle at that statement and my completely under-developed understanding of it as a child. I used to hear all the "old" women at my mother's table say it though, so it became part of my jargon. All married couples have their problems, but to hear anyone else speak of my maternal grandfather, he was an earth angel. I bet that would make any wife cringe when they have experienced differently.

It is usually the woman with the strongest of the personalities. The one that the whole community can make out to be the hard ass insufferable bitch. I supposedly came from a lengthy line of those same women to hear others speak of it. Now that I am older, I can clearly see how that happens.

He smiled a lot, but to sit in the silence of the present day and hear my grandfather relive stories of Gary in my mind was heartwarming. To visually recall this man, laughing from the bottom of his stomach ever so quietly just amused me. That amused me more than the Gary stories themselves; I think. I couldn't quite grasp the dry contented adult humor of it all in those days. Gary was a man of little education, and even worse little common sense. His way of relating to the world was beyond hilarious and if not for his wife being on the same wavelength, I feel she would have been one of those hard ass bitches that supposedly I come from.

Back to Gary and his lack of education and common sense. I guess that is what makes these people remarkably unforgettable, pure simplicity. Did he leave the legend he intended, or was he beyond simple enough to understand it was his job in the first place?

Gary was a tall lanky man who was just part of my childhood. Not as in daily reference, but as a fixture in my grandfather's life. I knew who Gary was, hell we all did. Like I said small town, even decades later, we all knew everyone.

Gary worked at the factory with my grandfather for years. The fish factories and piers were the staple of the economy there. My grandfather always accepted him and took him under his wing. He recalled a time when the bosses had needed some stairs built up to the upper level of the warehouse, so the women could dump the fish. Gary had proudly volunteered to complete these. He only requested a small price of a week's advancement so he could take his wife and daughter camping.

It was days later when the women all reluctantly had to go report the stairs to the higher ups. Standing there with all their nylons ripped and stained in blood, they all had complaints about how they couldn't balance on the new stairs. Concerns with how they were all falling off and getting hurt.

For "Christ sakes Gary, you built them backwards. These girls are having to tiptoe and jump at the same time." He smiled and agreed to fix them, but not until the return of his camping trip. My grandfather waved him on and fixed the stairs for him. I do have to give Gary one thing, family always came first to him, so that was admirable.

Gary was a friendly soul that undoubtedly had far-reaching beliefs in his abilities, beyond the normal. He was creative, but with the abnormal process of the average. He had a knack for combining the craziest of crazy. Solid in his own little world with his own little family, Gary somehow believed them to be absolute creations of luxuries for less.

Like the time he excitedly bragged about how he had finally finished his camper. He wanted to be able to bring his wife and daughter out to enjoy the great outdoors and he was bringing them out in style. Only the best for Gary and his. He had a stove for warmth and a smoke pipe vent to boot. My grandfather was ordered to be the first person to honor Gary's new luxury. With pride and complete hopes of male validation, Gary insisted. My grandfather, of course, stood by to welcome Gary's visit and the campers' appearance.

He spotted Gary's truck rounding his corner and couldn't help but notice there was no camper in tow. He had to turn his face and blow out the trapped laughter as he understood Gary had built a camper though. It was built in the back of his truck bed. My mother still recalls this event and bends ever so slightly to avoid pissing down her own leg. She was a teenager then but said watching them all try to squeeze through the narrow door opening was one of the funniest things she has ever seen.

The wife climbed in and sat up in the corner, daughter on lap to avoid running into the stove and its pipe. While Gary peeked out gesturing a wave from the family's cat. I bet that was a fun camping trip. No beds to sleep in, no room for a cat box and no room to even store food, but Gary and his family had a camper now, so that's that.

My family's laughter grew even more uncontrollable as my grandfather quietly reminisced about Gary's homemade shower. "God love him, he built it right over in the corner of the living room, all caddy cornered." "Don't believe he even measured it, and I know for damn sure he never stuck a level on it." An open shower unit in the middle of the family room. No door on this for privacy, just the damn shower, three walls, a curtain liner and a hole in the floor. Gary stood back in all his simpleton glory as he admired his newest luxury.

Beside himself with accomplishment and pride, Gary just had to be the first in his family to try this out. As he sang and danced, he lifted his long skinny white leg to soap the underside of his foot and lost his balance on the unlevel living room floor. Gary frantically tried to grab onto any stability he could find. His futile attempt at grabbing the shower curtain provided no stability and just like the fish he handled at the factory, he proved way too slippery.

He hit the floor and rode the decline out. Sprawled out, tall, lanky, powder white, with slight farmer tan exposed, frustrated, and cursing the Heavens. Gary floundered to turn his body to regather an upright position. His daughter, who by now was an adolescent and her one friend from school had just arrived home. They both stood in the middle of the living room clueless to what was happening. I am sure mortified, and now traumatized for life, but had no choice other than to look at his soapy, naked, body. Well, the scarring of more so the friend, I am sure. The daughter was probably well desensitized to his behavior at this point.

I could hear my grandfather laughing hysterically, yet quietly together as he reminisced. "He wanted me to come down on

Christmas Eve and help him take his front door out. I told him to leave it outside and that no one was going to steal it. He insisted that it had to be brought in and set under the tree for his wife the next morning though.

I remember overhearing this at my mother's table as a child. I could remember giggling because the adults were laughing their asses off, but I couldn't quite break down anything beyond the surface humor at that time. Apparently, Gary had thought nothing of disturbing his grown man friend and requesting help for his project. A project that he had illy prepared for. He was leaving it up to the last-minute hopes that my grandfather would have nothing else to do on Christmas Eve but help him.

I could understand as a grown woman how my grandfather's need to always help everyone with everything would add to my grandmother's rupture of irritation. If you're out helping everyone else, who is helping her? Anyway, apparently, he was available to help him, so at least Gary and his family could have a merry Christmas.

Now Gary was in a panic and his back was up against a wall. He could not fathom how he was going to get his wife's present in the house and under the tree. He had built this outside and worked on it for days. He was so proud of himself and so excited to be able to see her face the next morning. He didn't even want her to have to walk to the window and look outside, he wanted this front and center.

My grandfather stood on Gary's lawn with a flashlight and vehemently tried to talk some sense into him. Reiterating that the grand masterpiece was better off to be left outside. Gary wasn't having it though, his wife needed to see it first thing in the morning. With that, the demolition phase began.

Don't remark on how sweet this man was for wanting to surprise his wife on Christmas morning. Don't remark on how he just loved her so much that he was willing to go to any lengths for her. I want you to wake up and remove that romantic notion from your head. If you see it like that, then I want to applaud you for being able to escape any kind of trauma and I am going to brand you as a simpleton yourself.

Next, this was never about an act of love, this was pure ego. This grown man reveled in the thoughts of the validation and approval he was going to receive from his wife for a job well done. He wanted these first things in the morning. The validation was going to be his Christmas present, before anyone else got theirs.

As my grandfather ripped the door frame from the front of this poorly kept home, he recalled Gary squealing with pure delight as he hollered to his wife to stay in her room. Now mind you she had already been held captive for more than an hour and was forbidden from looking on the lawn most of the week. That's alright though, what's a few more hours? The wait will be worth it for her in the morning. She will know why and be super glad she allowed it.

My grandfather shook his head after Gary placed the masterpiece under the tree. Not only because he would now have to put the door back together, but to add to the grand present, Gary smirked proudly. My grandfather looked on as he watched Gary top the present with a carton of roll your own cigarettes and a pair of wool socks. Now I don't know about you ladies, but nothing quite says love, romance, and appreciation like a carton of smokes and a pair of itchy ass socks.

My grandfather shook his head one more time in dismay as he bent to pick up the wood to put the door frame back together. Gary valiantly released my grandfather at this time to go home and enjoy his own family. He had realized that putting the door frame back on would be a moot point.

Gary knew the grand present would just have to go right back outside in the morning but would call him sometime later in the week to help him repair the door. With that my grandfather just nailed up some plastic over the huge hole in the front of the house. Hoping that gesture would help combat the below freezing temperatures.

I mean come on, the front door being in shambles on the front lawn and the family freezing on Christmas morning was never a thought or an issue. This is the part where I interject and say, typically with this much enthusiasm and expectations for approval, a man-child of this caliber would surely use this line. "Nothing I ever do for you is good enough," and want to start an argument to pull the attention back to himself. He must obviously be able to see the damage and obstacles he has caused in his own egotistical pursuit of admiration. That present was never about her. However, I digress.

Gary shook for the remainder of the night. Ringing his hands and smiling as he glanced upon his grand gift of love. He couldn't feel the cold of the night or foresee the coldness of his wife's lack of admiration in the morning. In those moments, leading to the grand reveal, all he felt was the delusion of warmth on every level. Now this is where I must adamantly reiterate marrying below your means, I believe this is where this comes into play. Marry on your same level, be equally yoked, so they say, and in this case these two simpletons were definitely equally yoked!

As Gary sprang from his recliner prematurely in the wee morning hours of Christmas, he rushed down the hall and accosted his wife from bed. He couldn't take it anymore. The projected excitement in her face was too much to bear, and he covered her eyes to lead her to the tree. Not a word was uttered about the severe noticeable difference in the temperature.

When he removed his hand from her eyes, she was automatically transformed to the luckiest woman in the world. Her eyes lit up and her face revealed the biggest smile as she ran back down the hall to wake their child. She too couldn't contain her excitement. What a wonderful thoughtful man she had in her life. She squealed as she proudly scooped up her carton of smokes and wool socks.

Gary's chest swelled as he motioned for his wife with a head nod, and suggested she put on her new socks, she would need them to keep her feet warm. Gary had received the validation, admiration, and approval he so desperately wanted. It was now time for his wife and child to enjoy the labor of all his hard work.

His wife, quivering from not only the cold, but also the excitement, then plunked their underdressed child down inside her new extremely oversized wheel barrel. She stumbled to hold her balance as Gary lifted the plastic from the door frame and exposed the outdoors. He reassured her that by spring, when she needed it for yard work, she would have had enough practice balancing it. I mean after all practice does make perfect.

My grandfather's immense tolerance for everyone always allowed him to see the humor in everything. I am glad in a way I inherited that part, but I am a great mixture of all the women before me as well. Now I know as an adult woman how my Christmas morning would go over with a man like this. Let's just say this is where the police can be called. He expected to be showered with love, appreciation, and admiration for all his hard work and effort building this present for me. I expected that my children and I would wake up in a warm house and that I wouldn't have to cook the Christmas ham in a snowsuit and fucking mittens.

Regardless, if you want to be one of those people that preach that you should go into a relationship without expectations, they still exist even on the smallest of levels. You never thought about that one, did you? We all should have expectations, and I think at this point in my life the higher I aim, I may just hit it midpoint.

Now I can state two points of obviousness with this situation. One, Gary was a great manipulator. He understood that to remain happy with his position in life, that he would have to marry a woman with a much lower IQ. Or two, her IQ was normal when they met. Instead, he had consumed her with so many idiosyncrasies that she had given in and accepted her happily ever after.

So maybe, just maybe, we could possibly correlate the desire for expectations with the level of someone's intelligence? It makes sense to me. Anyway, what I am trying to say is, women, don't shack up with someone below your intelligence and comprehension level, don't marry below your means. It has a lot less to do with finances than most think. This will undoubtedly always lead to great disappointment, and a level of bitterness that takes years to surpass.

I think this is the very element that drives us to madness. How can you possibly exist, let alone thrive when the very person you have shackled yourself to, does not live to even exist on your basic, most elemental level of expectation?

I have heard it said more than once, to not have expectations going into anything, but fuck, we all do anyway!

Basic expectations like, I ultimately would like to be married to a man that can talk to me for five minutes a day. Abracadabra just like that, you will be with a man that does not feel you are worth five minutes of his day. It's unbelievable when you think of it. Does the universe think that is funny, or is it just testing everyone's strength and endurance? Trust me universe, I surely see why these women are so hardened. Smiling, while their husbands jokingly comment about their shrewdness to their friends. Do they think that's their way out? Still hiding behind mommy for protection? Kind of sick when you break it all down.

How about these women that want it all with their husbands? Business, the house, the children, and the family vacations. I bet you never planned to ask for safety and protection. Why is that? Did you just assume that was part of the package? Why wouldn't you? That is supposedly the very essence of what a man is supposed to be. Bet you never planned to lie in bed crying your eyes out, because everything you worked for financially, was irresponsibly gambled away at a poker table. That's all right though, just smile, otherwise you will look like a hard ass bitch. You will be poked fun at by the other men for being ruthless and the stupid naive bitches that haven't started their journeys of disappointment will side with them.

Although we will all take our hits, it's crucial that we learn and grow from them. It is imperative to the nature of a woman to not repeat the atrocities and to roll with the punches. Is that the expectation? Well, I counter with this, you didn't meet my basic expectations, so all bets are off big boy, I don't have to meet yours. Gloves off and I don't care who's listening. The wise will understand, and those yet to be wise, will look back on it in time and understand why. I don't care how "crazy" I look to the outside world.

Do we just have to understand that no one truly cares? Will they just meet us with the utterance of an emotionally disconnected heir of "well, you should probably just leave him then." That in itself will make a woman even more bitter. She's not looking for pity or advice. She already knows he isn't worth the paper it took to print his birth certificate. She is looking for commonality and a sense of validation, a little empathy. Apparently, the very thing she could never get from him. She knows she must either leave or accept, but some women stay stuck in the limbo state of the in between.

The amount of man children has become prevalent in our society, easily concluded when you listen. Women are left with the fairy tale belief that men will be our "prince charming." Someone we can share our lives with. That will devote himself to us and us to him and we will live happily ever after. The stark realization for many of us though is that they do believe they are princes, and they deserve royal treatment. They seem to be in their element as they order their loyal subject around.

We will share a portion of our lives with them. It will be the most eye-opening time of growth in our lives, as he remains in the same mantrum pose he was in when mommy wiped his ass as a child. He will devote himself to us when it is convenient for him. He will expect you to never question why. While he will inquisitively and from a very paranoid state, accuse you of doing everything that he believes he has secretly done to you. If he manages to beat you down enough and you give up, Wollah, a magical happily ever after! How's that, for a fucking fairytale?

I could still hear all the echoes of the past as I sat at the table trying to relax. Lost in the reminiscence of childhood memories. It seemed everywhere I looked would trigger conversations of the past. I could be thankful that they still spoke to me from beyond and be thankful for the wisdom they had imparted in me.

I never wanted to be back here though. I didn't even know where to start with any of this. I couldn't even fathom how to begin to pick up the pieces of what I had left behind. I couldn't even begin to understand the process of the greatest sabotage of my entire life. I couldn't try anymore, so I gave up. It wasn't in misery, and it was never with malicious intent. I just knew I was burning out, and I would not have the gumption to continue as before.

A serenity and a knowing that God had me through this part of my journey loomed. Just as always. The elimination of toxicity and all that didn't serve me was going to grab me from all angles. I was sure of it. I had so much left to learn. I guess I had to start over from square one, to fully understand the bricks on which my foundation was built. I stood there encased with all the thoughts of absolutely nothing but unknowing. Time to start over, like I had so many times before, due to anchoring myself to a directionless man.

I was awaiting the welcoming breath of fresh air that would certainly come with the elimination of needless worry. I only have to take care of my youngest daughter now. Worry still loomed over me with my oldest being so far away in college, but she was an adult now, I had to mentally readjust. This would be the "me" time I so desperately craved. I wrapped up what was left of my company, and in the years to follow never heard from either one of my previous business partners again. Regardless of their knowledge of my impending surgeries, there was no effort to care beyond themselves, just like always.

I realized this in its entirety when my ex-business partner's first grandbaby was due to be born. I tried to reach out to ask how everything was going, but I had been blocked on her social media. I am sure the other tiny troll I was in business with triangulated us to make herself look like an angel. Too bad for her. I felt worse about her pure naivety and her inability to navigate manipulation and wished her well in my mind. Another chapter completely closed thanks to the Big Guy upstairs.

In my pursuit of nostalgic yesterdays and the simplicity of my youth, I decided I would apply to a facility. One that I had worked at twenty years prior before I moved away from my small little hometown. I would reminisce and laugh at the good times. I enjoyed this place with the employees' years prior and thought it would be a relaxing piece of serenity again, simplicity. I could work a normal schedule of forty hours, go home, have time to eat, clean up, shower, and spend time with family. It was going to be my balance. Finally, my balance. No stress, no worries. I didn't have to oversee anything; I could just blend.

No one asking me questions. No deadlines, no attorneys, no banks, no amc's, no keeping myself a brisk on new laws. No more hundred plus hour work weeks. No more forgetting that I hadn't eaten in five days. I could just go do whatever and get my paycheck and be on my merry way. Maybe even develop some resemblance of a social life by hanging out with a few co-workers. Maybe a drink at the bar with some girls every other week or so, you know simplicity and for most normalcy.

My children's nana worked there then, and I reminisced about all the good times we had years prior. God, I love that woman. This was going to be great. It was going to be a temporary holding spot that I could deal with while the rest of the world just swirled on by. I was beyond optimistic and eager, while holding a slight state of nostalgia.

Childhood Closet
II

I cannot count the times I have wanted to reach out to another woman, touch her face, look her square in the eyes and tell her my story. Never because I want to "outperform" one of her concerns, or tragedies, but so she could relate to me. She could know I had suffered too, so she could find solace and safety in my validation, and me in hers. I never did it though, I kept quiet and just listened.

In the realm of some madness' circumstances exist that are so discernable that even the most adept and earnest would shutter in complete disbelief. I do not trust a smile much now. I know some people do smile to radiate happiness and light because they are genuinely happy. Happy to see you and happy with their lives and their day. I grew accustomed to the radiation of a smile but not for any of those reasons.

Sometimes I would question my own sanity. Maybe I am misaligned, maybe I have it all wrong. People flock to his smile and his victim lit innocence. Why don't you ever smile? You look so mean, are you pissed with me again? No one likes you because you look like a bitch. Come the fuck on, I can't ever do anything right for you can I? I will never be good enough; all you do is insult me. You never loved me, you never cared about me, all you do is use me. That's all any of you bitches are good for, you're after yourselves. Fuck you Cunt. Always a reaction of grand proportion, without me ever having to say a word.

I cannot possibly explain the disgust I feel when some woman believes he is a sweet guy. It makes me want to projectile vomit, yet I stand. I stand now and smile. Will it buy me time? Will it buy me dignity, will it buy me grace? Will it buy me out of an onslaught of insults later that night? Will it buy me sleep? Will it buy me refuge and safety, will it buy me a new life? No, but it does buy me the ability to not look like the miserable, unreasonable bitch that he so loves to tell everyone I am. It buys me the ability to not be used as a pawn and an excuse further for his victim mentality. Quite frankly in the moment, it buys me the knowledge that I am saving another woman's sanity and possibly her life.

What you see before you ladies is a result of my hard work. My sacrifices, my blood, sweat, tears. My silence, my torture, my demise, my very ruin, and all you see is his fucking smile. You want to listen to his sob stories about how I treat him so badly? You want to comfort him and rescue him? You want to be the hand that reaches out to help him up? You want to save him from the mean irrational woman he is running from? Be careful, this one will not only bite the hand that feeds him, but he will rip it out from the shoulder blade and dine furiously on your elbow meat. Do not fall for this shit ladies, be smarter, analyze the mind behind the smile. Stop taking information from the surface, because sweetheart you better know how to swim, or you are his next casualty.

Most times, it is just pure disbelief. Please understand, I beg of you, if anything is retained let it be one of two things, this one now, the second one later. There is a bird, the kildeer. It will mimic an injury to avert people and animals away from their nest. All this with the hopes that the predator will chase them down for an easy kill. Does this bird have the knowledge to distinguish between humans and animals? Does it have the skill set to understand human emotions? Does it understand that most humans operate from a place of empathy and would not harm their nest? Do they understand most would follow this injured bird to try and help it?

No, because empathy is a human emotion that is taught and fostered. They understand predator and prey drives. They understand how the very basis of the animal kingdom works. They must protect their most precious from danger. They understand physically they are no match for most animals and have had to adopt an ingenious method of protection and survival, that is it!

One of America's most prolific serial killers. He had no ability to comprehend empathy beyond the surface. He didn't feel it, he didn't know it, he didn't live it, it was never fostered. He, however, did understand that it was something he lacked and evolved to a dark thought process of believing it to be a human weakness. He used this emotion to lure women to their deaths.

He, much like the kildeer would fake an injury, knowing that most humans would offer to help, so at least he was one level above the kildeer. However, unlike the little bird that does it to protect the next, he did it purely for himself. He would give interviews behind bars and although he would exude that trademark charismatic smile, he could never evolve to the position in life of awareness of self. The very family he protected by proclaiming their perfection and taking all the blame on himself was the very family that neglected to teach him the one thing that was vital for his own human survival. Empathy.

Kildeer don't need empathy, they adapt on a basic level of survival. Humans do though, and the personality disordered, much like the kildeer, will adapt a strategy to survive. Survival from chaos, torment, instability, neglect, and abuse. Whatever and which ones they were dealt. Due to total individual neglect, they will not understand empathy and be left with only the ability to mimic it.

The ability to grasp and comprehend human emotions and to empathize with people is a learning process that never seizes. We are here to learn. We are on a path of discovery of ourselves, and we need this great ability to be able to do just that. I guess what I am trying desperately to convey is the need to look below the surface. Grasp on to the understanding that nothing is ever what it appears to be on the surface. That mud puddle has depth bitches, now strap on your life vest because the water is exactly right for a plunge.

Notice I did not say swim, there is no swimming. This is not about synchronized graceful swimming. This isn't about the breaststroke for a short distance, or the back float under the sun for leisure. I say plunge, because if you ever make it back to the surface, you can gasp for air and enjoy treading what everyone else sees on the horizon. You will get tired though, mentally, and physically, it is inevitable. You, however resistant to it you may be, will slip right back under the surface again.

I don't try to compete with twenty-year-old girls anymore. The surface, the superficiality, the need for validation of their very existence. The thought that beauty will hold the world captive and that their youth is all it takes to keep people interested. It makes me cringe. I have a harder and harder time peeking at social media profiles and these superficial little clips of videos that the youth make for likes. It perturbs me to no end. I giggle about them because I consider them to be sweet little bonding moments with my children. Their generation enjoys them, but still, I can't wrap my head around the why of it all.

Grown men wasting their time making videos of themselves meowing like cats, or mimicking toddlers on their tablets. Do they not realize they don't appear much more progressed than the toddlers they are copying? Just a few feet bigger? Kind of funny, the amount of wasted talent. All that creativity that resides at their core. Compressed down to fit a twenty second video of them dancing around in their girlfriend's lipstick and heels. The women of my children's generation are beyond a shadow of any doubt going to have it the hardest of any generation before them. Good luck ladies, try wrangling any of that in and raising it.

Raising it makes me giggle. I always heard the old women speak of how they had raised their man and children, and their job was done. I could never understand the magnitude of such a statement, until I myself raised two children and attempted to rear two men as well.

It makes me smirk sometimes, as I savor the thought of it all though. A little girl wanting and actually believing the ability to fill my shoes with this man, because of the way she looks. I will give her his meds and five thousand dollars, under the condition that she can never ever bring him back. No return policy. When she calls me crying and begging for me to take him back or to give her some fundamental tips on basic survival with him, I can see myself laughing and charging her twenty thousand to return him. Fuck, I should start pimping him out now, that in itself would be a wise business investment. The thoughts of that make me giggle, but in all reality, we all know that the true evil behavior that warrants the return comes after a couple of years. When you break it all down, it is not a worthy business investment.

Keep me separated, is the prayer you will send out, like a batman distress call. Keep me separated, give me clarity to discern the truth from the lies, from the mask and the real compassion, from the illusion and reality. Separated from the show and curtain time. Keep me separated. Keep me please, just keep me and mine.

Ahh my old bedroom. A grown woman back in her old bedroom, for the duration of, well who knows, that is up to God and only God. Hunker down bitch, you still have a lot to learn. It was humorous to me, as well as reality biting, to be able to clearly see my mother's least and most favorite child. Apparently by the size of my childhood bedroom, I knew I was in last place. The area I was afforded now as a grown-up was much bigger though. She and my stepdad through the years had decided to knock the wall out between my baby sister's room and my old bedroom. Rooms were still clearly marked for distance by the beams for ceiling support. I had three times the amount of room now.

As a child I had a six by ten bedroom. Well, we will call it a bedroom, I see walk-in closets with more dedication for shoes. The floors were different now though, new linoleum. Growing up I had an old thick linoleum, but the kind that would chip and crack from the freezing temperatures and it would slice your feet. I would be doing a great injustice to this newly designed room by not mentioning that it had a light now. Not a lamp on the other side of the room, but an actual light switch to flick on and off at the door even.

The whole upstairs, however, still had no heat. I figured maybe a space heater would do alright. I had severe anemia, so the cold hits my kind differently, and I am not a lover of cold temps. The winters are unbearably long and depressing here and I haven't had to deal with it in years. It was summer now so I could put that out of my mind, as I flung myself onto the bed set up in the corner. I laid there staring up and smiled thinking about the land time had forgotten, or as Mitchell so lovingly referred to it as "the place people come to die."

Ahh Mitchell, he was still very much a part of my daily life. I wondered if he was sobering up, if he was eating alright, if he was sleeping alright still. I was still wondering and waiting for his brain to dehaze from all his drug abuse. He had been in for a few months at this point and with our last conversations I could track his mental progression. I laughed at him telling me he had to get off the phone because he had to chase the craw dads down the hole. I think he meant rabbits, but what do I know?

At this point, I kept my phone glued to my hip in case he called. He was being held in county, and he and his cellmate were only allowed outside of the cell for one hour a day. Not outside as in the air, but outside the one-man cell for rec and shower time, to join the others. They held him up there with the murderers and at this time we had lovingly and sarcastically began referring to it as "Meth Row."

I would impatiently wait for his extremely overpriced phone call at this time. Another miniscule detail that alludes to the depth of the extortion within the criminal justice system. Anyone that has had to deal with this knows the exact phone system I am referring to. The extortion is yet disgusting again, and they should be ashamed. Of course, they are not, that is the lack of empathy and profiting from other people's emotions that perpetuate this system.

Let me cut into your thought process here yet again before you think. Well, they have committed crimes, and they deserve their punishment. I am fully behind that notion, do the crime, do the time. However, arrest and charges never equal guilt. Innocent until proven guilty, remember? Just the disgusting, irrational way in which they ruin someone's life with the callousness and apathetic approach they take to other people, makes me nauseas.

Man-made laws that allow for the payout of wrongly imprisoned people are great and fair. It will never ever come close to making up for the lost time, the sorrow, the anguish, but it helps cushion the insult slightly. Knowing that these laws only apply for the compensation of people that were found guilty and imprisoned wrongly, puts a whole new layer into this finely tuned machine of extortion.

I have spent a good chunk of my time learning about people that have been through these very same incidents. Although most appalling to the senses, I believe the one story that stuck with me the most had to be about that poor little nurse mother on her way home from work. She worked as a CNA, which we all know is among a very low paid, very underappreciated, and demanding profession. She had left her shift and was driving home to her five young children and her husband, when she was pulled over by a police officer.

I can't say I dare remember why he pulled her, something to do with the operation of her vehicle more than likely. However, she had a bottle of vitamins in her car's console. This man, maybe due to a mantrum, decided that these were in fact not vitamins and like a magical genie zapped the pills with his magical drug tester. You know the testing system that has been disproven in effectiveness several times in court, but they are still issued for police standard use. Things that make you go hmmm? Of course, just like always this magical genie test kit, turns everything blue and he decided through his recourse or delusionary power that he would arrest her for illegal drugs.

She spent five months in county jail, not being able to make bail. She lost her job, she lost her standing in the community, she lost time with her children, and her children were traumatized. Her, her husband, five babies and family on both sides were severely disrupted on levels unimaginable. They had no money to meet bail or to afford an attorney, so she sat in county jail, awaiting the worthless, bottom feeding appointed defender.

Oh, come on, we all know some of these people are not worth the outline of the buffalo's asshole on a coin. They are sell outs and a piece of the bottom rung in this intricate extortion enriched system. When the overworked lab finally analyzed the pills five months later that were confiscated, they were positive. Positively a vitamin, just like she said, and she was released. Where the hell is her compensation for false imprisonment? Well, she just had to sit there until they could prove her innocence. How about this, why didn't they await her results and then arrest her if they were in fact drugs? Innocent until proven guilty right? My heart went out to this woman and her family, and it was just another small insignificant story of someone else's life that no one cares about. Well until it happens to you.

So, someone like her doesn't count? She is not considered to be falsely imprisoned because she hadn't been proven guilty and sentenced yet? She and her family have no recourse. They can't meet the grounds. They would have to prove the arrest was unjustified. The arrest and imprisonment were found on the merits of this test kit. See how that works? The money that family had to scrape together just for the fifteen-minute phone calls and her commissary while she was in. More than likely with just one income now was probably a hell of a feat. They will never see the money back for the four-dollar phone calls or for the shampoo she was forced to buy at a place she never belonged at, to start with. She had her own fucking shampoo at home where she belonged.

All these man-made laws for the extortion of your money. I don't ever remember a ten-commandment stating thou shall not do drugs. Thou shall not run on the sidewalk. Thou shalt not collect rainwater for personal use. Stick to the ten, they were all we needed to operate successfully as a society under God's rule. You just must take them deeper than at face value. Let them encompass not only the physical being but of the soul. Do unto others as you would have done to you, in the same situation, always. Supposing the ability to empathize.

The things I think of in my downtime. Really? It was time to get off this bed and hesitantly start the slow arduous process of this journey. A journey that, like in past times before, I was not entirely looking forward to. I still had no interest in socializing just yet, and my mother would mockingly joke with me about hiding upstairs for the whole first year. I clung to the silence. I only went out to work, ran errands, and attended to my youngest daughter's needs and right back upstairs. No distractions, no drama. Nothing outside of myself that I didn't have to minimally attend to.

Uncle Cam
III.

The place I worked at during this time was without one shadow of a doubt, one of the absolute most toxic places I had ever worked. The nostalgia of twenty years prior was quickly swept under the rug. People with delusional beliefs of power, drama, and the soap opera style lives some of these people contended with. Some of them, no-where smart enough to grasp their own participation. I would just shake my head in disbelief. The toxicity at this place was so thick, you would chew it walking in the door. The saddest part about this whole situation was the fact that this was an old-age home.

People had placed their loved ones in this facility for care and this was just egregious to me. I knew in this desolate vacant land that time had forgotten, the choices were scarce. This was the only facility within a fifty-mile radius but still, this place was despicable. I can't ever say the residents went without care, they were loved and pam-pered by a few nurses, but the turnover in this place due to extremely apathetic administration was just deplorable.

How's this, instead of paying some of the administration their exorbitant salaries to hide upstairs all day and play on their computers or gossip about the ones working and busting their asses, you share that salary? Boost the morale of the workers that do something there. Greed and corruption, the worst addictions of them all. Even sadder was the fact that this facility, because of its location, was one of the biggest places of employment for miles. People needed this place.

This facility understood that they had power over the locals and absolutely abused this on every level.

This area that I grew up in was a complete and utter economic mess. A nursing home, a grocery store, two part time restaurants/bars and mostly art galleries. Very little of its original citizens seemed to actively participate in anything to do with the government of this town. They mostly just seemed to roll with the punches of outsiders who implanted.

Employment opportunities were not limited, they were pretty much non-existent. The couple businesses around knew they had people by the short hairs. They could be quite literally King Shit of Turd Island. Funny because my hometown is considered more or less an island. Don't get me wrong, this is my hometown, and I absolutely love this place and all our people. The people that reside here year-round are like no others. This is an island of hard-working bad ass survivors. The work ethic of the people that reside here is amazing, but I called it at this time the aisle of ill repute.

I would hear people detest the amount of art galleries in the area, I would giggle and say you all allow it. To be met with a reply ``they don't employ anyone, who wants to look at art all day?'' Well for one, a money launderer I suppose. The people of this community just fell naively to the honesty of their own perceptions though.

I mean for Christ Sakes can no one see the absurd amount of art galleries in this desolate economically barren area. This area is ninety miles off any major highway, you have to personally know about this place to find it. It's not like you will just happen across this area in your travels. This place is never going to be a tourist destination, without some legitimate effort. Anyway, they seem to roll with the belief that these art people are trying to make it a tourist attraction.

Anyway, back to the old age home that I reluctantly stayed employed at the whole duration of my mental retreat. Before being an old age home, this place was a hospital. I believe the doors of it being a hospital closed in the mid-seventies, 74 or so. Apparently, the downstairs cellar area where the kitchen was located now, had been the morgue area during its hospital years. I remembered the residents twenty years prior all speaking of the man with the brown shoes visiting them, before they passed away.

All us employees just chalked this up to the mortician's ghost that wore brown shoes coming to collect them. It was good to see an heir of this still being passed around the facility. I could listen to the new employee's stories of paranormal activity now. Apparently, his name had evolved to Charlie as of present day. "Charlie the ghost."

The years before this facility was a hospital or a community owned nursing care facility for the elderly, this grand home was actually the residence of my uncle Cam, my grandmother's uncle. She would detest much of her old extended family because they were of massive wealth, and it was misappropriated and gravely squandered. Squandered being that the rightful heirs were skipped over and one of the brother's wives and her children ended up with it. So, our family's wealth was given to people that were not even of the blood family.

My family would seem to agree and chime in with opinions of their own. I knew in my years that a portion of my family's money had been placed in a fund at a local bank to be used by the community. This money still to this day is used for scholarships of the senior graduating classes. Also used for people of the area that have fallen into extreme economic hardships. Although this was a kind notion, look around, ninety percent of this area would have a stake in extreme economic hardship.

I would hear references made to the fact that Uncle Cam had built way too many fireplaces in his home, and about what a prick this man was. Hell, I never met him, so I could only listen. Jokes about how he had to build the fireplaces to keep all his wives warm. What? Now you have piqued my interest slightly. How many wives did the man have? "Five, he was married five times but never had any kids."

Wow!" I giggled at this because I could only flash myself to my knowledge of that era. People had bigger families then, he must have been sterile, maybe? A side statement of "Poor man, never had any luck with women." "All his wives died in their early twenties, and he would have to remarry." This caught my attention further. I looked around waiting for a side utterance, a remark of sarcasm or something, but nothing. The conversation trailed into another, and Cam's predicament was not given another thought.

Hmm, Poor Prick Uncle Cam. He was wealthy, never had any children, and each one of his five wives died in their early twenties. Call me a downer but as I looked from side to side with a perplexed concern, I cocked my eyebrow and said it anyway. "So, my Great Uncle was a serial killer?"

Flabbergasted and dismayed at my reaction to the treasured family stories, they laughed it off and told me to stop being so negative. Alright then, but hopefully you have all accounted for the actual bodies of these young women. I was starting to believe the present-day Charlie at the old age home was one of these rogue wives. She had probably put Cam's brown shoes on to attempt to sneak her and her fetus away through the snow. Maybe this Charlie is actually a Charlene?

I felt led for a moment to take the time to investigate this a little further. I mean I understand I have a slight inclination towards what some people may detail as cynicism. I will check into this myself quietly later. Honestly, it's still on my to do list, for my own amusement.

Anyway, for the most part I was back here for surgeries I really needed. I had been to eight doctors throughout the past thirteen years. None of them were worth the money spent or my time to schedule the appointment. The ones I visited all had the same amount of ego as the others. I could walk in, tell them my symptoms, and tell them I believed this may be the problem, and due to pure ego, they wouldn't test me. Just dismissed.

They all charged me for their time though. How about a refund of mine? Did they feel they knew me better in five minutes than I knew myself? Anyhow, it turns out the very thing I was thinking I was suffering with for thirteen years was in fact the actual thing it was. It had just become a lot worse. The arrogance was just baffling to me.

I could get this procedure done here because my newly acquired health insurance was in a network up here. I knew the doctors in the area would be less skilled than other places due to the sparse population, but hell at least they listened to me. My newly acquired health insurance was a peace offering of sorts from my children's father.

He had moved back to our home state to be with his parents and decided that my youngest needed to be an emotional crutch and be held up there with him. I recall the first thing uttered about him when he moved back up there from NC. "He is so good; he climbed right up there like some superhero." His parents' roof was leaking and due to his father's elder age and back issues he couldn't move around like in previous years. So, my children's father had to come to the rescue and repair their roof as good as new.

Admittedly I was pissed considering he left our home's roof with eleven leaks. The water would pour down almost every wall when it rained and he repaired it with a neon, bright blue children's bed sheet. You could see this sheet coming down our road. Bright blue with a huge bright yellow square and a big pink star with eyes. The house was in such bad shape that I had three roof contractors stop and give me their business cards, unprompted. It was embarrassing. His family back home could not see it though, so I guess that's all that mattered.

The manipulations were many from him, but at these ages both our children see right through it all. Regardless of his actions all I can do is laugh it away, dear lord that guy for some reason just cracks me up. Have to love and accept him for who he is, regardless of the emotional manipulation. Honorable mention for his severe passive aggressive communication skills. I thought if not for that we probably could have worked it out.

You know you have lived in severe abuse when your first, looks like a safe bet compared to your newest. You start making excuses. Well at least he only neglected me emotionally. At least he was only extremely passive aggressive and didn't scream at me for communication. At least when he drank and got mad, he would hit the wall next to my face and not my actual face. At least it was everyone around me that was scared to talk to me because of his actions. It was not always just me scared to talk to someone because of his actions behind closed doors. At least when he stalked me, he was quiet about it, this new one you could hear coming down the street.

You start making excuses to romanticize the before. You begin wondering if you made a mistake by leaving? I mean I must have, but I talked to God about it first. God and I would have a lot of conversations about me leaving. Well, I had the conversations in my head, God never physically answered me, just signs. I just felt more at peace, believing someone was listening and validating me. God would not allow me to leave one man and go forward to another that was way worse. Would he? Maybe my children's father wasn't as bad as I thought? Maybe it was me, and maybe all relationships are supposed to be like that?

Maybe I expected too much when I asked him to repair the broken window in our newborn's bedroom. Maybe I expected too much when I asked him if we could have heat in the house, instead of a propane fueled grill in the kitchen, it gave us headaches. Maybe I expected too much when I moved both of our girls in the same bedroom and wanted him to help move the furniture in the room with less mold. Maybe I expected too much when I wanted him to fix the lawnmower so I could mow the grass. Our children couldn't even play outside. I feared letting them play in four-foot grass because of ticks and snakes. I was so scared that I ended up taking a pair of scissors and cutting the grass in sections by hand.

He grew impatient with this request every other day to fix the lawnmower though and decided he would just burn all the grass off the lawn instead. So now the grass was short, but it was soot black and our children still couldn't play. Maybe he was right. Maybe nothing he could do would make me happy. Maybe he was right, because I was not satisfied with the grass long or short. Maybe it was me expecting too much? Maybe it was me that was thinking he could magically read my mind. Maybe what I thought would be unnecessarily spoken common sense, would be my communication downfall. Maybe it was my fault.

In the ten years he owned the house, he never fixed the window. I had to get two previous owners of propane companies to inform him of the harm he was doing to his family by expecting to heat with a barbecue grill. He left the house full of mold with a sheet to repair the eleven leaks in the roof. Our oldest daughter was on seventeen different medications her senior year to combat mold allergies. He left for our home state after her graduation, but I stayed behind to get her off to college, and her medications ceased.

Anyway, I got tired of having to adjust my children and myself to his passive aggressiveness. We never communicated beyond the surface and mundane conversation of "How was work?" We were just silent, never fought, never raised our voices. I gave up years before on notions of a happily ever after and just embraced him as a friend and roommate. I slept on the couch for the last four years of our relationship and not once did he try to ask me why. He was comfortable in the bed, so I just made do with the truly little I was ever worth being provided for. Anyway, maybe I expected too much. Which is worse, who knows?

Trials and tribulations, looking back now I have to say the past four decades were a combination of both. We all have our stories as women and men, but I cannot help but to give it to us women, we are some strong ass magnificent bitches! Creatures of pure grace and determination, evolution, and elevation. Mind you I did not say girls, I said women.

You must earn the title of woman, Ms. Thang. It does not come from money, age, material possessions or your looks and societal standing. You earn it by defeating everything that was sent here to destroy you. You grab it by the face, you devour its head, and you shit it out! I'm not talking about stupid business deals at work, or by you believing you have accomplished something with your career. I am talking about shit that has been sent by the devil to destroy your peace. This is a whole different dimension of bad ass!

I had mentioned a dear friend of mine that lost her beautiful daughter at only sixteen in a car accident. I cannot see how anyone would ever adjust to that. I don't think that would ever happen. I just think as a woman you would be left with an indescribable void. She had her first brand-new granddaughter by her oldest daughter at that time, and I believe that grandbaby may have helped a lot. She forged on and through her pain and what I can only assume is incredible anguish, raised her youngest son still.

She was gifted with three more grandchildren from her oldest daughter and watched her baby boy grow into a man and get married. She had been gifted now too with a beautiful new daughter-in-law. Incredible moments in life. She seemed to be doing a lot better. She had accepted her daughter's loss, at least on the surface. Every family picture that they took she would be holding up a picture of her baby girl. She related her loss in spiritual terms, and you could just feel her strength radiating.

It was only three short months after her baby boy's wedding that they found themselves celebrating the new daughter-in-law's birthday. This same day they also found themselves mourning the tragic loss of her baby boy and this birthday girl's husband. Another car accident just two weeks shy of her daughter's death, six years previously. Unfathomable.

I had been back in Maine for only four months when I heard the tragic news. I could remember when he was younger and would play with my children. Just like his sister had. I could hear his little voice and remember how comical and just precious he was. I silently wept for her for days. There are no words. As a mother myself, what else can you do? You my dear are one of the bravest women I have ever had the pleasure of meeting, and I am honored to have you in my life. Know that God works through you in ways you can't even imagine, and I am in awe of you and your light!

I loved hearing everyone's different takes on other people that lived in the area or that had once lived there. Mostly cherished memories of people that had touched others' lives in some way or another. I could recall stories of years prior when the old women would sit around my mother's table and gossip. I would giggle recalling some of them. I could remember their faces. Their smiles and the way their lips would pucker before drinking from their coffee cup.

I could hear them say, "I have raised my man and my children, it is now time for me." As a little girl I couldn't see the anger behind their eyes or hear the pain in their voices. As a grown woman I could stand there and wonder, did we all endure some of the same. I could wonder if any of them put up with a man like Mitchell.

Sitting at the table now, I could only long to have those women back today. Generations have passed and now my sisters and our children are old enough to add to the stories and the hilarious warmth of contentment. My old family filled my heart knowing that everything was going to work out just fine.

The adage of its good to be home, strangely took on new meaning. I still oddly felt misaligned, but as though I was forming a place of existence. I knew with this notion I was giving in and starting to reestablish some resemblance of a new life. I still couldn't put down actual roots, my physical body may have been there, but never my heart nor most times my mind. I would appear to put my best foot forward with adjustment. I knew what people expected and I knew what people wanted to hear. Even on my worst days I hid my heartache, my anguish, my thought process and I tried to encourage others with all I had. Most days I had nothing left, so I am amazed with that blessing.

I spent a lot of time alone, which I am thankful to God and his universe for. I can't say minimal distractions, because there were many, they had just taken on a different form now. Mitchell still called me every night and by the grace of God seemed to mentally be coming around. Frustrations were many between us, but not with each other, it was more of an heir of everything else. I had so many things I wanted to say, but as we all know you can't say anything you want to on a jail call. They record it all and strange people will sift through it. Listening for any inkling of anything that can be used against you or pieced together for a case. Cherry picking in essence.

I was a very private person by nature. I didn't take kindly to the DA using calls concerning my period in front of a jury at the last trial. I found it distasteful and disgusting and could never figure out what my periods had to do with his charges. Following suit, I guess everything and whatever goes. Funny how many hats we must wear every day.

I instead opted to talk about the DA's weak ass heart balm lawsuit she filed, when her husband took off with her best friend. I started instructing on ways she could have given him a better blow job to keep him around. Sometimes I would mention my horrible menstruation too, because she seemed to love those. Never did I give them one iota of an indication about anything usable. Sometimes when he would begin to slip, I could foresee the road ahead and reroute or change the narrative. I know sometimes he probably thought I was the crazy one, when we would get lost in weird conversations, but he would follow my lead.

Most of the time we always spoke about how good and level-headed he felt being off from the drugs. He made a conscious effort every day to listen to me. He expressed to me although he couldn't be there physically, he could take this time to be there for me emotionally. Of course, Mitchell did not know the definition of either. He always wanted a commitment while in lock up but was not capable of one outside of it.

I enjoyed the phone calls though and for the first time in a long time, I could see there was more to this man than I was left to believe. He had a very toxic and enmeshed relationship with his mother. You know the type where the mother still wants complete control and infantilizes him to the point that he never needs to grow up. The type where they are still in love with their mother's validation and any other woman will never do. This will always surface as him being respectful of mommy, but he will secretly loathe the stifling inconsistent neglect and hate women. The sickest part about it is that the mother craves infantilizing them   too.

Most of them seem to rely on their mother as the main female in their lives. More than likely, this is due from the mother having no man in her life to fulfill her emotionally. She turns her son into her mini husband. Emotional incest. The mother will covertly feed this so she will always feel needed. Another woman for her son won't do either, unless she can manipulate her. I have found this parasitic relationship between mother and son to be common amongst the inmates I have spoken to.

He would now read books on spirituality, religion, and relationships. He made a concerted effort every day to apologize for past mistakes and beg for another chance to prove to me he was changed. Not the begging like prior times, but sober with confidence and conviction. He had a plan that was guided by God and God was first and foremost in his life. He would speak to me about God and how he was finding his way back to him. Although he had been wronged again by his parents, he was forgiving them and using this time to improve himself. Like I said though, I enjoyed his phone calls and the idea of being mentally transported back to the familiar with the possibility of a new twist.

I still had resentments; I was still angry. I still had questions, I still needed closure. The closure I was never going to get over a jail call and not until he was released. I had to put all that aside and just be present. Present for my children, my mother, my stepdad, my job, myself, and for him too. Did he deserve any of that by societal standards? Hell no, he didn't even deserve to have my phone number, but I was held to Mitchell by, I don't even know what.

None of this concerning Mitchell, made any fucking sense. I wasn't beaten as a child; I wasn't cast aside like a mutant. I did endure provocation and a lack of affection along with minimizing my needs, but I understood and was becoming even more aware of the role that shaped into my adult years.

This strange unexplainable feeling of an attachment to him. It was unwarranted and unjustified. So strong of a connection that it just kept me on the path of my belief in a Twin Flame Journey. This, as I have referred to before, was the only explanation I could ever find. Throughout the beginning of our relationship and up to present for what this connection was or why I would stay.

I mean how the hell else are you ever going to explain your desire to still care for and protect someone that treated you like absolute shit? (Minus knowledge of childhood, however, I was fully aware of the dynamics.) I mean I had to be tied to him for some damn reason. I knew I had learned a lot of lessons from him, and God must have placed him on my path for that very reason. If I was supposed to be done with him, I would have been released right? I mean shit, I released myself from people all the damn time at the slightest hint of abuse, so why the fuck him?

Before you try to draw attention to the fact that I was left imprinted with words from my mother of "You don't leave the mentally ill" reverberating in my mind. It still does not explain the Love at First sight phenomena that I experienced with Mitchell. Shit, I left them all, and they all had hints of mental illness, we all do. You will always hear a "professional" say, well they felt familiar to you. Familiar because of your childhood and you did not understand that red flags were actual red flags. Some could impose that you ignore the red flags.

I would say in a broad general sense this would be true for some. I however, fell in instant love with this man across a dark field. I had not even seen his face yet. A darkened silhouette, hundreds of feet away. I knew within my very soul he was the one. I was not drawn into Mitchell by his words or his actions. I did not ignore red flags; I saw them all. I knew they were red flags; I just knew I had to endure. Not to endure for the sake of receiving love, like a childhood cycle for some, but because something outside of myself made it clear in my soul.

Anyway, just know that whilst all these other events are running in the forefront, Mitchell was still there every day. As time marched on, I didn't have the time to keep a phone glued to my hip. Lessened time to impatiently wait for his call with some kind of news of release. I had no idea about anything going on with him, and neither did he.

His attorney had met quickly with him one time after four months of incarceration and said he would be back. His birthday, my children's birthdays, my birthday, and Thanksgiving had all come to pass. Not a word or a hope of even meeting his ghost attorney again had come to fruition. He knew he was being represented but had not heard a word from him or had the opportunity to meet with him again.

He left numerous messages with his office and was assured of a visit. Christmas passed and eight months of court continuance on his behalf and it still never warranted a reply. No form of any communication from the public defender's end. It, however, did appear to warrant new charges that were held in a misdemeanor light. We all know that shit was added for pressure. The police officer that was present during the mug shot for these added charges laughed and said, "after viewing the video I thought you would have been taller." Oh please! There is no video, or he would have been laid down in the beginning of this mess. Shut your face and stand in the placeholder this system has put you in. Shut your mouth.

As angry as I was for having everything in my life uncertain and up in the air, I very reluctantly moved forward. One foot in front of the other. I like plans, I like organization. Being in any predicament with Mitchell didn't allow for any of that though, not even organized chaos. I had in a strange way through the years learned to tread in a sea of uncertainty and unknowing always.

Constant disappointment was what I was accustomed to. Living in and coming back up to the surface. Most days bothering to exist was a feat in itself. Somedays I felt like I wasn't even connected to my own body. Sometimes I felt like I was living outside of it. I knew I had to put effort into the management of my own actions. Making myself perform tasks that would help me to blend into society. Admittedly most times I just felt like I held a remote control, and I forced the robot shell of myself to perform with it. I wasn't part of myself anymore and the detachment, although extremely alarming, was in part extremely freeing. Was this depression? It had to be. For the first time I think I could actually relate to what people would consider depression. Then again, admitting that would be admitting defeat.

Much like anything else in this world, I don't agree with labels. I don't agree with a good majority of them. I view them as just a lazy opt out and for the trap they were intended for. Society will have people believing that seeking the help of a therapist is a great thing to do. Hordes of people will tell someone they need a good therapist or to seek therapy. Especially when their actions appear to be outside of what that individual would consider normal. I mean great advice, don't take the time to open yourself up and talk to someone in need, but suggest that person go talk to someone else. On the surface it sounds contradictory as well, hell, but then again it is all by design.

I am not taking from the profession of therapy, most of those people that have been educated in that field are exceptionally perceptive.

They are not the ones that just rolled out of college with a degree, however. We know insight that would make a difference, is developed from years of pure interest, experience, and the desire for learning. They are the ones people should seek, not cookie cutter Joe.

Cookie cutter Joe works for some state-run facility. Cookie cutter Joe gets paid to tell everyone they are Bipolar within the first three minutes of meeting them. Those ones make me laugh. Understand now why the cases of bipolar seem to be so high among drug addicts? Many of them must go to state run facilities for the cheaper rates and woolah, of course they are bipolar. The label of bipolar, how much and in how many ways does that label destroy a life? A lot.

Cookie cutter Joe seems to get so insulted too when their diagnosis is questioned within such a short period of analysis. I personally have never been diagnosed with anything because I have never been to a therapist. I have often wondered though, how a psychologist with under five years' experience in the field can pretend they understand what is going on in someone's mind. You asked the person's name and what mood they felt today.

All these damn "Labels" all overlap for Christ Sakes. If you look close enough, every person on this planet would have a symptom or five of every supposed mental disorder in history. No, it's not an exact science, but you are either perceptive and insightful or not. You either have empathy and patience or you do not. No degree is going to change that honey.

Passing Through
IV.

I swear the things I think about at four in the morning when it is twenty below outside. I am just trying to punch my way through the two inches of ice accumulated on my windshield. Good God this place sucks. I don't know what was making my ears hotter, the frostbite or the anger I had for Mitchell because I was back here at all.

Still existing outside of my body but having to stay grounded enough to fit in. I only have to shovel through three more feet of snow and ice now so I can drive sideways down an extremely steep hill. Fuck Yeah! I can't wait to get to work today and make those scrambled eggs for the old people that are not even going to eat them. My irritation and anger for having to be back here grew by the day. The hatred for this place and the predicament I was living in caused me to join myself slightly again though, so I had to be thankful for that.

Want me to feel bad because you're in prison again? Like a fucking badge of honor? Do you ever look outside yourselves to see what you have caused? "Staking your claim" on women that you don't provide for. "Staking your claim" on women you can't protect. Justifying other criminals' behavior. No accountability, you all just accept each other as is. As sad as this is, I guess the other criminals teach at a higher level than your own parents did.

Your "women" have to step up and take on a whole entirely different life. Alone, directionless, relocated, horrible weather. Different people, no jobs, horrible economy, living upstairs from my mothers. Christ, I can't even go get myself fast food, this is no man's land. I work a job that I cannot stomach for one more day to pay for bills that you run up. Let's trade places.

I will lay on the pissy smelling floor with the kinder mat for a bed and read books all day. While everyone else has to run around and take care of my messes. I will have lights out at eleven and wait for my shitty fucking meals to be served to me. Hell, I couldn't stomach eating anyway so the zoo animal meat at the prison wouldn't bother me much. I am not trying to take away from the horrible conditions and abuses that occur within this system. My anger and frustration though, would get the best of me a lot of days.

A year into Mitchell's prison stay, no word from his attorney. I knew at this point; the DA and the attorney were playing "lets trade a pawn" and I was pissed. At least the prisoners are held against their will and unable to assist in healing the damage done to people. You are supposed to be the answers for people and there you are allowing people to suffer worse. If Mitchell and I only ever had one thing in common it's our persistent spite, so bring it on.

It was fourteen months before Mitchell's attorney came to visit him in prison. Proudly mouthing a plea deal that had been offered by the DA. The public defender expecting Mitchell to gladly take this plea deal due to the amount of time he had sat neglected and ignored, was hilarious to me. If you had taken the time to speak with him prior to this, you would have known.

Hunker down though, cause now your public defender who expected you to roll over for his pawn is pissed. Pissed that you did not take the classic bait. They are extremely used to ignoring the inmates and then having the inmates jump at any deal that is waived in front of their faces. Assuming they are tired of not knowing and the abuse. County jail is the worst, the inmates dream of going to prison. Just so happens that Mitchell loves county jail and I love living directionless with no physical man in my life though, so wrong couple.

His public defender was pissed when Mitchell did not accept the plea deal hastily. Instead, Mitchell instructed the public defender to email me and ask me what I thought. He said he was going to do what I told him to do. The offer was despicable and poorly thrown together. His email was unprofessional and had that same manipulative pressure of a police officer. Trying to manipulate my heartstrings not knowing they were dried up. Dried up for this situation anyway. Bitch, I find you and your tactics laughable. No deal. Tell the DA to do better, or we will go to trial.

They hate to hear trial; they are too used to forcing pleas to know how to perform at trial. They should be ashamed of themselves with their transparent and pitiful tactics. Making these people wait for them, like they will be some beacon of light when they finally decide to get around to them. They are so sure that these people are willing to get out of the mess of a county jail system that they will just roll over and accept anything they offer.

They are so sure of the conditions of the jail that they already bank on using them as a pawn. You know the "you give me this one, and I will give you these two". They work with the DA to assure their wins to make them look better at reelection. You, public defender are a fucking sell out. Go cry and gather your thoughts on how you can passively aggressively make him pay even more, go ahead we'll wait for it.

The anger I had for this whole situation, him, his family, his mommy enmeshment issues. The public defender, the DA, my living situation, my job, my new transition of life. All that anger, all that disgust. All that anguish from not knowing what or who I could turn to at that stage in my life. It would have normally been aimed at this worthless public defender. Luckily, I had way too much going on in my external life, outside all this other, to contend with him. I was out here taking way too much for the team, Mitchell could take a little more too.

I was under the exhaust fan at work when my children's nana came in. She cracked me up. Not only was she sweet and accommodating, but she also had a severe naivety about herself that would make the most serious laugh. She just took everything at face value and never took the initiative to investigate anything that was said to her. She would apply whatever logic she could muster up to a situation and leave it there.

This was the very woman that refused to touch a fax after the 911 attacks because anthrax was being sent through the mail. She didn't want to get poisoned. I know I can't even make this shit up. I remember all us women standing in a group outside during a work break. We had some in this group that were so crude and crass they would make a grown man blush. On this particular break we were all listening to a woman talk about her sex life. She loudly made a joke about her clit. My second mother quickly and inquisitively piped up to ask what the hell a clitch was and we all roared. "Clit," we said "Clit" and at that moment I knew she had no idea of that either and I tried to change the subject.

Just looking at her made me smirk and anyone would feel at complete ease around her. She came in at that moment to say something to me and looked confused as usual, but a different kind of confused. I couldn't hear what she said though because of the fans overhead. She was just coming back to work after having been the recipient of a new knee though, so as she left the doorway, I caught up to follow her out.

I asked if she was alright assuming it had to do with her knee and she replied with, "I don't know what I just said, it didn't come out alright." "I knew what I had to say, but it wouldn't come out right." I became concerned and as I looked up at the clock, I could see her shift was nearing end. I told her to wait thirty minutes for me and I would drive her home.

She didn't wait though and assured me she would be fine. I raced to my phone after my shift to call and inform my children's father that she was acting a little abnormally. I told him to be on the lookout for her. I didn't think she should be driving. I said she was acting like she was having some form of a mini stroke. As he went to ask me what I was talking about, you could hear his father's voice entering the background. "I am taking your mother to the hospital." I was relieved to know she made it home alright, but I was worried that something may be wrong.

She had just been placed on a new to the market blood thinner and we were concerned this may be causing some further confusion. I was informed that the hospital x-rayed her lungs due to some coughing spells that week, but the returned results showed she may possibly have a little bit of pneumonia. She couldn't return to work and due to me being a low man on the totem pole, I picked up a lot of extra hours with the shuffling of filling her shift.

I would gladly do this while she was resting. After all, not only was this woman a massive part of my past, but she was also quite what I considered a second mother. She was the nana of my children. I had massive love for this woman. Regardless of her son and I, she was still cherished highly by me. I didn't hesitate to cover any needed shifts.

My sister and I would drive up at night to visit her and check on her. An added kick in case I never mentioned this, my baby sister and I had married her two sons. Yes, our children were double cousins.

There was not much meat to pick from on this little rural island growing up. This woman who very easily was described by anyone that met her as a sweetheart was very energetic. Just two days before her knee surgery at seventy years old she was hanging upside down from her twelve-foot ceilings, stenciling apple designs at the peak.

She was growing very tired this week and was exhausted, but our real concern didn't start until the coughing up of blood. We didn't panic though because the doctors had just x-rayed her, and it may just possibly be some irritation from pneumonia. It was two days later when a bigger, more advanced hospital x-rayed her. They let us all know she had a massive tumor and an aggressive form of lung cancer, and she was terminal. I wondered quietly how a tumor of that size could form so quickly and silently blamed the new to the market blood pressure medication.

My baby sister works as an assistant director at a mental health facility. She for the past two decades has been alongside many terminally ill. Watching her mind switch gears and wear a different hat was phenomenal to me. While my baby sister and I had accepted the inevitable, well mostly, her husband and children didn't seem to ever grasp it. The reality of me being back home to watch my second mother die was not something I prepared for, but I strapped on my coasting hat one more time.

She lay in her hospital bed two hours from home, surrounded by an outpouring of friends and family. I couldn't help smiling when she whispered about the plans she had. "When I get out of here, I am leaving him and going to stay with my sister in Massachusetts." I laughed and thought about how she had talked to me twenty-one years before this about leaving. How she wouldn't know how to face her grown children. This woman was a beacon of light and had spent her whole life sacrificing her own happiness for everyone else. The reality of that just broke my heart into two.

Hearing my sister relive stories of them when I was away and have her tell me, "I know she loved me, but never like she loved you," would send shivers up my spine. I would have to pull over on the side of the highway between work and hospital visits and just cry and talk to God. I knew she was not getting better, but I just wanted God to make everything all right for her. I wanted him to give her peace and satisfaction with the life that she had lived. I wanted him to show her somehow how much she meant to everyone around her. She had been a Godsend to anyone that had ever met her.

The month and a half journey of watching her physical body deteriorate was one of the hardest fucking things I have ever had to endure. To this day, I still have times when the day will completely stop, and I have to regather my thoughts. My children's father stayed in denial the whole time. Sometimes I would have to interject, so I could be assured of his mental state. My heart broke many times during the end of her journey. Not only for him, and his siblings, but for her husband and her other grandchildren as well. It broke for me, and it broke for her too.

Mostly my heart broke for my baby sister. She was this family's pure pinnacle of strength once our second mother was sent home from the hospital. She sat all day and administered her meds at home to ease her pain and to help transition her to her final resting place in peace. Meds that would make this as comfortable and painless as possible for her, that her husband and children fought with her about.

They were all concerned with her getting addicted to pain pills. Like I said, the reality of the situation never set in for them, but my baby sister contended with it. Her daughter, our sister-in-law, made me proud though. I could see her starting to transition towards the end and accepting the process a little bit more. Not that it mattered at a time like that, but I told her I was proud of her and her strength through it all.

My second mother finally had gone home with a week of life left. I got to sit at her side and hold her hand and although she couldn't speak any more, I knew she knew it was me. I just stared out the window for more than an hour, her hand in mine, as we exchanged energy. I tried to smile, but I couldn't put up the front anymore. I sobbed about past events and could only muster up the courage to say, "Thank you for everything."

Everything! You were my driving instructor, my encouragement, my prom, my mentor, my advice, my confidant. You selflessly taught me your knowledge, you guided me, you lent me your material possessions, you included me. I thanked her for her son and our children, but most of all for always being a remarkable friend. I left that night knowing it would be the last time I would be honored with her energy.

My children's nana passed peacefully with her children and husband at her side. My baby sister wanted her to have just her little family that she had created in her last hour. She had had far too many visitors throughout this whole ordeal. With her prior knowledge of approximate life remaining one hour, my baby sister removed herself to finally cry outside on the porch in the dark alone. Fifteen hours later, her grandson graduated 8th grade and the day after that my youngest graduated 8th grade too. We all stood shell shocked, but we carried on for the kids. I don't know if they ever thanked my baby sister but thank you sweetheart for being an amazing pillar of strength and light, and for being an amazing woman.

People that naturally hold light are harder to find than imagined, but when you find them, you cherish and hold them with all you have. Much like my friend Lee. I had met him a decade before this, while Mitchell was in rehab the first time. We hung out quite a bit during that time and on and off through the years. Lee was a definite beacon of light. One of those people that just lit up a room when he walked in with his incredible energy and smile. He had the best sense of humor and could take a joke like no other.

I smile as I write this just to recall his nonchalant reactions to things. He had a bold personality, but never out of maliciousness or ill intent. He was just a very loving and fun light. You couldn't help but love life and everything in it when you were with Lee, just an incredibly fun aura.

Lee and I had the same initials and almost the same birthdays, only a few days apart. We had made a pact to have birthday drinks every year on our birthdays, but we would get busy and always be a couple months late. We made it though. He would karaoke and have a whole group of people with him and he would just radiate. We would all tease him and jokingly remind him to smile when we took pictures. Saying Lee no flash, smile so we can see you in the pictures. He would roar, throw some sarcasm and smile hugely. We could always see him fine in the pictures, but people just loved his energy, me included. He was a diehard sports fan, mostly basketball and he would rattle off players' names with ease. He just radiated light and would pull anyone into his warmth, without doing a thing. I like to refer to people like this as earth angels, and they are a blessing in anyone's life.

Lee had known about me going back to Maine for my surgeries, but not for my mental retreat. Lee and I would go out and although he knew about Mitchell, I never ever told him about Mitchell. Lee radiated too much light to learn of something like that. I used to like to keep everything upbeat and lighthearted around him. I would just state the obvious to him that Mitchell was back in jail, anytime we met up. I never knew how he would react to knowing the kind of relationship I was in with Mitchell. A man that adored me and would give me the world, finding out I was with a man that mistreated me on every level imaginable. It probably would not have been tolerated very well.

Lee had moved back from his temporary stay in California just a week after me going back to my home state. He wanted me to move back down with him after my surgeries and after all I had been through, I entertained the thought. I knew he would cherish me and treat me right. The thought of knowing I wasn't stuck in Maine. I had a place to start my life over when I was ready. Lee was reassuring for me, and I banked on that very thing. I planned on my surgeries and healing time being completed by the end of August, and I knew that it was going to be time to head down a new path, with a stable man that loved me.

I couldn't keep living in limbo with no stability. I needed to anchor my life, and plant roots now. No more of this wishy-washy inconsistent, abusive Mitchell energy in my life. My thoughts of what should be normal, and what society would expect from someone in my position, were the goals I was aiming to hopefully achieve. Of course, as we all know, we don't get to make our own plans, and we will be kept where God needs us to be!

I walked down the aisle of the church, to take my place among the family, for my second mother's funeral. I felt disconnected from my surroundings, and everything felt surreal. I knew it was me walking down the aisle, but I was just outside myself peeking in. I spotted my sister and her children and leaned forward to greet her, but all I could say was "Lee's dead."

I couldn't bear to sit up in front of everyone and allow people to greet me at my second mother's funeral. The reality and the weight of my world was crashing, and I just needed to be away from people. My mother followed me outside and we sat in my car until the service was over. I never cried, I never spoke, I just stared straight ahead. Reliving a series of memories and undelivered promises.

She was supposed to be able to travel, gamble and live her life and he was starting his own moving business. The plans these two had for themselves and their futures would never come to fruition. My plans that were interwoven with these two separate gems in my life, now had to be unwoven and cut away. All I could do was live with the memories, and I had to learn to process this all alone. As usual, I had no emotional support, no empathy, no understanding, and no rock to lean on. I just kept it all inside.

Over the course of the next three weeks to close out the month of June, I drove myself to a series of doctors' appointments and for two separate infusions. I sat in a room being pricked like a pin cushion to receive my treatments. I could see all the nurses. I could hear them; I could watch them all miss my veins. I could see the anesthesiologist come in to finish what they were trying to start. I could hear them say, "I always wondered how long it would take for someone to get this bad?" "How are you still walking around?" I could react by saying thirteen years and smiling lightly, but I wasn't really there. I knew I was the one still controlling this body and that I had to be present in it to at least interact, but it took a lot of effort.

I could flash to the synchronicities, songs and number patterns that had started being thrown my way again after a short retreat, but I couldn't even react. I spent time upstairs at my mother's house. Some of those nights with a drink in my hand, talking to a June bug that flew in every night for two weeks straight to visit me. Who knows if this June bug was even the same bug every night, but I named him Lee. I found a strange heir of comfort in this universal gift while fighting desperately to keep my mind.

Mitchell would still call every night, and I would fight hard to appear that I was there for him emotionally through his darkest times, knowing I have never had the same in return. I didn't feel like laughing. I didn't feel spiteful. The fight for the injustices that had been brought upon him had just all washed away from me. I was living as a shell. I knew he would never understand the depth of how tired and depleted I was. He never did. He would instead take it personally and just start a fight, depleting me further. My well was dry, and the scorched cracked dust was all that remained. Still for some reason God kept me going to give more, when I felt I had absolutely nothing left.

With my pre-op and infusions complete just three weeks after my second mother's and Lee's deaths, I could now prepare my mind for the state of surgery. I was numb to it all, but I knew this needed to be done if I was ever going to feel or live a normal life again. I not only had severe anemia for thirteen years, but the culprit was heavy, random and painful menstruation. This hysterectomy was unavoidable. I felt physically depleted and exhausted all the time. I could never make plans for more than a week in advance. The kind of bleeding I did didn't allow for much of a social life.

My friend Ace would call me randomly at odd hours of the day. He was always in trouble. The kind of guy you could shake your head at but always with a smirk. Just by talking with him, you knew he had an apparent mental illness, but I always liked to play the guessing game of "what does this one have?" He would call me when he needed to talk and always referred to me as his therapist and laugh.

Ace was never of a sexual nature. I think he just needed an anchor in his life, and I always seemed to be that for people. Funny, because I never had one. Anyway, I answered his calls most times, because he radiated an absolute positivity regardless of what predicament he found himself in. Honestly, it made me smirk. He would always talk about himself nonstop and the shit he was doing and then ask for my advice. Advice someone should never have to give to a "normal" person, but then again, he had a touch of flair, or mental illness so I just rolled with it.

He would talk about deep things with me, childhood issues and his family dynamics. He was more than willing to open up to me about anything and was always curious about my reply. I could easily see what had shaped him into his adult choices and he always was thankful for our conversations.

He was in massive love with the mother of his second set of children that he and this woman had together. He absolutely loved and adored this woman, but I knew why she left. Not to take from him nor her, but as a woman I could clearly see why she would go off with another man and restart.

As he peddled his bike through the mean streets of my former town, it was a guarantee that you would hear him jump from his bike and open a door. The door to the convenience store on the corner where she worked. He would hide in the bathroom and although he never said it to me in the beginning, I knew he was in there sorting out his delivery packages for his bike route.

He was elated to have been granted freedom from the affiliations he had been associated with for years and he had plans with the little bit of money he had saved. Sometimes he would call me in the middle of emotional outbursts, and I would have to talk him down by applying reasoning to his ex's decisions. I felt bad for her most times, but knew she loved him. She cared for him deeply, but I knew his behavior and instability had just taken its toll on her. Much like Mitchell's crazy behavior had taking a toll on mine.

Sometimes he would call just to taunt me into saying the word "about" because my accent with that word would make him laugh. He would say "thanks, now I can go on with my day," and would hang up. He was just so random. I couldn't help but pick up his phone calls.

The week before my surgery, we were what we referred to as sick buddies. He had broken his hand and was out of work and I was preparing to go into surgery. We knew we would be chit chatting being laid up in all. Ace wasn't the type of guy I could talk to about any of my problems. I couldn't allow that, but I could listen to him and help him. Helping others always helped pull me out of whatever hell I was swimming in.

He invited me to move down with him after my surgeries if I needed to be back down in that area. It was the sweetest gesture ever. Although he was never someone you could honestly be with or plan a future with, I felt a strange comfort in knowing I had a place to go to after surgery once again. I had to integrate myself back down that way.

The day of my surgery my sister drove me in the early morning and sat with me until I was out. The doctor let her know the surgery went fine and that I had lost less blood during my whole surgery than I did in the first ten minutes of my periods. I knew I was physically on my way to recovery after all these years of being ignored, cast aside and downplayed. I was thankful. I had a few people check on me that knew, but I had not told many.

Ace texted me to check up on me and make sure everything went all right. I remember I was too tired to really talk, but the thought of him checking was sweet. He texted me a few more times that night to check and we had slight interaction, but I was tired and lying comfortably in my bliss of narcotics at the hospital.

My children's father picked me up the next afternoon and dropped me back off at my mother's. He tended to me slightly by getting me drinks and pain reliever and off he went. I was thankful for him, because in all reality besides him and my baby sister, I had no one else I could count on with adult affairs. Two days later, while I laid in bed in slight but very bearable discomfort, I figured it would be a good time to text everyone back. I wanted to thank them for checking up on me.

I laughed and wondered to myself how Ace's raggedy ass broken hand was doing. I laughed at the fact that he still managed to text me with only one hand, and I hadn't heard from him the day before. I needed to throw him a line of sarcasm to check on him and his hand. This was not uncommon for Ace because he was all over the place. I wanted to thank him for checking on me anyhow. It was almost instantly that I received a reply. I grinned to think of how fast this reply was with only one good hand.

As I opened the message my energy of sarcasm and quick wit fell from my face. "I am sorry that you have not heard," his brother replied. "Ace passed away yesterday." I blinked a few times and adjusted my weight from the discomfort of surgery and responded by typing 'I am sorry for your loss." As I clung to my phone in a swirl of deafening silence, I knew no one would know of my loss, nor would anyone care. This was just one more punch in the face that I could apply ice to and wait for the bruising to disappear.

Although I could muster up a theory on what may have happened, I frantically sifted through online articles of the local news down that way. I was not surprised to learn of his drowning. I, however, could only smirk. Knowing that Ace was one of the few people I have ever encountered that would attempt swimming against a current, with a broken hand. I prayed that his family would find peace and prayed for God to soothe them all during this time. I even snuck a little prayer for me.

Breach of Duty
V.

My physical healing went well and from sheer boredom, and taunting calls from work, I even returned to the pitiful place I called employment early. Of course, there was never a thank you, but an expectation for me to perform duties that my doctor had not released me for yet was there. None of the restrictions that were on me were accommodated for. This just helped me realize no one really gave a good shit about anyone in that place.

The end of August was here. I would reflect on the plans I had made just three months prior on being back in NC by now, with Lee. Mitchell and I still hadn't received any correspondence from Mitchell's attorney. I grew irritated and restless knowing if this scenario had come to light that my plans on going back with Lee would have been my new life. All I could do was stand tall in a world of unfathomable frustration and disappointment, while I looked around at other people and their lives.

Why God? Why God? What did I do? I don't want to be here. I just wanted to start over. I wanted to leave the past in the past and move on. I knew when I spoke those words, that I wouldn't have the mental energy to move out of my space. Minus a rocket shooting me in the ass, I just felt stuck. Physically, financially, and mentally. I was back in the position of having to work just to pay my bills and never get ahead. I didn't even consider looking for anyone to partner with. I just wanted to be left alone. The thought of relationships once again turned my stomach. Even now that I would have the time to dedicate, I still had nothing left for me as I stood all alone.

I recalled my sister speaking of a little girl that was briefly at her facility, she was in her early twenties. She could never mention her name, but I recalled her tearing up as she explained her situation. She spoke of her breathing tubes and how, as this little girl lay in her bed void of the ability to do much for herself, how she would reach for her phone. A phone that was her one and only lifeline to the man that not only almost killed her, but to whom she loved. "How could she think she still loved him? ""What is the matter with her?" My sister would have to explain to this little girl that she wasn't allowed to contact him. It bothered my sister immensely to watch this little girl cry. My sister couldn't understand and had immense anger for the man that tried to choke this baby to death.

I remembered trying to appear present in that conversation and show empathy to her work situation. I, however, caught myself in a moment of thankfulness as I reflected on the day Mitchell had almost done the same to me. I could feel the pressure in my throat all over again and the pop sensation that radiated my ears. I could feel my eyes dry and burn from the wide-eyed fixated stare and my legs tire from trying to kick him off my hips. I could feel the burning in my throat as I gulped hard after an eternity of trying to gasp for air.

I could remember being on all fours fighting for air again after my release. I could feel my back arched, and frantically quivering. I could remember thinking about how evil that drug had made him, and I could hear the insults he was hurling at me from a couple of feet away. "Get the fuck up" "Shut the fuck up" "Get the fuck up if you want me to help you move it" "I didn't hurt you" "Why do you always have to make a big deal about everything?" "Look at you, acting like

I tried to hurt you." "You want me to help you move it or what?" "Where do you want it?"

That was the day I had asked him to help me move the couch out. He had previously pinned me against the wall by my throat and the greasy pervert neighbor overheard him raging. Believing this was his opportunity to finally get a date, he hungrily and excitedly called the police.

Mitchell's actions got us kicked out of a short term stay while I was looking at buying a house. He was upset that I had asked him to help me clean up his mess this time. I remember working hundred plus hour weeks and still having to make time to repair and patch all the holes he had knocked in the walls with my head. I couldn't risk not getting my deposit back. He couldn't even be bothered to repair the evidence of his own doings, instead he would just remind me of how useless I was. Such is accountability with a mother enmeshed man though.

My sister's voice trailing in the background brought me back up and I told her I was feeling tired and needed to probably try to nap. I can say after my infusions and more normal work hours, I got rest. I felt like if anything I spent the first year making up for all the lost sleep. Sleep I was not afforded with thirteen years of anemia, insomnia, and an onslaught of violent meth rages from Mitchell.

I flashed back to one of the nights he stood in my office demanding that I drive him home. Demanding like a toddler that I do what he wanted right then, regardless of what I had to do. He accused me of fucking the elderly man next door that ran a newspaper. He accused me of working late and not counting on him coming over. He stood indignant and righteous in his definite knowledge that he had foiled my plans for old man sex. Mind you this sweet man and his adorable wife were more than likely home sleeping. Like I said, Mitchell was only pleasant to me in the company of others.

He was more than pissed with me because I wouldn't be an accessory to a crime that he thought nothing of doing. His mother always allowed this behavior, so he couldn't understand why I wouldn't too. He became so enraged with me for telling him no, that he pinned me up against my work desk and slammed my upper body backwards. He then just started deeply and aggressively grabbing my arms. Standing over me screaming to the point of rabid froth.

I always knew to remain calm during his outbursts and to try to strategize my next move in my head. Never great plans, but little things you would never pay any attention to under normal circumstances. I knew he would grow bored with me being unphased and would resort to another tactic of abuse in a short time. As his screams and threats intensified, he leaned his body weight forward to bite my face. This allowed me just enough wiggle room to pull my legs up on the desk with me. At least now it wouldn't physically hurt as much.

After the second bite to my face and still no reaction from me, the back door moved just enough to catch his attention. He stood up to block anyone's view. He began to extend his hand as though to help me off the desk but then realized no one was there and began to rage verbally again. I was always confused by this notion. Mitchell could rage at me violently but could turn it off in the presence of others immediately. Like a button had been pressed. Yet, psychologists diagnosed him with emotional dysregulation and wanted to tell me he had no control over his emotions. His diagnosis of bi-polar and BPD made no sense to me.

I stayed motionless on the desk as he violently stormed out for a couple of hours. I normally would just carry on working after his assaults but for some reason this night, I barely slid my ass off the desk.

I plunked it into the computer chair inches below. I remember talking to God that night and asking him why. I told him that I needed a break from him. I couldn't mentally take it anymore.

I spoke to God about how I should have taken the opportunity to marry my best friend from high school, Sam. I recalled how much that kid adored me and how we were inseparable. We did everything together and how I should have just stuck with him. I had always carried a big soft spot in my heart for him, and no matter what, I always maintained contact throughout the first ten years after graduation. He had gotten in some trouble with the law after high school and I had visited him in jail. We wrote back and forth, but we lost contact after his release.

I had given birth to my youngest child by then, and he was a free man. Apparently, we had taken two different paths in life. I recalled his extreme intelligence and thought it was shameful to have wound up in that mess. He had so much going for him. I even wondered how it would have been for both of us if we had run off together. My children's father, before our children, had deterred Sam slightly from coming around me anymore, by trying to run him over in his car. I spent more than an hour talking with God and all the possibilities of roads I could have taken, and he just listened. Never speaking a word.

I walked to the mirror in the bathroom, stripped off my clothes and started counting the bruises. The bruises never hurt much, but the sensitivity the next day to the chest and rib area from having a grown man flail all his weight on top of you was always the worst. It's like you couldn't take a full breath for a day or two. I took down my hair at this point to cover one of the bites on my face, and although I told myself to smile it's not as bad as you thought, I just stood there in absolute disgust.

This is what the belief of love gets you. This is what doing everything for someone looks like. This is what hope does for you. This is what forgiveness feels like, again. Why bother? It was this night that my spirit to thrive totally tanked out. I had too much going on, there was no end in sight, and I must have deserved this. I never thought I deserved it before, and I would fight. I would break up with him. I would throw him out. I would be spiteful. I would play his game and laugh, but this time it was different. The realization that the police and the mental institutions were of no help and that I had to keep moving forward with him was devastating, and I had begged God for a break.

I endured more of the same abuse for a few more nights, but I had remembered at this time how my sister was on her way down for her divorce vacation. I looked forward to how she would be whisking me away to SC on vacation by the end of the week. That would be the break I needed. I could come back a little rested, wrestle him into the car and head for Maine to get him some help. I glanced at him, finally passed out, from pure hate and exhaustion from meth, on my cot in my office. I smiled knowing my sister would be there soon.

I reflected on the things he was screaming at me throughout that night. He had another personality that would talk to me. A different much deeper voice. It would tell me how much he hated me. This other personality would remind me constantly of how if it wasn't for me, he would already have Mitchell in the woods' dead.

He hated me because Mitchell loved me. He was going to let Mitchell play around with me long enough until he learned. I could only have Mitchell because Mitchell had begged him for a chance. I was going to be nice though, because if I broke Mitchell's heart, he would take him away and never let me see him again. He told me Mitchell was weak, and he was his protection. He couldn't see why

Mitchell was so easily duped by me and referenced how stupid he thought Mitchell was for trying to love a useless bitch.

I used to find this extremely alarming. His family and anyone else that saw him in the mental health profession there thought this behavior was fine though, even acceptable. I had no choice other than just accepting this as one of his meth personalities. "Aww you worthless fuck!" You have kicked my door in again just long enough to assault me and pass out on my fucking work cot! Not in the least bit worried about where I was going to sleep or if I would even get any rest. That's alright, I was exhausted, bruised, tattered and on day twelve of heavy bleeding but I would just get comfy on my desk. After all, only Mitchell's comfort ever mattered.

With reflecting on this it made me reflect further on the utter deterioration of his reasoning skills due to abusing high quantities of heavy drugs. I had him placed in a mental observation a couple of years ago, when I hit him with my car. This was one episode, involving the greasy neighbor, who wouldn't stop hitting on me. Normally Mitchell would jump on the hood of my moving vehicle or assault me at the driver's side. I was always alone when he attacked me any other time. This was the one time I actually had a passenger, and he attacked my passenger instead.

The hospital held him for three days but released him. I remember the doctor talking with me after his release and she reassured me he was fine. He was just suffering from psychosis. She assured me he was no longer a threat to himself or anyone else in the outside world. However, she did advise me to go get a restraining order.

So, which is it? Is he no longer a threat to anyone else or do I need a restraining order? Never made any sense to me. Why would you release someone under psychosis? Why would you think for a minute that a restraining order is going to stop someone under a delusion? "Why would that be beneficial information for me now after you have released him. You couldn't tell me that while under your care? Maybe a little head start?

He would dare me to get a restraining order all the time. He would laugh in my face and tell me to go get one. He would provoke me to get one and then laugh at how little it would matter. I thought, "what can I expect?" Those doctors don't want to be there anymore than the patients. Trying to get a real answer out of any of them was going to be pointless. Maybe that's what they were used to normally telling people, and they just thought it sounded good. Maybe the bare minimum to cover their asses. Who knows? Yet again, she sounded like an incompetent idiot to me.

I did a week physically away from Mitchell but not his massive onslaught of horrible accusations and verbal assault. Only through text though, I wouldn't answer the phone. I couldn't fully relax on this vacation and be present for my middle sister like she needed. Instead, she walked into a world she never had a clue about, so I tried to shelter her as much as possible from it. I knew if he was there in person, he would have been a different version, a nice version. He wasn't though, and so believed I was fucking someone that my sister had smuggled down on the airplane with her. I had to let her in on some minor things. I am glad I got the time with her together, but I still feel bad that I couldn't be fully present for her.

It was the day before my return with my sister from vacation that I awoke in the hotel bed. Gearing up mentally for having to move him back home with me to Maine. He needed help and he had not, nor was he going to get it there. I knew if I could just survive the trip with him, that his personality would be altered around people there. This was the day his mother texted me slyly and she had him arrested, once again.

Arrested for the same crime, she had willingly allowed him to participate repeatedly in at her home the whole time. I was pissed because I knew why, and it wasn't for the reasons anyone else would think. It wasn't for the right reasons at all. She knew about us leaving to get him help. She had financially fed his addiction and would drive him around to score drugs. She would speak of the financial drain set upon her by her criminal son. She didn't want him moving away from her, or to get help. How would they get their money back? How would his parents cash in on their fraudulent life insurance policy on him for profit, if he gets better? In a way I was beyond furious, but in another way, I knew God had extended my vacation.

I really did live in a shell now, but I was still giving the strength to forgive and to slowly move forward. I could still socialize but seventy-five percent of that was done online through my social media. I still spoke to and encouraged others with advice when they asked and wished them well. A good majority of my interactions were with "throw away men " who would send me a line or two to feign interest.

Feigned interest, quickly followed up by pictures of their penis's. I would block a good majority of these men because they become obsessive. I had already learned my lesson of obsession. God had granted me these lessons through my children's father and Mitchell.

Just for a side note fellas. I know that men sexually are visual creatures, you are turned on by naked women. That is because the female form is beautiful. We have beautiful bodies. Men, one more time, women are emotional creatures. We not only possess the beautiful form that you long for, but we also must be turned on with our emotions. That is our key. Women find nothing emotionally enthralling about a picture of your dick, and men you do not have a beautiful form.

Now by no means does that entitle you to emotionally manipulate a woman, this is where hurt, and toxicity will come into play. Use this wisely. Say what you mean and mean what you say always, and you will have a woman's love for life. Do the opposite and you will meet her scorn! We all know hell hath no fury like it. Depending on her birth sign and the length of your manipulation you will face your music. You will not escape it.

You can run to the arms of another girl for her pity and validation. You can tell people she's crazy. You can call her a bitch. Just know your karma will be to stay in the rung of low hanging fruit girls that are probably never going to level up. Even if that woman you manipulated walks away, God is your karma, and he sees what you have done. Don't neglect your woman emotionally and then complain that you worked your ass off for her and she left with another man.

How is verbally abusing her or stonewalling her and neglecting her emotionally holding the key to her emotions? What did you do to keep her hanging in there with you? Men, do you understand the priceless value that a grown woman adds to your life? Your dreams, your goals, your ambitions? How about your self-esteem and your existence? If you do I beg you to remember this.

The demonic low hanging fruit girls will allow you to run to them and validate your one-sided view. They can easily be sucked into your triangulation. Maybe they will even give you some ass because they are desperate for validation themselves. They will temporarily comfort you because they are tempting and easy. They are meant to take you from your path as men, that you must walk. You will watch your divinity walk away, while the foul mouth gutter trash you ran to for your temporary comfort will teach you where you belong now. The evil of the world always comes packaged as everything you want in the moment.

Be a real man, and you will be given a real woman. Nothing worth having is ever easy. I am not saying by any means that you can't be just granted a real woman out of the blue. God will send one as a test, if you mess it up, it was meant as a preview to what you could have, when you level up. He could be sending you a real woman as a lesson, so you learn in the process, the testing of your strength and endurance. Or you could just receive one as a reward. God knows when you have leveled up enough through life's trials and tribulations to deserve one. Remember men, walk in your integrity, a real woman will follow!

I could only have these conversations in my head, not even with the couple of men that I felt would grasp this. Sadly so, I had to keep it mostly surface. I spoke to a few men that naturally would delve deeper by instinct and these are the ones that would hold my attention. Never attention enough to warrant a future with because God had not released me yet. I still apparently had some more work to do myself.

I still couldn't see beyond Mitchell and my quietly affixed self-described "Twin Flame Journey. " Although I had spoken of needing breaks and we took them; I knew God wasn't allowing our finish. I was held there in more ways than the surface human mind could ever imagine.

Completely healed from surgery, I never cared enough to reach out in a victim mentality mode for help from other men. I sat and did my time right along with Mitchell. I still held myself captive. Pretty much outside of work, I stayed upstairs at my mother's away from anything and anyone that could physically revert my state of mind. I enjoyed the solitude. Still no word from Mitchell's attorney, and I figured God was holding me here to work on myself longer. Mitchell sounded frustrated, but we kept in daily contact. He had been doing a lot of inner work on himself. I was so happy for him and admittedly proud of him and the things he appeared to be starting to understand.

Seventeen months after Mitchells latest arrest, I had packed myself and I had moved myself to a different state. I had closed my company, and I had started a new toxic job. I had witnessed my second mother's journey's end, and I had lost a dear friend and an opportunity for the future. I had undergone bloodwork, infusions and surgery and I had then lost another friend. I had returned to a toxic workplace unhealed from surgery, but now I was healed and maybe feeling physically better, but I was still adjusting.

Seventeen months after Mitchells latest arrest, he had been transferred to another county jail after one year in the previous county jail. Apart from their pitiful plea offer of Class C Felony charges and 58 further months, we still had not heard from his pathetic pawn piece of a public defender. One would think that after all that I had endured in the years previously with Mitchell that maybe I would get a break from the universe? With the past seventeen months of events though, apparently the universe did not think so.

Even worse, it thought it should fling some more on to me, because why not? I was so used to doing everything with only the help and direction of God. I never had an earthly man I could depend on. God knows his warriors can take it though.

Pa's Protection
VI.

The numbers were random now and this may have been because of everything happening and that I was severely distracted. The 555 I was seeing quite a bit before my second mothers' sickness and Lee's death, but I only knew they signified change. Let's face it, I had been through some changes, so I dismissed these. 1212, 1222? What the hell were these? I could barely lift my head to start another day. Most days I would wait for the boot in the ass from any direction to carry on. While I appreciated the appearance of these numbers in my life for encouragement and a little direction, I barely had the energy to carry on daily. I did the bare minimum and hid upstairs when it was all done.

1212 Finding balance in life after facing inner turmoil or overcoming challenges. 1222 Devoting time to the family circle and true friends. Communication must continue to improve with your twin flame so the relationship can be strengthened, and both may advance spiritually. Oh please, I had been doing this all as far as I was concerned.

I did a lot of thinking upstairs in this combination of childhood rooms. I had my computer set up on the side of this room that used to be my baby sisters. The bed in which I slept now literally took up the whole width of my childhood room as it existed then. I could sit at my computer desk, and I could always hear the creaking of the floor. Immediately followed by an obvious sound of someone getting on my bed. You could hear the pressure exerted on the box spring and hear the metal bed frame move. I had rearranged this bed to have it extended out into my baby sister's old bedroom area. Although the floor never appeared unlevel I figured this would have helped. It never did. The series of noises were present no matter what direction I moved the bed in.

I had become so content in my comfort of being alone. Mind you I didn't say happy, I said content, two different things there. I had become so antisocial and so accustomed to my own little haven of space, that the thought of even a fucking ghost using my bed, perturbed the shit out of me. This noise never greeted me at night though, or not that I ever noticed. It was always in the late afternoon. After my work shift was over and I picked my youngest up from school. The time when I wanted to be by myself, hide away and recharge. Sometimes I would wait for this noise and jump on the bed. Hoping that I was going to kick whatever the fuck it was out. I know it sounds crazy as hell, but hell comes later.

I was hesitant to ever mention this to anyone because just like with most things concerning me it would have been dismissed. I was learning to accept this ritual as stability. I would sometimes laugh and think, this is about the only pace of man I can handle right now. He is perfect.

Quiet, yet a commanding entrance. Consistent and stable, I could count on him visiting every day. Yet never disturbed what I had going on, never hollered at me and never berated me. Never tried to start an argument and never tried to zap my energy or get in my face. Never got in my space that I was aware of, and he never made a mess. Hell, he was so perfect, no one even noticed he was around.

Best of all, if he was in that bed when I got in, he never stole my covers. He never kept me up at night on crazy meth binge psychosis rages. He never demanded sex and never took up my side of the bed. He never excessively sweats sourdough smell out of his pores from withdrawals, and he never smells like cat piss from manufacturing meth. He apparently always left quietly in the morning, having enough respect for me to let me sleep.

Ahh he was perfect. I will keep him. Now if I could have gotten him to go get a job and help pay some bills, I would have married this fucking thing. Like with anything in life though, you can't have your cake and eat it too.

Mitchell had no idea how little I even thought about another man, but I knew inevitably he would accuse me of fucking around with someone. The only time he wanted commitment and stability was when he was locked up, and that was for his peace of mind. In the past the only time I could go out and socialize, pretending everything was fine, was when he was locked up. However, that felt like a life-time ago.

I was accused of fucking around on him constantly. Even when I kept myself locked away for almost a year during his last stint. He still accused me of fucking around on him. It was part of his disgusting, disturbing ritual of childhood chaos and this time would be no different. I guess in a way not only was I understanding the energy and life this relationship had stolen from me, but I also knew I had to rest up for a fresh perspective. I would need an abundance of energy and goodwill to make another chapter with him.

On Fridays, my baby sister would most likely come visit moms. I enjoyed spending time with her. She was just starting her wee little beginning of understanding awakening. She was a deeper intellectual conversation than I had been used to in a couple of years. We could all sit around and listen to stories of the "old islanders" that we mostly knew of and had sometimes met. Sometimes they were before our time but either way, our table time now was priceless with our own mother and her stories. Things in life that can never be bought or labeled with any monetary value. Wisdom and love.

My mother spoke of my great grandmother who I had met when I was a little girl. The home my mother lived in, and we grew up in, used to belong to her. She would reference pa, who was great gram's husband, but I had never met him. Apparently, he was quite short and that's who mom believed she inherited her height from, only 5'2. He was quite blunt, matter of fact, and spewed out random insults to people he felt deserved them. He lived to be 99 and only died because he fell from the post office stairs on the unattended ice. He was quite set in his ways and stubborn.

She would speak of how funny he was and how he would tell the bear where to shit in the woods. I smirked to think of a little man complex. She said he and the man two houses up would have a friendly race every Sunday to see who could get their whites hung up quicker on the line. I laughed to reflect on that time. Even in that era, my grandmother did as she pleased. He could cook his own meals and wash his own laundry. He would walk to town late every afternoon and go to sleep upon his return, every day like clockwork. She then said, "matter of fact, he slept in your old room."

What? Figures, my imaginary prince charming that I had grown accustomed to, was Pa. I felt a little incestuous even though I had never made a move on him. I guess now I could at least call him by name. I guess that would explain those weird pokes to my stomach that would wake me from a dead sleep as a child. That is something a grandfather would do. Well, if anything I felt bad that he had to be so quiet now. He probably would have made a great lighthearted soul to banter with.

I began calling him Pa and after fourteen months of visiting he just never came back. Did I call him out and release him to a better spirit world by acknowledging his existence? Did I offend him because he wasn't my PA? Maybe he felt I was too much to try to haunt and he should just give up while he was ahead. Anyway, a partial mystery was solved. Kind of.

Ahh, I had many, I mean so many internet perverts that would make their so-called moves on me from behind their computer screens. This is not to take from the sincere, good-hearted, well-intentioned men. They do not go unnoticed, and I sincerely wish they have all found someone to love and appreciate. The perverts amused me though. I would often wonder if there was any depth too low for them. I had to giggle at them and not take offense. They all helped me transition to a more elevated mindset, during this time. They unknowingly let me take my disgruntled frustrations out on them but would always come back for another round.

The men that would come at me with requests of threesomes for their wives and themselves always entertained me the most. I knew about these types of people. I would never willingly hang out twenty years ago with anyone associated with this lifestyle. However, I had grown immensely through the years though, with individual acceptance for people. We are all on different levels of understanding and we hopefully all strive to get to the same goal one day. We all just take different paths. I personally would not ever have an interest in partaking in this activity, but behind a computer screen most people have more courage. If they had known anything about me, they would know to never ask. I am a one man at a time type of woman, even if I prefer that to be a short time.

Anyway, although you men believe that a threesome is going to spice up your marriage, your woman wants to feel the most desired in your life. If you are showing an interest in this type of thing, apparently, she is not the most desired by you. She will more than likely go along with this in an immature mind state because she is trying to bend to become more appealing and desirable for you. You are manipulating her emotions by lying and you will have Karma to pay. Trust that!

It wasn't, however, my time to reiterate tidbits of facts to these people, I just needed the mental vacation. Five thousand dollars? You are offering me five grand to sleep with you and your wife? Let me check my schedule. I'm busy this week but if you are going to pay the airfare and for a week of hotel accommodations and a rental car, I could probably put you in my very overbooked sex schedule.

I would then fling in some weird request that I knew could not be accommodated. "Oh, I am sorry, normally I would require a gift card for food at Bobs Discount Grocery, but I see your area doesn't have any." "Can't do it, no deal." This pitiful shit kept my mind busy and helped me to crawl out of my abyss of despair and darkness. Hopefully you didn't get your threesome for your wife's sake, even if she somehow thought it, was her idea.

When I first moved to NC in my mid-twenties, I had a peculiar sense of naivety from living in the bubble of my own life. I did meet two women via my best friend that I embraced that had this very lifestyle with their men, but I never really pried. I grew to have love and appreciation for these women regardless of their extracurricular activities. They both had personalities of full acceptance with their choices. So much acceptance that I got front row seats to the after show in complete detail.

No discretion with these two, so I knew more about this lifestyle than I ever cared to hear. Apparently, they swung with each other and would switch out husbands frequently, while the other watched but they were a best friend duo. They somehow managed to maintain the best friend relationship through it all though. One would get mad with the other through the years for some indiscretion of the other and want to vent to me. While I was all ears, I don't know seriously how much help I was in that situation. I never seemed to grasp the etiquette involved or the boundaries you could offensively cross or even uphold when fucking your friend's man, but it entertained me anyway.

The older one was a sex toy representative when I was first introduced to her. Let's face it, a good percentage of people that decide this is a good profession or a good side hustle are not introverted characters to begin with. I mean don't get me wrong the products themselves many of us women can be thankful for. Either as a fill in or an additive to our sex lives, but we can order those online. We don't need you peddling your newest dildo line while we are out trying to eat as a group of friends. There are other families with their children there. Either way this one was particularly accustomed to her lifestyle. Although they like to describe themselves as open-minded and sexually confident, we all know they look like the guy that buys the sports car.

The sports car guy is trying to attract attention from lower-class gold-digging girls, just for validation. Then they whine after she leaves and accuse her of only wanting money. Insecurities we all have, I guess. I am open minded and very sexually confident; I don't have to sell sex toys to make people view me as that. The things I thought silently to myself while trying to enjoy my chicken wings during girls' night. Tit for Tat, I guess, we all learn in our own time.

Speaking of chicken wings, my short friend had a boyfriend, well never mind I will tell you later. However, these swinger friends of mine, were in my life for more than a decade. Not by a manifested choice, but via my best friend. So, while my interactions with these two were always maintained by my best friend, they somehow managed to dance along in the background as strong acquaintances.

For discretion's sake I don't mention their names ever, but I will instead refer to the older one as the sex toy girl. They were full participants in helping my best friend plan my surprise baby shower with my youngest. Sex toy girl had taken the time to make me one of the most adorable cakes I had seen. She did an amazing job and honestly surprised me. She was creative and through the years I watched her evolve and transition to acceptance of things in her own life. You could see this creativity more and more.

She eventually divorced and began dating and married a different man that held the same name as her first swapper husband. When we spoke, we had to refer to them as Tim one or two. My contact with her was limited throughout the last few years, due to my busy life and Mitchell's drama. Her new husband, although committed and monogamous, was by all definitions an alcoholic. I knew she loved him and put so much of her effort into helping him get better. We last spoke about eight months before I moved back to Maine. She was expecting her first grandchild then, and although she looked broken and much tamer now, she was uncontrollably elated.

It wasn't quite six months after moving back to Maine that I received the news of her death. Her new husband felt he was more powerful than God when he made the decision to murder her and then turn the gun on himself. You never know what goes on behind closed doors, is what the old ladies used to say, and with Domestic Violence this rings particularly true.

Often, I have noticed the truly abused, the truly beaten down, the women that endure like no others against a tornado of hatred, will get back up and smile at the world. The women that find the strength to go on and endure even more in an attempt to help are never going to say a word. There won't be any police reports, there will not be any evidence, a word will not be uttered, but their smiles will be different.

Both our smiles were different then, but I was so busy trying to tread my own water, I could never have pulled her to safety.

So, a big obvious question that you may have known was coming. Why would society describe this woman, who gave all of herself to help another as broken? Would they describe her as codependent? Would they describe her as being trapped in the savior role? Would they describe her as an enabler? Yes, to all those. Society would try to downplay this woman's selfless act of helping another as a mental defect. They would paw and grab on to anything to validate beliefs that this shouldn't be done. Yet, require this very same trait in personality to fulfill roles within the system.

They want compassion, empathy, savior complex, enablement, and selflessness for many roles, or so they say. Doctors, Nurses, Social Workers, Rescue Workers, Mental Health workers, give of yourself, help another. Yet shame that very trait in a person when it leads to a tragedy? Her efforts will be labeled and cast aside. A police officer sacrifices his life to try and save someone, he is a hero. Which is it society? Do we want people with these traits, or not? Or is it we just want people with these traits in a neat little controllable box?

Either way, that is everyone's journey to walk and their own path to travel in life. Don't tell me it's OK to do it as a profession supposedly but not live it to its entirety. Otherwise, you're looking at a false mask and narcissism on a grand scale. Societal narcissism, whose veil are we living under? Who would want to deceive so many into thinking this? Wake the hell up! We are not in this because we need validation or love or acceptance from these people. We are placed here to give of ourselves and help another soul. We go where God calls us period. Doesn't mean we always enjoy our fucking assignments!

Women, you were a godsend to these men, because you were warriors and had the strength to endure it all. Not what society would have you believe. You knew your fucking worth; that's why you stayed so long. Most of them are not capable of an element of life that we share unconditionally. I think we stay in the beginning because of the intrigue. Not the intrigue most would think, but a different kind. A simplistic, empathetic kind.

I don't care what anyone says, physical attraction pulls us all in at first. Does what I find physically attractive make it so for everyone? No, not at all. We as individuals all have our own ideals. The overall personality pulls us in further. The little quirks. The little jokes. The little misunderstandings. It can start as simply as this.

A man on your first date getting you an ice-cold glass of water. As he hands it to you, he remarks on how hot the water is. You laugh believing he is being sarcastic and thank him for the cold ice water. He laughs at you and calls you cute.

After a couple of more dates, you grow to understand you do not have the same views of hot and cold. What you found so attractive about him is what he found so attractive about you. Although you both had a weak spot for quirky humor, one of your perspectives was correct and the others was not. You can't argue this with him. He had learned what he had learned. He was taught what he was taught. Bringing it up again is futile. He is going to stand his ground and think you are insane. You are going to do the same, because to you he appears insane.

The whole world knows the difference between hot and cold. It is taught to us at a very early age. "Anyone that lives in society understands the difference between hot and cold." You stammer this to him as you leave out his front door. "He has to be still fucking with you, there is no way he could be that stupid?" "Right?" You get into your car and call your best friend. At least she can laugh about this while you passively aggressively blow off some steam. You need her to unknowingly validate to you that your perception of hot and cold is right. You are starting to seriously question which one of you needs help.

No wonder he is single, and you thought he was perfect for you. Damn man doesn't know the difference between hot and cold and he is trying to make you seem like the crazy one. Like he has any right to judge you. We always have to look deeper, sometimes to our own detriment. Well, let's call a spade a spade, it's always to our own detriment."

` I mean was he raised in the swamps by the banjo people? How could he be so blind to not seeing the difference? Poor guy, he really does need help, but damn it, he is so perfect for me in every other way. Can you live the rest of your life calling your freezing cold water, Hot? Besides everything else about him, you really liked. We must take the good with the bad, right?

You know that you know what most people know. You do not have to question your sanity when it comes to that. The rest of society will validate you at any time. Who will he have to validate him? Who is out there that will tell him that hot is cold and cold is hot? Who in hell is going to do that for him? Who the hell did he talk to in his world that encouraged that?

Maybe anyone that he talked to just ignored him and laughed about his ignorance. Maybe people that spoke to him regarded it as him initially being a smart ass, or being jokingly charismatic? Maybe they brushed it aside thinking he had odd humor, just as you had. Or maybe nobody cared enough about him to even tell him the difference and help him learn. `

You simply say to yourself, "no one is perfect." "Everyone on this planet is their own brand of crazy." "I owe someone else that same courtesy." "After all there is no perfect person." "He is the closest thing that you have met that is perfect for you though." We are taught overall that if someone truly cares about us and for us, they will never try to change us. "You won't change them, instead you will change that about yourself." "Afterall a relationship is supposed to be a compromise, right?" "People are not always going to see eye to eye on everything."

This isn't something as superficial as asking him to change his hair color because you really wanted it darker. If that was the case, you would have been dating someone with dark hair. It's not like he was perfect for you in every way except for a lack of humor. If that were the case, you wouldn't have felt he met what you needed in the first place. You would have looked for a man with a sense of humor, that's important to you. It's not like you met him, and he was boisterous and arrogant. It's not like you thought, oh he would be perfect if he was quiet. The chances of any of us trying with someone that doesn't match our list of needs and desires is at a minimal chance in the first place.

This is just a little thing. He just doesn't understand. No one ever took the time to explain to him. Maybe people had just ignored this because they didn't want to be bothered. Maybe at one point he believed this benefited him in some way with someone? No, everyone alive knows the difference between hot and cold. You just know he is still messing with you.

As time rolls on, you start to question your own perception of reality. You start to lose yourself from bending too much to someone else's beliefs. You start to wonder why it couldn't be as simple as hot and cold anymore? You are made to begin to see life through someone else's eyes. If you bent on the obvious, what else have you bent on that you didn't see?

We question our own sense of self, who we are and all our beliefs. We wanted their surface appearance. We wanted their work ethic and their drive and motivation. We wanted the whole package that was presented. We are all told that no one is perfect and we on a grand scale all hold that belief.

I could watch a basic mating ritual with something as simple as my angel fish. I could watch them swim in the tank, and I could tell when the females were ready to mate. The male and the female would interlock lips and pull. If the female could overpower him, she wouldn't mate with him. That female fish doesn't want some weak ass male to mate with, how strong will her offspring be? How will he protect them? No woman truly wants a weak-minded wimp man that she can be the alpha of. She doesn't want to live in her masculine energy permanently.

"What did he just say?" "I can't believe he just said that to me." The kind of inquisition and disbelief. We don't even begin to understand that he is scratching the surface of a boundary, we don't understand there is a game. He laughs, we laugh, and it's forgotten about, until he does it again. We think enough of ourselves that we will object and argue with what's been said. Now you're longer and a little deeper. We will argue a little more. We will stand our ground, "you don't speak to me like that. Oh, we understand our self-worth plenty, that's why we stayed. We had something to teach, and we did it out of love.

Fragile egos, difference in perception. Woman are endowed with compassion and understanding emotionally, Men are endowed with physical strength. Ego in a personality disordered or misaligned is all they have. They cling to what they believe of themselves and the world around them. They will resort to their strengths when threatened with that being stripped down. He needs to feel in control at any cost when faced with that. No matter how nicely and lovingly you present it. He wasn't taught to have healthy coping skills. He will just keep beating you down, until your well is dry. You will never get the empathy you need in return. Minimum return on the emotions you need replenished, and the breadcrumbing from them begins to angrily sustain us.

Excuses, are we enabling their behavior? Are we enablers? Or are we desensitized to it all now? We are not making excuses for them; we are making them up for us. How much can we endure? The problem was never you and your love. It may have been in the technique you implored, don't stoop to their level. We don't need their approval. They feel less than you and they know it, that's why they can't love you as society deems appropriate.

They feel unworthy of love. Especially yours, they were never shown any love in a healthy fashion. All they know is their families' distorted love. They will want you to feel the hate they have for themselves, as they project all their insecurities and issues onto you. They are threatened. The illusion they have created of themselves to sustain is being questioned. They are what they have told themselves they are, they don't understand any other way. They feel so uncomfortable being loved that they must pull you to a place they are comfortable with. They will force you to take the plunge. Can you swim? Can you tread the surface?

Can we force someone to hold our reality? People's words and actions are supposed to match. The older I get I can see that they seldom do. Unless one is in perfect alignment with their own feelings. I began to understand the manipulations of one can echo within millions.

This is never to say you should stay. I would never urge a woman of any standing to stay in this. Understand the severity and silently plan to get out. Know that it can happen to us all. You can always tell the women that have never endured. They will always pipe up with, "I would never stay" "How could she stay with that, she's an idiot." I would Never. I urge people to rephrase the word "Never" because I guarantee you, you never know. You never know what you would do until the opportunity presents itself.

Would I ever stay around a man that I just met that hit me or insulted me? No, not at all. Why would you? With that simplicity in thinking I can understand. It never starts out that way though. It starts with emotions. It starts when we as women want to create a bond. Our own views of normalcy. We can see the issues, we know the cure, but they lack the ability to compromise. Men rule physical and as such see only their physical needs. Women will accommodate this to appeal to men, ie sex and food. Women rule emotions. Emotions are not physical, and most men will dismiss our needs.

Would you stay with your man if he incurred a bodily or brain injury? What if he gets violent from there? Is that his fault? He was the kindest, sweetest man before. I can't leave him now when he needs me. Why? Why can't you leave him then? Do you do unto others as you would have done to you? You will grapple with that. You will put your toes in the water of hope. If I work hard enough, he may return to the way he was. Same principle.

Love is never blind. To fully love someone, you need to be open, aware, and perceptive enough to see it all. Hope is blind though. And hope will take you to hell and back. Until you have followed hope there, you will more than likely never question its existence.

A woman's empathy is exploited, always has been. When that can't be exploited or we have taken too much, we are the unreasonable bitch. Double edge sword. Was that our burden as women to bear? Compassion and empathy. Or do we embrace this within ourselves and carry it on anyway?

What do we learn through these occurrences? Do we learn we are flawed? Do we learn we are the bad ones? Do we learn to be at their beckon call to calm down his reaction before it happens? Do we learn to run around trying to keep peace? Walk on eggshells? Do we learn over a series of mishaps and occurrences to become more in tune with the man we are with, then ourselves?

Yes, we do, because we are trying to survive it on one level or another. I know my situation was nowhere near as drastic or abusive as some other women, so I can't speak for us all. Sometimes it's in the subtleties of understanding, if we can just help him see this one thing, it will make it better for us all. It is seldom one thing though.

Any good mother knows, we were not designed to put ourselves first. We all know this. We will come home from work. Get the kids, get them home, help with homework, cook supper, serve supper, clean up supper. Do the laundry, fold it, and put it away. Kids want to talk, they need advice. The husband wants to talk, and he needs advice. We bathe the kids, because we cannot go to sleep until we know everyone has been taken care of. Our hours of sleep are less, and it falls on us. We mop and sweep, we pick up and we read bedtime stories. If we are lucky and don't develop insomnia to have our own quiet time, we are perpetually cranky from not getting enough sleep. Yet again we are the cranky, unreasonable bitches.

I remember the dilemma that I transitioned into with something as easy as buying myself a pair of socks, without having to buy the kids anything. It was a huge hurdle for me. Learning to put myself first with something as simple as that. Any mother knows this.

Yet, there are women that will lecture on putting yourself first or living as though they do. Are these the inexperienced ones or the ones that have leveled up through the milestones of raising their own children? I am not going to tell you to stay or to get out. Only you know your situation right now. What I will say is if you are to be his help-mate, if you are there to help him achieve his dreams, he should be helping you achieve yours as well. Ask yourself where he is going. Where is he leading me?

Are you putting an endless amount of your own energy and hours being devoted to a man because he is working on a plan or a goal? Are you taking his shit because he is sleep deprived and cranky because he is working on an actual plan? He wants to do a certain thing to lift himself up out of poverty, to secure his children's future and yours. Or are you just expending your energy on a man barely working a 9-5 that wants to be served and treated like king of his castle when he decides to come home? Spending all your precious energy on a man that has the end goal of coming home, eating a cooked meal, leaving his plate behind as he silently goes about the rest of his night? Look at your situation ladies, if you are with a man that insists you stay by his side so he can merely exist in his own comforts, how will he ever show you life?

Our jobs as women are to uplift our men. Encouragement and support. We are the ones to see them when the world can't or refuses to. We do not come from a place of wanting to change them, to entirely meet our perspective. We encourage them to respect themselves so that the world that views them will change its perspective. We want our men to thrive and excel. We want them to reach their full potential.

We are emotionally superior, and they are physically. Unhealthy men that can't allow themselves to accept love, will forever see a woman's emotional input as a threat to their perceived existence. Some of them can't see the truth of what they are within themselves. They will resort to their superiority of physical strength to quiet what their egos cannot bear. We as women make sacrifices of ourselves every day. Silently.

I think when you realize that your man is leading you nowhere, you will look to a man that does. I decided to follow God. No matter how crazy I looked, and I made a game out of it slightly. Fun adventures.

Little girls, are you with a well put together, good looking, rich businessman? Are you enjoying his position and the ease it has afforded you? Are you walking around smiling and dangling what you have acquired? To raise a man, a desirable man, it takes a lot of work. Work that you do not understand. Did you build with this man? Did you lose sleep with this man? Did you put any of the work, blood, sweat and tears into this man? Or are you just enjoying the free ride of what he is today?

Either way, understand that to build a man of that caliber, it took someone's encouragement, hope, sacrifices and beliefs. They were not yours. You have no idea the amount of suffering that was endured to get some to where they are today, for you to enjoy. If he is a great man today, you must be thankful for him and respect the ones responsible.

Respect his mother. Respect her only if she respects you and your boundaries. Afterall she was supposed to raise him to be a self-sufficient aid to society not to keep tethered up her own ass for her needs. If you live with a man and he still calls his mother to talk about you and fill her in on his troubles during the day, please know that man still craves his mother's validation. He may be with you physically but emotionally he is still with mommy. If he has an ex-wife, then you always respect her. He will not tell you the whole story, and it will only be from his perspective. Rest assured she endured on many levels.

Back to the surface for most. After Pa's mysterious departure from my afternoons and with an insurmountable amount of time left on Mitchell's jail days, my days just went on boring and mundane. Nothing to look forward to and no hopes of having that anytime soon. Just two months after my surgery, I was anxious and ready to move on with my life, but I was still being held by God. Right where I couldn't foresee that I was needed.

Uncanny
VII

It was mid-September and standing in a topsy turvy of no direction, I was picking up quickly enough to understand. If I didn't have a goal or something else to focus on, I was probably going to end up sneaking into the deep woods and waiting for someone to find my lifeless body. I would spend some time thinking about how I would do it and then realize I never could. I have children, that would be the most selfish thing ever. I did have long moments where I could perfectly align with how someone could and would romanticize suicide though. I couldn't help but feel so bad about the depths and time of depravity someone would be subjected to, in order to make that final decision.

Just three months after the passing of my second mother from cancer, our personality-deprived department manager fell ill with a cancer diagnosis as well. Not the same form and nowhere near the same prognosis, she had a chance. I became extremely empathetic for her position. While pulling together to work extra hours at a job that I couldn't stand, I could at least use her illness as an excuse. An excuse as to why I would extend my time doing something I didn't like.

It was not like years prior when I would do things just because I didn't think I had any other options. I knew better now, even if others around me didn't. The days were one after another and nothing outside the normal routine. Mitchell was still calling with no word of communication from his lawyer and giving off the appearance that he was transforming.

I woke but I was frozen, I couldn't move. I lay there stiffened and staring at the cursed slanted walls that were only designed for a good head smack. I couldn't even move a muscle. I was more than frozen. I couldn't even blink my eyelids as I lay there staring. I could feel it behind me in the dark of the night. No words were uttered, but I felt it. I could feel it staring at me. A sense of evil terror like I had never felt in my life. I never saw its face, I never saw even a reflection, but I could feel it and the void of space that it filled. It didn't speak, it never touched me, but I knew immediately it wasn't there for good. "Gods got me, God's got me." The same thing I would repeat before I had to go in for another round of Mitchell. Gods got me, God's got me.

I have seen evil in someone's eyes. I have seen the dark descent of emptiness in someone's eyes and though I never saw its eyes, its presence radiated this feeling throughout my body times a hundred. It was all consuming and in the reality of probably one minute, it's all I could feel for countless days after. Matter of fact it was so profound and evil, It still commands shivers within my body to this day.

I mean what are you going to do? Kill me? Gods got me, so do your worst. As much as I would have loved to roll over and confront it, you are frozen for a reason. I must believe that some things are not meant for us on this plane to ever see. Still frozen with a sheer all-encompassing panic, I could feel it distance itself and then a noise. I shit you not clear as day, no mistake about it, noise. It never spoke to me, it never physically touched me, but instead I heard my window open.

This wasn't one of those vinyl easy track windows either, it was a stubborn window and force had to be applied always to open or shut it. A massive force of freezing air rushed to the back of me. I could feel then, I could feel the freezing air. I could hear what sounded to be the flapping of clothes on a clothesline during a windy day. The hollow extremely loud sound of wind just echoed off the walls. I could feel the blanket that lay on me begin to flitter and then it lifted. It was repeatedly lifting as though it was flapping on a line.

I laid there in sheer fucking panic and just waited for the window to shut. I hate the cold, and this thing knew it. When the presence left, I still lay there frozen just from the sheer horrific occurrence of it all. I had never in all my life felt a presence of evil like that. I gather they can't mess with your free will, but they can try to change your mind. Even as embarrassing as this is to admit, I woke the next day lying in a puddle of my own piss. I hadn't drunk, I hadn't been under any extra stress, and I had not been researching anything of this sort at all. After this I became inquisitive as to if other people had ever had this happen.

Of course, not inquisitive enough to tell others, but instead quietly research it for my own sense of understanding. I could see the medical references to night paralysis and attempts by the medical community to dismiss this as a sleeping disorder. I could see the psychologist's references to having it relate to trauma. I never found anything amongst all the research to explain this occurrence away that set right with me though. I took surface level comfort in talking to myself and explained that these two professions must be correct and soothed myself eventually with the surface explanations.

It was roughly three to four weeks later I woke frozen again, but this time in pure ecstasy. I didn't want to move anyway. If something was making me feel this damn wanted, desired and aroused me this much, why would I want to move and disturb it? I figured as I laid there frozen in a climatic thrill that was never ending, that this was a long overdue sex dream that I very much deserved. If this was the so-called night terrors of the medical community, I had not read anything on feeling this damn good during one. I will take it; please can I have another? I didn't even know this level of ecstasy existed, I want night terrors like this, every night. Medical community with your sleep disturbance shit, all I would do is sleep all day long, if I thought it was going to be like this.

I could feel its presence; I could feel its touch. I could definitely feel its touch, and everyone was another dimension of pure ecstasy. Intense orgasms of unmeasured proportion. I was so aroused I didn't care who or what it was, just give me more! Honestly, I wouldn't have cared if it was old Pa back for a visit, and making a move on me, I would have let him keep on rolling.

As I lay there frozen, I could see the top of his head moving closer towards me. As he pulled the cover back to reveal his face, I was so relieved to see it was Mitchell, and with every touch it just intensified. I knew I missed him. I knew I was gravely sexually depraved, but this was too intense for a sex dream. I have had sex dreams, and I may have gotten close to an orgasm or possibly had one, but this was other worldly. I didn't know what I had done for this conjugal visit, but I was more than ecstatic to have him greet me this way. As he smiled at me and drew closer to my face, I wasn't scared. I was strangely at an odd peace and awaited my hello.

It was the moment that Mitchells face met mine that I realized those were not Mitchell's eyes. I began to try and move slightly to indicate uncomfortableness. I wanted to put distance between Mitchell and I until I could reassess. Hopefully If I could sit up and view him overall, I would know for sure. Maybe just waking from a sleep haze had me second guessing. He didn't take to me trying to move in my frozen state though. He leapt to begin choking me and panic began setting in. I could feel the intent and he was trying to kill me. I tried to move; if I could just move my legs I could kick. He may lose his grip. I was frozen, I knew what I needed to do in my mind, but I couldn't move.

I was released as I sprung forward straight up in bed. He never said a word, and there was no prior indication of evil intent. Like it is said though, evil comes disguised as everything you want. I started sleeping with a lamp on after that. Too much in this room for me to handle as of lately.

All I was left with was confusion and an inquisitive state of mind. Why is this happening now? Why do I keep having what the medical world would describe as night paralysis? Apparently, this is such a big thing they have a diagnosis and label for it. I must take the time to investigate this further now. I was left with a feeling of unease and panic with the first "attack", this second one was eye opening and frightening. This kind of thing is not meant to sit easily with people. It is so out of the norm and so disturbing that people actually talk to doctors about this. Of course, this community has a label for it and its disturbed sleep patterns, sleep disturbances, possibly from stressful events.

Now if I wanted to look at this for a quick psychological evaluation, I could simply say this. Well, it is a form of a nightmare that I have manifested in my dream state. Possibly because of the undiagnosed PTSD associated with my former/current relationship. I could be reliving the horror of almost being choked to death by a man that I had loved and had immense attraction for. I would normally find this to be a plausible explanation for this occurring.

The question I had that I could not find an explanation for was why so many people all had the same dreams? Attacks from these manifestations in all the same positions. Mostly on the chest constricting airflow. Men and women alike. Explain that to me?

I knew then I had officially been pulled into a darker side of the world with spiritual war. Except now I wasn't just on the outskirts of questioning its existence, I was being shown its existence. An incubus. Apparently, I had spent too many nights alone without a man for physical protection and maybe all the time before, Pa was politely protecting me?

My mother hollered up the stairs, she rarely came up over the stairs. Much like in childhood, she would stand at the bottom of them and holler. I would giggle to feel the same sense of annoyance as I did as a child when I had to answer her back. Amusingly so in my 40's.

I would like to have believed that I answered her a lot more maturely now though. I took her to the store and ran her errands daily. She never renewed her license after her mental diagnosis of anxiety disorder and agoraphobia decades before. She kind of just blended into the background and used slight tactics of manipulation for her sense of enablement, but we all did it for her anyway. She is our mother. Even so, I was living in her space for my sanctuary, of course I will do it, annoyed or not. Her boyfriend, whom I consider my stepfather, absent from marriage, would also need rides to and from different places. I was a constant taxi service. I knew a lot of weight was going to be placed with others demands coming back here, but I did it anyway. Distance makes your heart grow fonder, and time has a way of convincing you that things were not as bad as you had remembered.

She needed to ask if I would be willing to bring my stepdad for another doctor's appointment. He had previously battled prostate cancer in the past few years and had been in remission. He still required biannual checkups for this. His doctor's appointments were almost two hours from home. Of course, I wasn't ever going to say No. How could you honestly look at someone and say, no? No, I would rather lie here and look at the walls, than travel two hours one way and sit at the doctors for someone else's peace of mind for their health? No one could or in my opinion should. Do onto others always, as you would have done to you in the same circumstances. God always gave me enough strength and umpf, to get up and still do.

She wasn't quite sure of his appointment date as of then, but she would update me when they found out. Thanked me and asked me if I had enough time to run to the store for her. I had to leave to take my youngest to the movies to hang out with her friends. Per usual I always made the time, annoyed or not.

As I sat outside in my car listening to music behind the movie theater, I looked at the time on the car's clock. Ten more minutes and she and her friends will be out. The movie should be wrapping up soon. My gas light popped on to signal an empty tank. I thought about sneaking off to get the gas quick but did not want to miss her. On the way to the movies, we had a great discussion about her friends. My heart just swelled to be able to measure her maturity at the young age of fourteen. My children just amazed me.

We joked about one of her good "guy" friends. They had known each other for years, throughout the summers when she would go home to Maine to visit her grandparents. My mother babysat him, so they went way back a good nine years. Born the same week of September and he was just an adorable little boy. I had grown up with his parents, and I always knew because of the combination of those two, their children would be good kids.

She was having a moral dilemma, because he had gotten a little girlfriend, and the new little girlfriend was jealous. You know the typical teenage crap we all encounter. I chimed in reminiscing about Sam and me in high school. I told her all about how we were inseparable and how much I just adored him as a best friend. How we had kept in communication through the years and how important friendships were in our lives. I giggled and said "Who knows, baby girl, maybe you two will look at things differently when you are older. I said, "shit maybe you will figure out that is the boy you should have married, but it may be too late by then." I was referencing the conversation I had with God about Sam the night I had taken enough abuse from Mitchell. I never let her know that, but the conversation we had was very deep for me and I think it touched her the way she needed it to.

I spotted her departing from her friends and looking around the back of the movie theater for me, so I honked my horn and beckoned her to hurry. Momma was running out of gas. She filled me in on the movie and as I was about to pull into a gas station, she piped up with "I'm hungry." I decided in that split moment to divert my travels to the gas station up the road. This gas station was situated slightly next to the only fast-food place within a sixty-mile radius. I said "Woolah, let me get some gas here and then we can go right there to the drive thru." She smiled and I said I would be right back. I must prepay and grab a soda.

As I hastily walked up the ramp to the convenience store, I noticed a man coming in my direction and heard him mutter something to me. He quickly jumped to the door to hold it open. I made no eye contact with him as I believe he was slightly intoxicated, and I was not in the mood for one sided drunken small talk. I hadn't combed my hair in close to two days, I wasn't flirting either. I looked like a mess. I scurried to the back of the store to the soda coolers. Hanging out there, for refuge from being hit on by a drunk any further.

I stood by the cooler for what felt like way too long waiting for him to make his departure. He kept talking loudly and was dragging his visit out a little too long. I decided for the sake of the cashier; I should probably go push him a long in line. At least the cashier could use me as a convenient excuse to rush his annoyance out of the store. I stood in line never looking up or directly at him or the cashier, because like I said I was in absolutely no mood to socialize. As the man loudly left, belligerent, spewing some perverted reference to me, I stepped further in line. I placed my soda on the counter and stated I needed twenty-on-pump two, as I stumbled through my pockets looking for the debit card, I knew I had just placed it in there.

"Do I know you?' Still distracted by finding my debit card, I looked upwards. "Don't I know you?" Oh my God Sam? My heart flatlined for a moment and he said my first name followed by fucking and then my last name. I started laughing and "Sam fucking Jones" was all I could return. "I was just talking about you to my daughter." "Hah?" "Yeah, my daughter is out in the car, well my youngest." I got pregnant with her the same month he was released from prison, and he never knew about her. We had just lost contact. He knew about my oldest and had seen her several times when she was a baby and a toddler, but he hadn't seen her in close to eighteen years either.

"Oh my God, can I meet her?" "Yes of course" as he abandoned the post and followed me to my car. He peeked in to say Hi, and quickly pulled away, remarking on how pretty she was. "I know Sam and both my children are gorgeous." We hung out for about ten minutes outside the store and gave each other our big life rundowns. It was like I had just seen him yesterday. True friends can always pick right back up with you. No sense of judgment or having to ease back in, it was like no time had passed. We exchanged phone numbers, and I mentioned us having to get together sometime soon for a drink or something. Like we all do with old friends, but we all know most times it's just an empty statement with no real intention behind it.

I was baffled with the uncanniness of the universe, and as I pulled away to bring my youngest to the drive through, I just couldn't get over what had just happened. My daughter just laughed to witness my reaction to something of this magnitude.

He and his wife had divorced, and he had reluctantly moved back to the area. He only planned on it being temporary and, much like me, felt stuck. He had a ten-year-old son, who he got on vacation and was working at a crappy convenient store job. Much like with me, there is nothing around there for employment opportunities, but bills still must be paid. Five days after meeting at the store, we met up for Halloween drinks.

This beautiful man that meant so much to me in my younger years was in front of me. He was divorced, single, a great devoted father, had his own apartment, a job and was very respectful. I still couldn't allow my mind to see him at any point as a relationship interest though. I used that night as a catch up, an opportunity to finally come out of hiding and begin socializing. Used that time to just live in the past.

I had mentioned to Mitchell the circumstances I found myself in with meeting up with Sam, I giggled about it, because he had known of Sam. I had referenced him here and there through the years, but he had never met him. I downplayed my beliefs in the bizarreness of the universe because he had no idea of the conversation, I had had with God that night. Not only for that reason, but I knew in typical Mitchell fashion he more than likely would become enraged with jealousy. I could never be excited about anything around Mitchell. He would seemingly do anything within his power to make sure my happiness was short lived and drawn back to center around him. Even if that was by abusive means.

I had begun noticing the numbers 1212 and 1222 within the last several weeks and I couldn't help wondering if the universe was trying to alert me to this happening. I laughed silently with my own amusement, almost like my grandfather did all those years before.

The following week after Halloween drinks it was what I jokingly refer to as my birthday week. I had never in a million years celebrated this all week, nor did I expect anyone else to. Honestly, I barely celebrated the actual day, but for emphasis's sake I liked to call it my birthday week. Mom had let me know previously my stepfather's appointment was scheduled for my birthday. I had agreed to drive him two hours one way on my birthday for his doctor's appointment.

I figured I would take this opportunity to invite Sam along for the ride, just to get him out of the stifling area we resided in. It felt good to have him there in the backseat, just to aim my conversation at someone besides my silent stepdad. A two-hour car ride with a man that can only converse when he is drinking is uncomfortable as hell. Sam going would distract from at least the unease of the car ride. My stepfather was noticeably nervous hoping this appointment was not going to be the outcome we were all dreading. I grabbed his hand in mine, squeezed it slightly and said, "I got you". Sam was such a good sport the whole ride, sitting up in the back seat, hood up, nodding off, but he never fell asleep and was available to pipe up and talk to me about any conversation I started.

My stepfather was not great at understanding or relaying information to my mother. She felt she had more control of the situation if I or one of my sisters accompanied him. Especially with something as important as his health. We would sit in on his appointments to give her the information she needed to help take care of him with any future medical issues. His cancer was back, and I sat there listening to options to fight his cancer again, two hours from home.

I could glance out the glass and see Sam still sitting up in the waiting room chairs for us. I knew that more hospital visits obviously would be needed. At the same distance with more frequency, and I geared up to the thoughts of it. I can take him on my days off from work, and my sister sometimes and possibly his brother. I listened intently for instructions and follow up call details. Listening while they gave him the option to join a trial.

I could see his mind shift gears and although as normal he had been quiet the whole appointment, he did speak up. "Well, I would like to live a few more years." The nurse explained to me the trial options and honestly from my understanding of it, if he wasn't fortunate enough to be assigned to Group C, then it wasn't going to be worth his time. However, that is not how trials are directed and it's the luck of the draw. We left the appointment with my stepfather quietly and then followed his directions of wanting to eat out for my birthday.

The ride home was slightly somber, but we tried to make jokes to distract us from the elephant in the car. I was driving in my own thoughts of wondering how I was going to tell my mother about trial options for his revisiting cancer. I found my mind floating to the cynical sarcasm that I comfortably live in for a coping mechanism. Happy birthday to me! I have spent my whole birthday finding out my stepdad has cancer again and worrying about him, and my mother, how could this birthday possibly get any better? Well, let me tell you, God and his universe answered me with a quickness.

Rounding the corner for homestretch, with only fifteen miles left to home, my most prized possession gave way. My best friend, my freedom, my life, my shelter, and my private refuge to get away from it all. The place I sat quietly to gather my thoughts. The one thing that had been there with me quietly through all this just lost steam. With only five payments left on her, Carole the car, decided she couldn't take any more of this dreary existence, and unbeknownst to me quickly bowed out.

I could see the perplexed looks on both Sam's and my stepfather's faces, as we drove the rest of the trip at a top speed of ten. I knew there was only one shoddy car dealership within a ninety-mile radius. A place I would never buy an overpriced vehicle from. However, it was going to be my last resort and at this time a very much needed service.

Was this God and his universe's way of showing me, it could be worse? At least the car was still barely drivable. He didn't allow us to get totally stranded. Was it a way of forcing me to get rid of everything I valued? My home was already gone and my business. Ninety percent of my belongings were over twelve hundred miles away in storage. All I got to keep was my car. My love. Or was this yet another test of my strength and resilience? What was I going to do? Walk in subzero temperatures to work at a job I couldn't stand? Was I then going to walk to my daughter's school and piggyback her home? Better yet, was I going to walk around to do everyone's errands for them? The expectations on me were not going to just miraculously end. I could already feel myself getting prematurely angry with the projected scenarios in my mind.

No garages or let me reword that, one garage within this whole county. The great country of Canada would be able to replace her transmission though. It was going to be sixty-five hundred once I got her over there. They could replace it, but with no guarantees. After replacing, I would then have to have her towed three hours away to a dealership where they would have to reset the computer. They, however, couldn't guarantee upon resetting the computer that it would even see the transmission. I reluctantly had to go deal with this damn car lot. So damn reluctant, I continued to drive her anyway for another five weeks at a great top speed of ten.

I was so unattached and apathetic about having to take on a new car payment before the new year. I ended up with a payment on a car

I would never have looked twice at, on any other lot. Honestly it was the best option there. Just not impressed at all! So unimpressed and so unexcited that the official ritualistic naming of the car by my youngest daughter just didn't have the same appeal. Through the years I always let my youngest name the new vehicles. The first one was Penny, because every time we went around a corner the change in the console would fly out. The second was Carole, named after an absolute redneck couple, we liked to giggle about. Now the third, welcome to the family, Shitbag!

The car itself was fine. It was just my attitude and my reluctance with having to forfeit the last piece of safety from my old life. I was like a child misplacing their security blanket. I think for a short time I may have liked having a semi disabled car. It provided me with a great excuse to force people to only request errands once daily and I could passively aggressively project some of my disgruntled anger on it. Best yet, I didn't have to make the effort to even go visit anyone, including Sam.

Slapping Shuega
VIII.

The trial my stepfather had joined for cancer treatment would be for thirteen months, and I knew I would be driving him more frequently to appointments. My jovial department manager was undergoing chemo, and my hours had increased. Now I was also upstairs at this facility working in the business office helping. I absolutely adored the business manager there and had known her for years. Her bubbly cynicism and sarcasm were a match with mine. This woman had also battled breast cancer a couple years prior and thankfully was in remission. This area just has a massively high amount of cancer, it seems like everyone there gets it.

I could stare down from the third-floor center window of the office. I would stand there with the business manager and chit chat awaiting my next work order from her. She had passed me a salad as she was adamant about eating lunch. This was never on my list of priorities but for her I would force myself to eat half of a salad just for the company's sake. I had oddly zoned out, while I munched my rabbit lettuce and stared out at the road below. There in my peripheral view, walking solely, she caught my attention. Another memory from childhood. Shuega.

Shuega was a woman of vivid personality and ten years my senior. Growing up in this small area, we all knew from a very young age of Shuega's disabilities. Shuega was a mentally handicapped woman that loved Dire Straits. You could often find her rocking back and forth to her favorite song when we were younger. We knew we could interact with her, but to not disturb her. Always very friendly but with limited mental capabilities, the whole community embraced her, and we all accommodated her. She was very well known and loved within our community.

I could peer down at her now in her fifties, walking alone and very much appreciate all the hardships she had endured in her life up to this point as well. No longer appearing vivacious and talkative like when we were children, and I had no idea what her favorite song was anymore. It had been years since I had seen her. I could only stare down at her now and begin humming Money is for nothing and the chicks for free. I smirked and silently relived an occurrence between us from when I was nine.

I remember at this ripe old age for me, I was already damn near a pro at grocery shopping and looking for bargains. Like I had said before, my father never came home to live with us until I was ten, I was the oldest and my mother was agoraphobic. I had some adult responsibilities. I remembered standing in the store in the checkout line one day, with a few groceries in my hand. I remember reaching up to put the items on the counter and looking over as the old-fashioned bell on the entrance door caught my attention.

There like a child half my age bounced in Shuega, mind you ten years my senior. I remember at this age knowing of her condition, so just smiling politely at her and placing the last item on the counter. I wasn't even halfway to my eye contact with the cashier when I heard "Money is for," and the rocking began. I never looked her way, I never had time. Like a sting from a wasp, unsuspecting and totally caught off guard, Shuega reached over and slapped me right across my face. I could feel my nine-year-old face bounce, and I steadied my head.

I could look back on this moment and wonder why I never resorted to crying or becoming alarmed? I never felt bad for myself at that moment. I could only feel bad for her. As the cashier reprimanded her, I could hear her say sorry and watch her rocking become more agitated and profuse.

As I zoned out at my current age munching my lettuce, I could wonder why? Why did I not think about myself in that situation? Why did my feelings not matter? Why did I not holler or scream at her? Why did I not speak up? Why did I not slap her fucking face back? There were no societal expectations for a nine-year-old in that predicament. I never thought once, If I slap her back people will be mad. No thought at all about a repercussion for her on my behalf. Totally blank slate of just not caring about myself at all in that situation.

Wow, have I always thought like that? Did my mother just do an incredible job of instilling empathy in me? Was I just taught to put everyone else's needs before my own? More than likely the theme. Who knows. However, I had to slightly smirk at the thought of slapping her back now. What would society think? Hah? I laughed to myself as she trailed out of my eye line.

I could hear my grandfather again, quietly. "Nothing good will come of that." His words were about a power plant built relatively close to the area, just across the water. If his words were accurate then he already knew, while he himself at the age of 67 lay dying of brain cancer.

It's not the asbestos that some of these men were forced to work with or around. It's not the power plant across the water, or the 4+

radon levels that this state is marked for. It's not radio waves, cell phone towers now or hormones in food. It's not pesticides, medicines or vaccinations. It's always cigarettes. Do you smoke? No, well who around you smokes? Come on, the whole projection of shame onto an individual has long overstayed its welcome. Give the public something else to keep them angry and misaligned with the truth.

I suppose instead of naming every pharmaceutical medication ever prescribed to a person. Every job safety data sheet with a full list of chemicals and every household cleaner ever used. Any pesticides used in one's time, a complete study on any external obsolescence of their residencies throughout life, and a list of vaccinations injected into their bloodstream. Every food ever ingested, and a complete log of hours in traffic and their travel history, it probably is easier for all involved to just type on the death certificate, cigarette smoker. There goes the proverbial black sheep. Another maze on playing with people's emotions.

As a child, my best friend and I would go down behind her house to the water. We would battle the thick droves of slippery seaweed and the infestation of sand fleas. We could hang out in private and collect sea glass though. I would sit on a huge rock in the water and dangle my feet while I scanned the water and counted seagulls. Slapping the saltwater waves was a comfort and a peace of mind away from my insane family dysfunction. Now that I am older I could long to be able to do the same again someday. Slapping at saltwater without a care in the world, or even the idea of needing one. A simplistic ideal.

It had been close to thirty years, but I could still look back on this day with my childhood best friend and remember the innocence. The mind state of trying to figure it all out. My children now had surpassed the age I was that day. Funny how fast life passes us by.

Could I ever have sat there on that rock at fifteen and even imagined my life today? No, we cannot even begin to fathom the difficulties that await or the levels of maturity we will reach. We cannot comprehend the efforts, the struggles or the strength and reserve we will require in years to come. We just know at that moment, the little that we know. We know that we don't want what we have right then. Our lives will be different. We won't do the same that has been done to us. We want something different, without ever having a clue as to how to get there. We feel big beside the water, and we feel momentarily free and limitless.

It was this sunny afternoon that I spent with my childhood friend walking along the beach. Like I said this was a retreat for us, we did it semi often. This beach happened to hold one of the last dilapidated enclosed fish piers from the sardine canneries of my grandfather's and Gary's day. Although we had seen this dozens of times, it was this day that we decided to explore it.

Psyching each other up and grappling with the morality of it. We knew it had to be done. Nothing of any interest to a fifteen-year-old child. Absolutely nothing. The amount of effort we exerted to clammer on up and explore this, and it held no mysteries of the unknown. No massive riches and absolutely nothing that would be of interest for a typical fifteen-year-old child. In the far-left hand corner sat one lonely cardboard box, with papers inside. I guess just because it was in there, we had to peek.

The old papers it contained were receipts for jewelry stores, expensive dinners and travel receipts. Like I said nothing that would be of any interest to a fifteen-year-old child, until I caught the name of who they belonged to. J.N. I call him this out of respect for any of his remaining family and for his infamous role within our community. My best friend had never heard the stories, yet again her mother didn't host the neighborhood for coffee, and she didn't grow up privy to the "old lady" talks at her table.

J.N, it was always rumored that this man was from New York. He would come into town dressed lavishly, adorning a black trench coat and carrying a briefcase. He was eerily quiet and everyone that recalled being in his presence would describe it as "Evil." "Just pure evil that man, you can't describe it any other way." My mother would still get goosebumps to this day. To hear most recall him in my youth, they believed he had affiliations with the mafia, and believed he was responsible for several deaths within the area. "They could never prove it, but he was always the last to be seen." "We knew when we saw him, someone was going to die, we just never knew who."

"He was always the last to be seen with these people before we found them." "He was the last to be seen with several men, your dad's father included." I guess knowing the possibility that this J.N. character had murdered my paternal grandfather, always put a spin of interest on him for me. "He was never sloppy, they could never pin anything on him directly, it was cleaner and cleverer." I guess this may have been why J. N's notorious smirk was so entrenched with evil for those in the area.

I could stand here today reflecting on finding that box and really learning of the horror that loomed around this infamous character J.N. Everyone in the area from my mother's generation knew of him and he had affected everyone's lives on that island. None of the stories were "good." Not to make too much light of evil, but remembering the stories always made me think of "Rich."

Rich, if there was one person from my childhood that earned a spot as family it was this man. This man was a total pillar of strength, and I can honestly only reflect on him now and understand what I couldn't comprehend as a child. My mother and this man were best of friends. He visited all the time for coffee and was sometimes part of the coffee gatherings at my mother's table.

Rich was known in the area but not accepted by the community on a whole. He moved forward anyway to live in the truest authenticity that was allowed. Rich was a gay man before it was all right to be "Gay," but we all knew anyway. I always accepted him because he was a part of my mom, and she absolutely thought the world of him. Rich loved all of us and had begged my mother to give him my youngest sister to raise. His argument was always, "You can have more, I can't.

Although humorous to think about, I know that the sheer torment that this man lived during that time was more than likely unbearable. He would fix our hair for beauty pageants, and he just had a talent with hair that was indescribable. He was natural. He even cut my hair for my baby shower when I was pregnant with my oldest.

He was a fixture in our lives throughout our childhood years. Although he never asked me to give him my child, he would tear up in anticipation of being able to meet her when she arrived. He was so excited to meet her and my mother's first grandchild. He couldn't wait to hold her and would get giddy at the thought.

I could remember in my younger years Rich visiting my mother at odd times in the evening and he would always have a flask. Rich liked his drink, but who wouldn't, having to deal with those societal pressures? He had to cope with life somehow, feeling trapped and unaccepted by most. My mother just absolutely loved him and just rolled with whatever crazy predicament he found himself. She was always there to offer solid advice. I could see now where I always got it from. She raised me to always fight for the underdog, and I guess in this case, during that time, Rich would have been considered an underdog.

He had come to the house one night, intoxicated and looking for a shoulder to cry on. Like usual, except this time when he lifted his leg to cross the threshold from the outside porch to the kitchen, he slipped and broke his heel. Legs dressed in fishnets and his wig crooked from the impact, he began to cry out. He wanted to be a woman, he was trapped inside this repulsive man's body, and he could not take it anymore.

I believe this was the only time I heard my mother get irritated with him. "Richie damnit." I love you, and we will talk. You go into the bathroom, wipe that makeup off your face and put on some of my pajamas. What are the kids going to think if they see you like this? I am going to make you some coffee to help sober you up and you are staying here tonight. No more driving. Her heart broke for his predicament, but she had to shield us too during that time, so I understand why she did as she did.

Through all the hardships he endured, throughout the years he was part of my family, I learned a lot just by observing my mother's acceptance and love for people just as they were. He was so excited when I had my daughter, he went to my mother's house to see if he could catch me there and called to see how everything went. Rich never did get to meet my daughter; he died of an overdose before she turned three weeks.

Fifteen years later when gay marriage was finally enacted, the one person I mostly wanted to congratulate for his struggles, was not there anymore. I knew he would have rejoiced on that day, and I did too in his memory. Oh, how I wished he was still alive to finally live his life. It has been 23 years since I last saw his face, but I can see it clearly like it was yesterday.

I think about Rich when recalling J.N, because he too had a brother that fell prey to the "Last to be seen." Rich would chime in with the stories just like all the others had. He too joined in with the consensus of "evil." Like my paternal grandfather, his brother and all the others, he had the strong belief that he had been murdered in an unlikely way.

His brother, much like my grandfather, was last seen with J.N. before his death. His brother had gone out drinking and someone had slipped something extra in his beer. J.N, apparently worried about the amount of projectile vomiting Rich's brother was suddenly inflicted with, found it would be best to drive him home safely. He put him in his own backseat, laid him on his back and let the man choke to death on his own projectile vomit. I suppose one incident of this could easily be written off. He was only trying to help. If paired with others that's when the true evil intent comes into play.

Another resident was last seen drinking in a boat alone with J.N. He jumped over in his intoxicated state and just never resurfaced, or so it was said. Another man left to freeze to death in an open field. My paternal grandfather, although last seen with J.N, didn't get the same kind of sendoff. My grandfather, much like Rich's brother and all the others, was drinking too. My grandfather's remains, however, were found inside a half burnt down home, wrists still bound to the doorknob with a bed blocking the doorway.

They say in life we get our karma. They say we leave the legend we choose to leave. Do we though? Do we all get that luxury? Avery, a little frail shell of a man. Having dementia and the absolute inability to recall his past or even acknowledge his current surroundings. Lively though and I must admit, quite cute.

He would holler from his wheelchair. "What are we going to do? Where are you taking me? As he frantically rolled away, never waiting for a reply. I must admit he was one of my faves. He would be adamant about the fact that he wanted Jesus to take him now. "Get me the fuck out of here, why do I have to stay here?" His eyes would be intently fixed but with a dazed effect. He would holler in a demanding and disgruntled way. All the residents of the old age home had ankle monitors so they couldn't wander outside, but this man couldn't have if he wanted to.

Are the elderly acknowledged for their pasts? Do we know their stories of the incredibleness that they experienced or what we learned from their existence? Do we know how they touched previous lives? Do we know of their accomplishments, their failures, their regrets? Do we take the time to learn from them? They are after all; all we have that links us to our past. Please take the time to understand what you can from another's life.

I could watch Avery forcefully and feverishly holler at all the younger nurses that passed him by. I could watch him try to stand from his wheelchair. I could hear his frustration. I could hear him holler at God and I could hear him sob and beg for God to take him home now. While I could watch the nurses smile at him and ask if he wanted to go lay down, all I could do was just stand there in awe. They never had a clue. They never had a clue that Avery in his younger years had a beautiful sixteen-year-old daughter. They never knew that this daughter was much desired by pure evil and that J.N. would advance on her sexually any chance he got. They never had a clue of the fear this little girl felt as a target by this community's most prolific, and they never knew the incredible lengths that Avery went to protect his baby.

My mother can still recall standing on the railroad tracks above Avery's home, the day they zipped the body bag around J. N's corpse. One single shot to the back, it dropped him. Avery told him not to come around his daughter again, but he did anyway. The whole town looked on cheering for this momentous occurrence, but Avery went away for murder. They never knew that this feeble, frail and dementia ridden man had not only been responsible for the death of J.N, but also the sigh of relief for this town. They never knew in his younger days that this man was deemed a hometown hero. Avery, as I stood there looking on, didn't even know it himself, anymore.

Working there always had me question life. The fickleness of it, the chosen over the unchosen. Live long and prosper, only the good die young. As I looked on most days at the residents, I would question those notions and I would always be left to wonder. Why these people but not others? Were they left to linger for a life lived wrong? Did they still need to learn lessons before God would take them home? Or were they chosen to stay longer for the rest of us, so we could learn? Who knows the why of it, only God. I choose to believe they are still here because God needs to use them to help other people learn. We need to do it quickly though because most of them are not happy about it.

Mitchell still called every day, but another Christmas had come and gone and still no communication from his angelic well-intentioned public defender. I had been forced to let go of my old life all together. Right down to most of the materialism, and with the most recent being my old beloved Carole car. I wondered if I was supposed to leave him completely behind too. Was this what God was instructing me to do now? I still felt a massive connection to him, but I was tired. I didn't have the same gusto as when I first arrived here seventeen months ago. Another round of snow, ice and freezing temperatures was upon us with the new year, and I was losing steam again.

The maximum of three months of fairly decent weather made it hard to sustain a jovial go-getter mindset. Especially when the dreary snow and ice rolled back in. I felt like a broken solar panel. It can't help light up shit, if it's been sitting in a dark closet for seventeen months, and I couldn't either. I missed the sun and good weather so much. Every time I heard the abnormally loud snowplow turn our corner; I could envision all the snow it just stacked up behind my fucking car in the driveway. Great, I can't wait to shovel that out with my 120-pound ass in the wee hours of the morning. The old people need eggs to stare at and complain about though.

I would become so annoyed that I would discreetly ask other people about the disarmament of heavy equipment. Fantasizing fondly of laying out booby traps to blow off its tires. I would think better though when the realization that it was actually a job that employed someone in that area hit me. Those around here were like tampons at a rest stop, hard to find. Instead, I settled on the fact that he was probably just as miserable doing it, as I was of hearing it. So, I would just smirk and wave at him from the upstairs window like some old obsessive psycho.

You know through all these years; I never did drugs. Never had an interest, had opportunity upon opportunity to try them all, never interested me. Mitchell was always high on something, and I fought with him constantly trying to get him to see my viewpoint. Trying to get him sober. I had been through damn near any scenario someone could think of with a drug addict, and I never caved. Never once said, if you can't beat him join him. Never once appealed to me. I could honestly see very clearly why people would cave to drug abuse around this dismal, lackluster area, but that would be just my luck too.

I can see it now; I have already lost thirty pounds from surgery and anxiety. I could barely eat anymore; the food wasn't appealing. I could visually see my face sunken in, but the thought of food just made me sicker. The thought of eating took me some time just to get in the mood for. I was now trying to force myself to eat at least once every day.

I could envision it now, trying some drug for the first time ever in my life and overdosing. This area was notorious for overdosing. I had lost dozens upon dozens of acquaintances and schoolmates from this through the years. I can hear it now, poor girl, I never knew she was a heroin addict, that explains her weight loss. Those poor kids never stood a chance with a mother like that. Her poor mother and sisters. It's too bad really, she was so pretty and had so much going for her when she was younger. The drugs just took their toll through the years though. No, I am too stubborn to give anyone that satisfaction. I guess I will have to stay sober and ride this dog turd of an existence out.

I would spend a chunk of my free time talking with Sam on the phone. We could talk for hours and although it never fostered any feelings of sexual desire, it emotionally comforted me to know someone was there to listen. Just like high school all over again. A deep love for this man just out of respect for his emotional support throughout a good portion of my earlier life. We could be that for each other now. We were both trying to recover from a hailstorm of shit in our own individual lives. The dynamic hadn't changed one notch, we were still heavily unified on the friend front. Although I would have loved to have had that with Mitchell at that time. Our monitored fifteen-minute phone calls never allowed for discussions on anything besides surface beliefs and the ignorant grovel between us both.

My family had made remarks on my dating status. I could tell they were concerned. I mean what mother wants her 40+ year old daughter living upstairs? Knowing she had to come back because of the games her ex was playing with her youngest child. Knowing she needed a mental retreat from toxic business partners and her felon inmate boyfriend? That doesn't exactly scream stability, and as a mother we are comforted knowing our children are comforted.

I knew where she was coming from. I got hit on constantly but would always find some excuse as to why I couldn't date them. No fault of their own, I just wasn't directed that way. God still had me on reserve for Mitchell apparently. I didn't even want to start dating. More constraints on my time. I just don't want to play the relationship game. I got me buddy, I am fine!

"You are as stubborn as your grandmother, you know. She wouldn't even put her glasses on to pass her driver's test." "She said there is no need for anyone to see that good, and she failed." I would chuckle because I did inherit some stubborn staying power, but that had nothing to do with wanting to stay single.

I don't need drama. Someone else's problems, drama. They have a baby momma with controlling demands of the kids, because she is jealous, he is moving on. Drama. Their kids running to momma innocently creating more drama. He still wants to do his thing, while he takes for granted, I am going to watch his children, because I am a mother myself. More drama. All the shit that goes on! Who wants it? Not me but thank you. I mean honestly who wants to date a woman that is going to call you out on every drop of your bullshit? Most times without blinking. Not going to be very fun for them either. Plus, I will just get annoyed with their inability to step up to my level. I will just have to pack my shit up and leave them and their kids. I already see the end, so why begin?

Sam and I bouncing our problems off each other through the phone was fine enough for me. He in a strange way helped restore some kind of resemblance of my old self. Not a resemblance of hope or prosperity in that area. I still couldn't see in front of me, but I always knew who I belonged with. That knowing never wavered, physically there or not. God wasn't going to allow me to divert from his path that he had for me.

It was a couple of months prior to this, when I had taken my step-father for his cancer diagnosis, when my beloved car shit the bed on my birthday. This is when more drama had entered the overall equation. I can clearly look at most other predicaments and see that life's little trials and tribulations are thrown their way for the betterment of one's soul. I also realize most people do not view life in the same way I do. We may not be happy with it, but things are done for us, not to us.

My birthday week unbeknownst to me, would be a week that would go down in infamy. One of my mother's dearest childhood friends had moved back to the area. She was living with her sister after a separation. She would circulate between a thirty-mile radius of old friends and family and was very sociable. She was still out partying and still living the lifestyle of a teenager. This woman would draw you in with her wildness and her stories, but you knew she was a barely recovering addict with a sorted past and flourished in instability. Pretty much the same energy as Mitchell. Either way we loved her. Her re-appearance in my mother's life was not just for joy and nostalgia. It was for pain, transformation, and a little lesson for me as well. I could never understand the depth of this at the time, it is always one of those hindsight twenty-twenty jobbies, but I appreciate it no less.

My mother's childhood friend had happened to dance to the correct social scene. She was there at the right time to overhear some information that may be of concern for my mother. So apparently as I was driving my stepfather back from his cancer diagnosis, my mother was learning of his infidelity. Knowing a woman's blind fury and scorn, I think she is probably the reason behind my beloved car's transmission dying. She didn't aim her lightning bolt of hatred quite far enough. A few more feet behind the transmission mom you would have had him, but poor Carole had to take one for the team.

This was clearly a test of resilience, forgiveness and self-love, but my mother didn't see it that way. What do you do? What is the correct thing to do? Do you put your own feelings of betrayal and absolute rage aside for his betterment? I did it for Mitchell.

Every day when he called. Even when he would provoke me with his disgusting insults and sheer unfounded jealousy, I never caved. I never said a word over those jail phones. I held steady for his own good. I could have raged enough to put him and numerous others away for a decade or two. I put Mitchell and his doubts, fears and worries before my own. Sometimes all I wanted to do was drive down there and punch him right in the throat.

Do you hold back your own perspective of hurt and betrayal? Your absolute disgust and rage to show concern for his cancer diagnosis? Do you lovingly help him with everything needed? Do you just not say a word, so as not to upset him in his newly found delicate state? Do you want to put more stress on him? What do you do? You more than likely do what most do and so did my mother.

The energy in that home was absolutely tension fueled and so were the countless arguments. It would break my fucking heart to hear my mother cry out like a wounded animal in pain downstairs and equally so to hear a cancer stricken, quiet man sob all alone. I made it quite clear it was not my battle, and I would not take sides. I loved them both just in different ways. What has happened has happened between you two. I can talk with you and offer advice. I can try to help you see things from the others perspective. I can be there for you to vent, but I will still be available to take him to doctors' appointments and run errands when he needs me. I was not taking sides, and my mother never expected me to.

"I just want to leave, I never wanted to be back here." I miss my old life, I miss the nice weather, I miss my own business. I miss when my kids were younger, and it's so bad, I even miss that shitty ass moldy house. I had been back in Maine now for eighteen months and Mitchell had been in the county for twenty-two, with only two visits and a plea offer from his attorney. We still had no information or any nearing signs of being able to figure out the future. We were still very much up in the air. No plans and no end in sight.

His court appointed knew if another plea offer couldn't be offered then a trial would be where we were going. Just like the last time his mother pulled this shit. He won in trial last time though, so I know the slimy DA was not willing to take another hit to her record. The malicious intent of the DA was more than obvious. It had been months since the plea offer and still no communication of any kind from his public defender. Never mind a strategy for trial, but no worries, public defender. You are home at night eating food that isn't marked for zoo animal consumption. You are sleeping on a mattress not a kinder mat on a concrete floor. You are taking a shit in a bathroom with a door, no one holding up a sheet for you. I suppose under your comforts none of it would bother you. This is how people with charges are treated, relevance to them or not, they get to you when they get to you in that county.

I could check the time spans of other inmates held with him. Most with arrest dates after his and they had all come and gone. Child molesters, rapists, murderers, small time drug addicts, dealers, assaults, breaking and entering, and theft. The whole gamut of crimes had been sentenced or had pleaded out. Some of these people had pleaded out, done their time and were back in for another crime. Yet, there Mitchell sat, with no communication out of pure maliciousness from the DA. The biggest whiny, passive aggressive, immature, childish criminal of them all.

Who needs to sue on those grounds, the odds are stacked against you from the beginning. However, try as you might, man's law holds absolutely no weight to God's law. You will be dealt the same as you have dealt. I don't give a shit what you have accomplished in this earthly realm, or who you believe yourself to be. You do not get final judgment, God does, and you will be judged accordingly.

Everything is a test, and you are always the student. Most people are not going to be aware of that while they are running around. Ninety things to contend with and shear stress. They are actually sitting down taking a damn exam. We know the simple answer to a math test placed in front of us. 11 +21 = 32, simple right?

How about if you are hanging upside down from a swing with an eyepatch on with a blow torch to your feet? While a gang stands around throwing rocks at your face, and your kids are screaming because the other one ate the last chicken nugget. Your family's dog is stricken with parvo and you're about to lose your family home. Your husband has been running around with the neighborhood tramp because he can't take the stress. You have no employable skills because you gave up college to be a wife and no other family to turn to?

Either way, you get the idea. Your external circumstances can make it a lot harder on you to come up with the right answer. Especially while you're lost in a moment of self-preservation. Most people are going to fail a simple test when too distracted in their own thoughts and perspective.

Let's make a deal though. I will take the blowtorch away from your feet, if you let me kill the dog in front of your children. Look at that, it will take the heat off from you and you will no longer have to worry about the dog's problems. The shock to your children having to witness that will stop their foolish argument over a chicken nugget. Is it easier for you now? Those are the deals the devil offers to make it easier on you, but at what cost to you and others? At what cost to your core? He doesn't make it happen; it's your own choice. He always gives you a choice. God expects his children to concentrate on the test, regardless of obstacles. The devil draws more attention to the distractions. Choose wisely.

No man is free from sin, it's never going to happen. Religion preaches the elimination of sin. It's not going to happen. People are people and they are imperfect, by design. Where does the line of sin stop? Is breaking a man-made law a sin? If that is the case, the amount of sin increases every day. Spirituality teaches the eradication of ignorance. All people are born to be imperfect, and they have the capability of learning. Children absorb like sponges, and they are going to learn what they see, and are told. They adapt from there. The amount of awareness can also be increased every day.

Pink Flam-a-goes
IX.

I could feel my level of anxiety increase as she leaned into my ear. I couldn't move as usual, but I knew. In the dark of the night as I lay there frozen, I could feel her breath in my ear. I could feel her face against the back of my head. I could hear the whisper of "I love you and I am so proud of you." "You are not my mother; she wouldn't say either of those things.' As quickly as it appeared it left. Trying to come to me in the form of my mother's acceptance. You have got to be kidding me. Weak.

The arguing grew louder and louder as my days of mundane existence carried on. My stepdad being present and trying desperately to regain my mother's trust and approval while fighting cancer. Her anger and despair grew deeper and deeper. I would have discussions with my sisters on their thoughts of the situation, but I was there every day. They didn't have to live among the repercussions of our stepdads and mother's actions. They actually were afforded the stability of a home from their husbands or ex-husbands. Due to pure exhaustion, I couldn't handle any further confrontations in my life. As such I never pursued or got the luxury of other women.

I would empathetically and logically try to get mom to see his side, while I aimed for her to learn her own lessons. I was exhausted and it felt most of the time like I was throwing a match into a dried out well. Just drying my well up more. Still God allowed me to endure and keep trying for her to see. I like to think she may have retained some of the self-help I threw her way. When I was way too tired, I suggested videos on other women that had been through the same thing as her. I figured in her own time, in private this may help her to evolve.

My mother never did drugs and barely drank through the years. She was never judgmental and was willing to help anyone with the little resources she had. Her likeness had been instilled in me. I still remember the very statement she hollered in agony when my dad was packing up to leave her, "How can you leave the mentally ill?" Kids, you don't leave the mentally ill ever.

I know in modern day psychology this could be a spin of en-meshment and manipulation. However, I always chose to see this as a good-hearted well-intentioned woman feeling completely abandoned. I know a good majority of mentally ill, will become completely erratic emotionally when faced with this. I would hear her voice echo some-times when Mitchell was in the heat of the moment. "You don't leave the mentally ill."

I could see Mitchell and I one day as if a mirror was being held to my face. The boundary was laid down by my mother. "No more drinking in here." Her old high school friend, enraged with a boundary much like Mitchell always was, became hostile. The hostility that was displayed towards my mother as she stood tall at the bottom of the stairs was uncanny. Much like the way I would stand when Mitchell would do the same thing.

I am absolutely within my rights to demand sobriety in my house, especially for the sake of my children. As my mother was well within her rights to demand "No more drinking in here." We let the behavior go on for a bit, but someone has a limit to how much they are willing to watch a loved one self-destruct. We can only help for so long and then you need to take the initiative to help yourself. We have provided you with support and a stable environment in which to do that and you are just taking our kindness for weakness. Do not take what I am offering for granted, that is not why it was offered. It was offered out of a genuine interest in helping you. People that had to learn to manipulate for childhood survival, are usually still manipulating in adulthood though.

This high school friend stood within inches of my mother's face threatening to call the police on her for trying to kick her out. She stood there threatening to physically hurt her. She stood there demanding her money back that she gave mom to watch her dog and called her every name in the book. I just stood there looking down the stairs and realizing I was being shown my past through another perspective. I never said a word, but I stood by to make sure no fists were thrown. I would have to step in then.

The high school friend stormed out angrily and my mother just looked at me with a perplexed look of sadness, anger, and confusion. I hugged her and said, "She will be back; Mitchell does the same exact thing." She didn't like being called out on her behavior & her lifelong coping mechanism. She learned that because of the horrible childhood trauma and betrayal that she endured. She drinks to numb herself to it.

Blowing up like that assures her that she is slightly in control of her own decisions still. It also buys her some time for you to feel bad and try to invite her back. I know who is right, but that's how they measure love. If you love them enough you will want to make amends and justify your thoughts, hoping to receive a resolution. They then believe they have you hooked enough to keep emotionally manipulating, except they are not even aware of their own cycle. Hence the massive amounts of apologies and I didn't mean it pleas. Her high school friend's behavior was a mirror to Mitchells. They had both been diagnosed with BPD. If we are receptive enough, God and the universe throw us signs and lessons all the time.

My newest crazy thought during this time was the Pink Flamingo. I was leaving my direction to God and his universe at this time. I willy-nilly threw out my intentions to follow the Pink Flamingo. My true happiness will be marked with a pink flamingo. I rarely see them and the thought of one had just popped up due to a prior conversation of its mispronunciation. Flam a go. I giggled about this and thought, Perfect Flam a go can direct my path. I know, but hell at this point who cares!

My manager at work was luckily just wrapping up her Chemo treatments and was doing amazing. The rumor mill buzz word was that she would be returning in no time. My stepdad had luckily been accepted into the trial, group C, and I felt a lot better about his chances. Although they still constantly fought, and the high school friend was there for added drama's sake, I knew I had the option to escape if ever I needed it.

I had decided prior to all the drama and misfortunes that I needed to take classes to advance my prior career field. This gave me a direction and a goal to work on. Something so I wouldn't feel so mentally stuck. Trying to take classes and exams in the middle of all the demands and fighting is impossible though. I found myself having to escape.

With the numbers 1212 and 1222 being the only ones of significance, and never in excess, I found myself trying to weigh out the proper road. Continue putting my needs aside? Continue putting what I need to accomplish aside? Continue doing it for everyone else and never doing for myself? Apparently, the universe didn't want me leaving this God forsaken land of shit.

My second mothers' death, both of my dear friends' deaths, no release date for Mitchell within sight still. My department manager's cancer and treatment and my stepfather's cancer diagnosis. The transmission blowing in Carole. The strange and coincidental run in with Sam. A former confession to God, with the regrets from yesteryears. My mother's heartbreak from my stepdad's infidelity. Apparently, I am supposed to be here for some reason. God and the Universe knows damn well if there was any predicament it could put me in, it would be this. Forcing me to reanalyze my love for Mitchell with an opening with Sam.

"He would be good to you." "He would work his ass off to support you." "He worships you." "He has loved you forever." "You can't keep waiting, what if he gets ten years?" "You will be an old damn woman still waiting for him to get out." "We know you love him, but you don't know when he is getting out." "This one is here now, and he loves you and worships the ground you walk on." Ughh, is all I could mutter. I don't give a good crap about love anymore. I can't be bothered. He is a friend; a great friend and he always will be. Can he engage me mentally and stimulate me conversation wise? Hell yeah, he is super intelligent, I love talking to him. It's so refreshing to be able to have a little piece of my past. Someone intelligent enough to connect the dots and be self-aware and engaged enough to offer me advice. I used him almost as a mini psychologist. After so many times of being everyone else's, I got one for a change.

He had offered me several times his apartment space to take my classes in the quiet. I wouldn't take him up on it because I preferred working from my desktop. Moving that up there was somewhat of a chore and not of any interest to me. My mother's house was a half of a mile from work, his apartment was thirty plus. I liked my odds of getting to work at 5a better from my mothers. The home rental options were scarce and with every heartbreaking encounter of wailing and fighting, I could feel myself talking to God more and more about going to Sam's.

The visual of Sam smirking insanely and stating "I am not the same kid from high school. I have changed, I am not as you remember." The conversations I had within myself justified the fact that it was not my job to judge. We don't all live the same. Just because I have no criminal background, doesn't mean that others are necessarily bad, people make mistakes. Just because I don't sleep with a sword next to my bed and a baseball bat across the room doesn't make me better. I don't know the trauma or the state of mind he obtained from doing prison time. Just because I don't use heroin doesn't make me better by any means.

I could relive the night I stood in his apartment and watched his dealer drop off his goods. I could see the angst in his eyes and the shame behind his disgruntled smirk. Anxiously hesitating as he stroked his leather belt hanging from the back of his chair. "Go ahead, don't let me stop you."

Although extremely hesitant to do so, he knew enough of me to know I wasn't going to judge his choice. I have found that addicts are ashamed to shoot up in front of people they have respect for. He bravely talked his situation up enough to be able to do this in front of me. He kept his body angled inwards though and never looked at me as he leaned into the wall. You could almost feel his shame radiate, but I had been gone out of his life longer than these drugs had been in it. His loyalty at that time was going to be to self.

This man lived for his son. His insanely intelligent, dare I say autistic savant son. There was no drama with the ex, they co parented beautifully and why would they not. She didn't want him anymore and quite frankly I understood why. Sam, an extremely intelligent, motivated, and ambitious mind. He could have very well been a psychologist with ease or a great philosopher.

He was now divorced, living back here with a criminal record and a heroin addiction. Seriously universe? Why would you go through all this trouble of granting me a second chance at life, with this? Slap in the face! I trusted so much in the universe and its direction that I began to talk myself into this possibly being my new destined reality.

Do I want to bother with a heroin addict? Seriously, do I? Do I want to start over with a man that has far more and way worse felonies than Mitchell ever thought of committing? Why would the fucking universe do this? Was this one of those careful what you wish for jobs? It had to have known I didn't have the energy to put in to this one, or even the notion of desire to. Maybe it was one of those silent understandings of the universe baiting me. How much do you trust the universe? How much are you willing to put yourself through? This is a test, if you leap into something that logically makes no sense to do, it will show your loyalty to God. It will show God that you mean it and that you truly follow him.

As reluctant as I was with any of it knowing his current lifestyle, I also knew that God would not have coincidentally set this up. There are no coincidences, just opportunities. Maybe this was my opportunity in a logical sense to void my prayer to God from a little while back, or maybe it was a test. Who the hell knows, but apparently, I was being forced to try to find out the why behind it all.

Grocery shopping seems like a pretty neutral friendly thing to do together as friends, but it was more than fucking painful for me. Even the thoughts of grocery shopping with someone were more attachment than I was willing to budge on. Mitchell and I used to do that together, well once upon a time before meth took over. Grocery shopping with another man was just too much of a line to cross. I will take him in my mind, because I don't want him starving to death and he needs a ride. I am helping him out, we are not a couple, so I have nothing to worry about.

As I sauntered the aisles of the grocery store, I could count his paces in front of me. Long strides, no interest in walking with me at all. He was on a mission, and this made it so much easier for me. He didn't want to be with me anymore than I wanted to be with him, so friends it is.

Ahh thank you God. I looked down to gaze upon the contents of a food cooler. Behold, I hadn't seen one in a long time. A frozen alcoholic beverage like I used to sip upon at the beach. I started reminiscing and then I focused more intently. There on the front of the bag standing in all its one balanced glory, the Pink Flam a go. Freezing for a brief nano moment, I knew the universe was either signaling to me about Sam or the booze. It let me know I was on the right path. I decided though, I would probably find more happiness sitting outside on the porch in a snowstorm, sipping off a frozen alcoholic drink. I bought two, not to share, but why not double my happiness?

At this point I must begin to question the so-called norm. Apophenia? It amuses me slightly. Not because of the name or the belief in this, but the stifling belief by a community of so-called experts that believe this to be of the abnormal range. Range of mental illness? I found moderate amusement with different articles throughout this time on various subjects. I prefer to think of this as the ability to see patterns. The ability to look deeper to predict future patterns.

Everyone has an opinion, much like everyone has an asshole. They both have different openings for shit. Seems to me the released impact of another's opinion is the heaviest of the two shits. Not ever to deny that "It takes all kinds' ' Everyone is going to have a differing opinion on all subjects. That is what we consider uniqueness and individualism. We have to be open to another's perspective and not to the point that we stifle or invalidate, but to the point that we question. Stir another's mind. We must not live to force our opinion on another. We all acknowledge what we will do in our own time, in our own way, on our own journey.

However, some of you social justice warriors, hard core feminists, and pro or anti-abortion people, are ruthless. Although I respect your opinions, understand that you appear to have anger issues. Anger and passion are not the same thing. Using a basic form of manipulation like shaming another into your beliefs is a far cry from having an intelligent conversation or healthy debate. Some of you are illogical.

Am I going to go to a gynecologist for brain surgery? No, no more than I am going to listen to a twenty-two-year-old little girl holler at me about women's rights. I don't care how much you think you know about the subject. Baby, life will teach you more than a book ever will. Am I going to go to a proctologist for a heart issue? No, no more than I want to see a man standing in the streets hollering about abortion. I understand and respect your opinion. I can understand your beliefs, but I don't see your solution to the problem. There are no solutions you are willing to provide with your "Angrily passionate opinions." None of you! Where are your solutions?

Are you going to be those little girls emotional support? Are you going to be there through thick and thin? Are you going to physically be there to comfort her through the pain? Are you going to be there to financially support her and her future goals? Are you going to be there tonight to relieve her, so she doesn't have a mental breakdown? Are you? Or are you hoping to make the change one person at a time with your act of shaming?

Even if you are willing to do that for a girl, that is one girl. That would make you a man. The problem lies with the fact these boys are not willing to do any of that and she needs a lot of support. Not only physically during and after, but emotionally as well. She already understands that a baby isn't going to keep this boy with her. That is her path to walk. Her horrible decision to have to face. Her trauma, while the little boy shames her and escapes all accountability. Some men are even the driving force behind these abortions, insisting that the girl must have one. Unless you have something better to offer her, she doesn't need another dose of shame, anti-abortion man!

We already understand as a society that the supposed statistics for domestic abuse are one in three. Of course, this is only the reported cases, I personally believe the numbers to be higher. If a man has no problem punching a woman in the face and breaking out her teeth, what makes you think he would have a problem with raping her? The ultimate control for an abusive man, eighteen more years of this woman having to put up with his abuse. She can go nowhere now.

She will be forced to raise his children in an abusive environment and the children will grow up in complete instability. Repeating the same cycle. Seems to me, it is much easier for an abused woman to escape with less children. It has never been about women's rights. Stop with the levels of misdirection and the fighting. It is about population increase and control. Like I said no one on this earth understands what these women must endure or the difficulties of their own stories. One mother enmeshed disgruntled man's delusional view of all women does not make it so.

Do you have any children? Have you sat at home at night and had to comfort and nurture your child? You wouldn't want anyone else in the world to take your place then. That is your job and you do it with ease and desire. Have you sung to your child, have you kissed their boo boos, have you helped guide them on their most down days? Have you been there to hug them when they are questioning their self-worth or why the little boy in the cafeteria keeps being mean to them and pulling their hair? Don't be angry with just these little things that you don't understand yet, Hardcore feminist!

Social Justice Warriors, with your full gamut of things to be angry about. We see your point; we appreciate your opinion. Just because people don't get as equally angry as you do does not mean they don't share the same or a semblance of the same. Most of you are younger. Different priorities. We birthed you for Christ Sakes. We birthed you to take over where we were too tired to continue. Go forth, be the change we need, but know, we are fucking old now. We admire your fire, and we can relive our fire through you. Do us right, do us proud, but for fuck sakes do it better than we did!

Anyway, it made me think about the "professional" opinions of Jesus. I remember reading articles on Jesus' Christ's mental health being questioned. A man that was idolized for being the son of God. A messiah, a prophet, a man that did nothing but give and help. I burst out laughing. The audacity of these people. Not because of who Jesus supposedly was, we could argue different avenues with that all damn day. Instead, I laughed because of who they thought they were.

Every person on this planet would have a trait or two of just about every so-called mental disorder. It is nowhere near an exact science. Yet we applaud its broadness and apply it every day to a self-centered state. A man that existed centuries prior to any living man on this planet today. He exhibited signs of "niceness" and the belief of kindness and humbleness. Regardless of the obstacles, people followed him and helped to spread his word. What fucking harm was it doing?

Oh no this man who is nice must have been mentally ill. Why because the complete norm at the time was to walk among douchebags that didn't know any better? Is that how people are measured today? The nice are mentally ill because they stand out from the range of normal douchebags. Seems to me the mean ones are abnormal too. Outside the median of the range, makes for either or. Does it make them abnormal? Well, look we are all well within our normal range and rights to be indecent douchebags, I guess. Too nice, mentally ill. Too much of a douchebag, mean psycho serial killer. Got to be just the right amount of indecent douchebag if you want to cut it within this world.

A cult leader? Change in perspective? What if you live in shit town? Called that because the residents of the town decided it was all fun to mimic the animalistic behavior of monkeys and fling shit at other people. I come into town and decide I don't want to fling shit; I want to instead clean it. Now I would technically be abnormal, wouldn't I? Outside the range of normal behavior. What if twelve others decided with me, they would rather clean it than fling it? Am I now the leader of the anti shit flinging cult? What if everyone in town decided they would all rather clean it? I have started a revolution of sorts have I not?

We have all decided we are not going to participate in the shit flinging required of the town. Are we now all sovereign citizens, because we believe the man laws of flinging shit no longer fulfill us? How about if one man gets mad that we are not flinging shit anymore and continues his behavior. Is he not the abnormal one now? He was normal last month.

How about if we have equal shit flingers and equal shit cleaners, and one person comes into town and wants to roll in the shit. Who is outside the norm now? How and which one has mental illness? Which one's thinking is not aligned with everyone else's? It's still all centered around shit, isn't it? So still all normal, no one has veered from the shit yet. Now, what if I waltz into shit town and want to spend my Saturday nights making quilts for the homeless? Now I am really disturbed, because my life has nothing to do with the shit others focus their lives around?

Gladiators were considered normal. When was this marked for normal and what was the central ideal when discovered? How about the people that found it bothersome, were they abnormal then, because they would be considered normal now. The enslaved men of those days were considered property and trained to fight to the death. The race of the man was not a factor. It would almost make a person wonder why the entire history of slavery is not taught in public schools. Does it suit a better agenda of propelling hate and distractions to only teach on one time?

The psycho serial killer of those days was considered normal. Civilized society now? Who decided this was civilized or whose behavior marked a new wave in respect for others? Seems that mental illness or not, Jesus had a massive effect on society as we now know it today. Always discounting the actions of others, in your race to prove that you are unique. It's pompous.

Introversion, a mental illness? Does it interfere with your everyday activities? Does it affect your life? If so, it could be considered as such. We all know that to study and understand the human mind that a severe amount of introversion is implied. An extroverted person is not going to have the desire to analyze to that degree, nor the know-how. They are more validated with people and centered in a different idealistic. Some of the very people that preach mental illness are the very people of introverted status. However, when it applies to them, it is not a mental illness, just an energy. It doesn't affect their life or their ability to hold a job, because it is their life and job. Ahh thank you professionals, keep shining your professionalism, we would be lost without it.

It would make sense to me that if a heart can reroute an artery due to being clogged for survival, then the brain can rewire for survival due to trauma. Where do the new wires go? Some would insist on mental illness, while others would insist, they reroute to a higher understanding.

Chili Cook off
X.

After everything that had kept me stuck up here, I was ready to venture away. I didn't know how, but I had to start gearing my mind up towards leaving. The excitement was there, just not the plan. I had countless offers to move with different people, but my heart wasn't in it. I am not going to go shack up with someone with their insistent demands just to have a place to go. I could stay where I was if that was the case. Misery here or misery there, is still misery.

Within a week's time, I was talking to people back in my old area and beginning to recirculate my brain's deadened activity. I was starting to get excited again, finally. I was so relieved. I had been through so much, just since my oldest graduated high school, three years ago. I was coming out the other side though. I was just excited to be able to get excited again. Then it hit. The fucking covid!

Oh my God, you really do want me stuck here, don't you? You really don't want me to leave this damn place. You really don't want me to be happy. Why? What did I do? Not to make light of a pandemic, and I never under any circumstances believed this to be centered around me, but I had to frown at the irony involved concerning my situation. Apparently, I hadn't served enough time in my own reflection. Either that or the universe was keeping me stuck here.

Forcing me to either wait for Mitchell or to force me to spend more time with Sam.

One thing was for certain. If I was supposed to be here with him, if the universe was keeping me trapped here to force me to try to love someone else, then it would have to be a lot smoother than anything with Mitchell ever was. I envisioned niceties, and respect for each other. You know like they say relationships are supposed to have? I knew we had respect, and we were on the same page depth wise. We could have long conversations pertaining to the surface and the deep. I wasn't in love with him, but perhaps with a lot of time I could learn to be? I wasn't happy with this prospect at all, but I guess people were right. I did need to start amending my mind to a prospect. Why not?

Mitchell could be in for the next ten years. Sam already knew a good chunk of my past. We wouldn't need to figure that out anyway. We were open with each other about pretty much everything, and we were complete idiots with each other. Maybe that is what a relationship is supposed to be? Far for me to guess. I just knew I wasn't going to tolerate any disrespect or abuse. No hollering in my face, no forcing your demands on me. No belief that I am here to serve you. I will walk the fuck away. I wasn't going to have to worry about that with him and that gave me a huge sense of relief. Expectations yet basic and very minimal again.

As the popular phrase circulates "Go into it with no expectations" I am yet again going to state that even when you don't think you have any, you find out some damn quick that you actually do.

"I just bleached in here." "I work at an old age home." "One case of covid would destroy the whole facility." "You are quite aware of where I work, and I don't want to be responsible for making anyone sick."

I was considered an essential worker. No unemployment for me, no using this for an excuse to be lazy or to collect benefits, like some. "Well, they were only here for a couple of hours." He assured me he bleached behind them and that they wore masks, so it was all good.

So, let me get this straight? You bleached behind the two strange men from out of state that you allowed in our apartment while I was working? They had masks on. That's great, I appreciate you making the effort. Can you explain to me how you believe a mask is going to make a difference, when you have low level Susy skank in the bathroom stuffing drugs up her nasty twat? Did she have a fucking mask over that? Like I said, no expectations, guess I still had some anyway. Never seize to amaze me. Do I dare ask what drugs she was smuggling for your two upstanding buddies? To which I got a reply of, "not sure, they decided not to take her and got the drugs back from her."

"Oh, my good God, even better. She then pulled them out of her nasty twat and the packaging is in the trash in the kitchen. Oh my God, like I said, only the simple minded would say go into something with no expectations. Should I have to tell a grown man that what he did when I was gone to work was unacceptable to me? Or am I the one with too many expectations? Which angle do I approach this scenario with?

Should I be upset that strange drug dealers from out of state during a pandemic thought where I stayed was a trap house? Should I be upset that drug deals were going on while I was gone to work? Should I be upset that some nasty girl was in the bathroom stuffing drugs up her cooch? Maybe I was being unreasonable.

Well, I have said my piece, so let's move on, it won't happen again. He knows my boundaries now. Let me bleach again and start over. Now of course this is wishful thinking, with the beliefs that this man due to being different from Mitchell would be able to learn from his mistakes. Possibly amend his behavior. Not all men are the same right?

Aghhh idiot, this is why I don't date or get in relationships anymore. The energy I must exude just to tell someone what I consider to be basic common sense and human decency. It is just too much effort for me most times. I mean you know I don't live that kind of lifestyle. I made it more than clear I don't use drugs. Yet I guess in a relationship my needs never did matter. Or maybe I am just being one of those unreasonable fucking bitches that men like to remark on? Or maybe if I just learn to give up altogether, I could be as charmingly accepted as Gary's simpleton wife. Which is worse? Expectations or none?

I was feeling like I had dropped a lot of my expectations through life. Requiring the bare minimum from a partner, but for Christ Sakes how much lower do you let the expectations go to accommodate someone else's life? Mitchell was a complete and utter whirl of destruction, chaos, and instability, but his ass knew better than to conduct anything of that nature in our home. I have some of my belongings here now and most importantly my desktop for my classes. It was very quiet while I was here, and I could accomplish what I needed to. I guess take the good with the bad.

Throughout this short time, Sam was inconsiderate, rude, and extremely self-centered. I would spend a good majority of my time in my car contemplating why? Why would God set up this chance meeting in time to realign me with this man? What purpose was it serving? It certainly was not for happily ever after. Although I could understand his switch up between friends and a relationship, I am not putting any more of my precious energy into directing a grown man in his life. I am not holding his little hand and telling him how to treat me, he either knows or he doesn't, and this mother fucker didn't.

I was extremely disgusted, and I shut down and began living totally in my own head. Ahh, I had the expectation that God was trying to do something good for me. I expected that if I pushed myself to do something that I never wanted to do, that it would be me living outside my comfort zone. I expected that this was my new path and that I was just being reluctant to change. I expected alright, but it wasn't from Sam, it was from God.

I expected him to do me right this time. I took the leap of faith. I tried to start again, no matter how reluctant I was. I knew if he gave me energy to pull through other days that he would do it here too. Guess what, I did have expectations, but it was never from Sam. He was what he was, who he was, and as lost as he was. I had fought this so much in my mind, that I was exhausted from the thoughts.

He would take my car to work and leave his child at the apartment with me. He had the expectation I was just going to stay there and watch him, while he would go meet up with the lowest of low, under the guise he had to work. He would shoot up and drive their dirty asses around in my car, while I was stuck at the apartment.

I would listen to the history of countries. Play a never-ending series of board games and make angel hair spaghetti. Comfortably numb? How was I achieving what I needed to achieve with these distractions? I mean everyone had expectations of me and what I was supposed to do for them always, but not one fucking time did anyone ever consider what I had to do! I didn't exist and apparently, I wasn't supposed to.

I always heard it said don't allow the present to force you back to your past. I will tell you what, that is a hard fucking thing to contend with when your present is just as bad as your past. At least Mitchell never left me to sit at home watching his child while he ran around in my car carrying on life. Almost like he had no responsibility to anyone other than himself. Mitchell always did all of that, but no child was involved on his end.

I ended up taking my desktop back to my mother's because at least there they would just want me to run their errands and not take my car. Although my mother, stepdad and the friend were there fighting, at least I could hear something different. Something different than the continuance of an ever-looping list of every country in the world, all the capitals, the flags represented, and the currency they used. Like I said, highly intelligent, with the selected interest, but it wasn't one interest of mine. If I was dating a man with these interests on a continuance loop, I would leave, so what makes this any difference?

I would let everyone in the household know that I would be taking a proctored timed test on a certain day. I would adamantly remind them daily of the time. I hoped that enough respect would be granted for quiet during this two-hour interval, but no. During my test the arguing continued.

My stepdad decided to place himself as far away from the fighting as possible by starting a construction project in the hallway right outside of my door. After my failed test, no one asked if I passed or failed. Not one care in the world. Now I had to repay to take this over and it set me back another two months on my goal. I moved my desktop back to Sam's. Maybe I could implore Sam to take his own child out of the house and although his child was a homebody that resisted change and routines, something has got to give for me, please?

Waking up to find out drug deals had gone down in the apartment while I was asleep, made me understand how very little I was respected. Respected by a man that stated he had loved me his whole life. Finding out that for three days I had walked around an apartment that had a shit load of drugs stored in it for safety, infuriated me even more. Was the universe trying to get me to give up what I needed to achieve? Did I not matter at all?

I would just mosey off and live in my car. Sitting just ten feet away from the bottom of the apartment stairs, I could look up every so often to see him or his child staring back. I was comfortable though in my car now. I will take my classes on my little phone screen and have my own space to write notes.

What in the hell was the whole point of this? Was this to teach me to completely put my past beliefs in a different perspective? Was the point of all this so I would stop living with the nostalgic beliefs of yesteryears? Believing people ever had love or respect for me? Was that what this was all about? What was God trying to tell me? Maybe this. Look, I know you thought that coming back here was going to make you feel safer with your miserable existence, but no. I am going to show you how miserable you were before. Maybe you will learn to take the abuse of Mitchell like I have blessed you with and bend to a simpleton Gary's wife. I mean what the fuck was this trying to teach me.

Perseverance of your dreams? No, enough had already been thrown on me and I still persevered, still accomplished. I didn't need that past test again. With every new disappointment of the expectations, I believed God had put upon this "relationship" with the realigning, the more it kept me emotionally with Mitchell.

I missed my old life, but there was no turning back. This was now my fucking disgusting reality. Maybe I should do drugs? Numb myself like everyone else around this God forsaken shit area. Ahh Pot Gummies, perfectly legal in this state, and a Godsend to keep me hanging in and detaching from reality as much as possible.

I know it wasn't anything as cool as "heroin" but fuck, I can only bend so much. Gummies helped me to detach and accept my reality. I could now at least go sit inside and pretend to watch the anime that this grown man so much enjoyed. Fucking anime, I am a grown woman with goals, sitting in this situation surrounded by anime. It calmed my anxiety and helped me feel like things were not as bad. Just accept the fact that no one cares. Accept the fact that there is not happily ever after. Accept the fact that no one wants to see you achieve, encourage, or motivate you. Just because you do it, doesn't mean that anyone else does. Maybe you are the abnormal one.

I am the crazy out of normal range one. Surrounded by douche-bags in shit town but believing that I and others mattered. Sit down bitch. Understand your desire to accomplish anything for yourself or to help others feel they could, is delusional and abnormal. Sit down and line yourself up with the rest of these idiots. Your expectations are too high and at least these pot gummies will let you drift on auto-pilot until God throws you another fun packed adventure.

Pot gummies? Ahh while I am stuck here like some damned soul, you will be my answer. God sent these to me to make it through this little holding spot. Or was it the devil trying to tempt me to be a useless lazy unmotivated Gary's wife? Who knows, but I ate the fucking hell out of those. I think at this point it just allowed Sam to think he could continue with his self-centered way of life. I would look at him some-times and realize how narcissistic and possibly sociopathic he really was. Why would God do this to me? I barely had any energy, and you wanted me to waste it on this?

I followed God and I had allowed all this through his instruction or my inner knowing that I had many lessons to learn. We all do. I had learned to let most things go, but my inner knowing was not some-thing I was ever going to allow myself to bend on. My morals, my beliefs in right and wrong and I knew this was all wrong, but why?

Was this God, or was I amid a spiritual attack to grab my soul? I never investigated any of this societal believed mumbo jumbo until after it happened to me. I sat there zoned out and awaiting the universe to kick me back to something I could grab on to, as the same symbols from months ago reappeared on the tv screen.

Now I had stopped watching television approximately three years ago at this point. Not because of any movement or belief that I had, but because it was just a bombardment of noise and clutter to me. The shows that they aired were somehow insulting. When you actually sit down and realize that this is the way big money thinks about the rest of society. We can be complacent and entertained by fuck hole drama like tit jobs and cat fights. Sam would watch alien stuff and anime and the alien stuff when I was zoned out became the lesser of two evils for me.

The symbols across the television screen took me back to a couple of months prior upstairs in my old bedroom. I remember waking again and not being able to move, frozen but staring. I did not have any feelings of unease during this session. I was in a strange sense of calmness, so I had almost forgotten about this one. Peaceful dreams don't seem to have the same impact on your mind as an outright horrific one.

I remember laying there frozen with paralysis and watching a shape write something on the half-slanted wall on the other side of the room from me. Ahh the old half slant walls, good for something after all. The shape appeared to be a man, but I couldn't make out a face just a human body form. He wrote shapes on the wall and pointed to them. I didn't know if he wrote these with his finger or a long stick, I couldn't make that out either. I remember seeing a triangle looking shape, some circles and maybe one that looked like an A, but I could never remember the series written out for me. I just remember it being quick like he was trying to teach me something and I was in a class-room learning.

I never really gave this episode another thought until right now on this day. Hmm? What the fuck was that dream trying to say to me? Was I supposed to be learning about this? Was this going to be some kind of key to get me up out of this? Anything was worth not having to live in this shit anymore. This night paralysis had come to me with a sense of peace and not horror, so let me focus on this alien crap.

How do you explain to anyone the thoughts that cloud your mind? How do they come across in society? How would someone view you? A schizophrenic, antisocial? There is no shame in my game because I am fine with my decisions. I know others are not granted this beautiful piece of the world and they live on the surface of life. Believing almost that this is all that exists. How do you tell anyone differently? How do you explain it to others? How do you try to instill a gift in someone that can't connect the dots? They don't slow down enough to look at the universe, they run like a rat in a cage.

Delusional? I dreamt about these things before I realized their existence, so no delusion involved. I am not out here in other people's faces forcing them to heed my warning or advice. I am not crazed and attacking anyone. I am connecting dots from the universe and mental illness in society's eyes or not, I rather quite fucking enjoy the hunt. I always did like a good challenge.

Sam would share with me parts of his childhood that I never knew before. Happenings within his own family dynamic. It would help me to understand why he made most of the decisions and had the lack of empathy imparted with him nowadays. He was mostly blank though when it came to emotions. He could carry on conversations, highly intelligent conversations. He was engaging, and he could crack jokes.

He could take care of himself on a fundamental basis, and he could survive just fine.

Surviving in the sense of existence and his feelings emotionally were never going to get in his way. He came from a sense of logic mostly and had very little feelings. Emotionally he kind of operated from a psychotic animalistic nature. As sad as this was, the only things he really did care for were his son, his drugs and sometimes very little towards me. I understand that men are naturally prone to operate from logic as women are more emotional, but we are supposed to have a pretty good mixture of both.

I would take the time to explain to him my side of things and my perspective, but it was like the same loop of Mitchell, and my children's father. They only seemed to pretend to understand at that moment and had every intention of carrying on in their own way, after. No ability to care about compromise. The very roots for a successful relationship. Entitled to their own beliefs that they need not change, and their woman just needs to tolerate it.

We have several roof leaks and a mold infestation. Our children are getting sick, we can't fix it with a sheet. I had offered to pay for repairs several times, but the outburst of male ego would always prevail. "No man is coming into my house and fixing things that I can fix. " Always translated to me as, instead my family will just deal with my laziness and accept me for who I am.

Mitchell you can't scream in my face and physically attack and beat me, because I won't help you commit a crime. Somehow was always translated in his mind as "You hate me, you never cared for me, get out my face lying to me." "Nothing I ever do is good enough and I need someone that is going to accept me for me." Sam, I am going to tell you this once and only once, I do not live this lifestyle. I don't do drugs, and I don't hang out with these people. I don't want them around me. Somehow translates to O.K. gotcha, I will just wait until you are sleeping so you are not consciously aware that they are around you.

Maybe I had too many expectations? Maybe I was the unreasonable one? Maybe I was the fucking ruthless bitch they all made me out to be. Don't act so aghast when I leave and beg for me to come back. You all beg and pretend for another few days and then its right fucking back. Maybe I have too many expectations? Maybe I am unreasonable? Or maybe just maybe, I see too much and need to carry on the rest of my life alone? I don't know but shifting out of my own mind to interact with anyone was just becoming an immeasurable amount of inconvenience for me.

Another day another, well not quite a dollar in this area, but I was done with work. I am going to make some dinner, sit the hell down and work some more on my classes. I would like to consider this a mundane, simple and reasonable series of relaxing tasks. No stress other than the cleanup and the studying, but for the most part normal. A normal expectation of myself to require and achieve? A normal expectation in a relationship? Come home from work, talk a little about your day, while you make dinner and then eat? Good God I am starting to see what an unreasonable bitch I am now. Maybe they were all right. I am far too expectant. I just wanted too much from a relationship, and it was never going to happen, apparently.

What the hell is this on the floor I just bleached? No, and before you believe I am being a demanding clean freak, it wasn't food, it wasn't drink, it wasn't vomit, or even blood. I would have accepted any of those and gladly cleaned it. No, the crinkling and cracklings of little pieces of copper chore boy aligned the floor in front of the stove. As I stood in the silence of this tiny kitchen, I then scanned the countertop. A countertop I had just cleaned before I left. "Oh, what's this? A burn mark that wasn't there this morning. I deduced unreasonably and from my bitch like posture that this burn had to have occurred while I was gone. Possibly along with the tiny copper pieces? I know to some that sounds illogical, but I was pretty convinced it happened while I was gone to work that very day.

There I go with my expectations. I unreasonably expected that after I had a conversation about this very thing with him that the behavior would perhaps be slightly changed or amended. Even more unreasonably so, stopped? No, instead when confronted about what he did that day, I got a line of bullshit about having a couple of his guy friends over for a chili cook off. They wore masks though.

No chilly or mess from it in sight. Not even a fucking splatter of sauce from three grown men in a tiny kitchen. My big mixing bowl was gone from the strainer though. "Oh, O.K., did they take it with them in the big bowl?", I asked. A bowl I knew I never wanted back. "Yes, they took it with them."

As I stood there listening to his splay of lies and his ridiculous explanation, I couldn't help to start dissecting that for self-centeredness as well. "So just to recap Sam, you had some friends over for a chilly cook off?" "You made all kinds of chilly?" You made so much that you couldn't possibly save any for me to try?" "I didn't matter because you were full?" "Instead, I have to come home from work to cook and clean again?" "How was that being thoughtful of me?"

Even the lie he was telling to make himself appear more endearing was making him look like a fucking dick head. Can I just call him out now, or do I make this more challenging and amusing for me? I always go with the latter. Try wiggling out of your lie as I question what a self-centered prick you are during that too.

After that argument was ending and he had apologized for being self-centered and not thinking of me during the great chili cook off, I smirked and said, "Thank you." He smiled, assured me it wouldn't happen again and hung his head like a beaten dog from an apologetic state. He looked so relieved with thinking I was that fucking simple, and I couldn't let it lie there. I had to call him out. Maybe I am an unreasonable bitch?

"So, was it before or after the great chili cookoff that you guys had the great crack bake? Like a deer caught in headlights, he was silent. I couldn't help to question loudly "Who in the fuck have you been with in the past that allowed you to believe that women are this stupid? "Do you honestly believe for one minute that I thought you made chilly?" Oh my God the dating pool just gets narrower and narrower, well for me anyway. I am not going to reiterate the conversation from just a few days prior. It should be pretty fresh in your mind about my boundary, that you just leapt over. Unplug my desktop, pack up my clothes and away we go again with this fucking instability, and back to my mother's house, for the second time this month.

I can't accomplish anything I need to for myself amid all this. Still no word from Mitchell or his ghost attorney on a trial, sentence, plea, or release date. The suicidal idealization started to rush over me again. As I lay on the floor of my mother's listening to the fighting, I began wondering if I could overdose on pot gummies. An overdose from those wouldn't be as bad. I could take a fist full of those and woolah. Much like my grandfather's search back in the day, someone could stand on my body and wait for the great spring thaw.

Chicken Wing
XI

Pink Flam A Gos were everywhere now. Saltshakers, cups, towels. What the hell? Now knowing that society considers these and the upside-down pineapples as a swinger notion. I am not going to allow my mind to go there. It would make me think back to my old life and remember my sex toy friend. These had to be bombarding me for a reason suddenly, I don't know why, but I was supposed to follow them for my happiness. I am not buying these things, a waste of my money. Strangely it brought me back to my frozen drink at the grocery store with Sam. I still had a couple in his freezer. I am a cheap bitch, so I went back, eventually.

I had used this time at my mother's house to correspond with Mitchell's attorney. I cited laws and time restrictions from my law books and general statutes. I nicely let him know that he was in clear violation of not only the written laws that he took an oath to abide by, but he was also in violation of many ethical codes. Although I never threatened any action to be taken further, I simply tried to appeal to his empathetic side.

I have been up here for over two years now, and he has only corresponded with his client two times. I called the law office, and the girl assigned to handle the public unpaid clients answered. (if that doesn't scream discrimination, I don't know what does) She assured me that they had gotten Mitchells prior phone calls.

She had placed the notes in his file, and the last entry was from July. She assured me that the attorney was supposed to see him in July and nothing else was noted in the file. So, when then? That was over two months ago. It's not these assistants' fault. They are underpaid to be the front line of enablement for their bosses. Yet society wants to lecture on how being someone's enabler isn't a healthy behavior. Half the jobs that exist wouldn't if you were not having to pay someone to enable your behavior.

Empathy and the court system don't exist together. It was election year though and the slimy corrupt sheriff had been around the jails giving out his candy bars. The insult of simplicity. Yes, you got my vote now. You feed the inmates meat marked for zoo animal consumption and steal via means of misappropriating funds without a check and balance. Thank God for that candy bar though. You got my vote.

Nothing better than the quiet vegging out of anime and a pot gummy for tolerance. As I scrolled through videos, there it was again, a video on pink flam a gos. What's my happiness? This pot gummy or sitting on the opposite side of the room ignoring the fact that I stay with another sociopath? Must be the pot gummy. A pot gummy and my frozen drink. I must admit that both together did bring me a new sense of happiness.

Oh my God what the hell are these? They had a little weight to them as I tried to kick the two boxes further under the bed. I needed them out of my eyeline. Let me peek. Two boxes, side by side. Hastily and unevenly thrown under the bed. One with a picture of a model holding on to a life-size purple popsicle. The other model, holding up a huge slice of pepperoni pizza.

As I crouched lower, I could feel my forehead shake and my eyebrow zoom up. The all too familiar inquisitive mindset that we have when discovering our child's half eating snack from last month under their bed. This was with a grown man instead. Ahh the feeling of living with Mitchell all over again, except this wasn't Mitchell. This wasn't some insane half project that he drug home during a meth binge to clutter my space. Heroin apparently has a different taste.

A purple popsicle and a pepperoni pizza pool raft. Ahh, pool rafts? He had mentioned no such purchase, but then again how could he explain this purchase? We had no pool, there wasn't one around for two hours. I just had to ask, didn't I? Umm, did you get some pool floaties? No, those aren't mine, those are Fetters. Fetters, his dealer. "Oh OK, well can I ask why Fetters has them here and not at his own house?"

Fetters had grown on me slightly, for as lost as he was, he had a knack for coming through when it mattered. Probably due to his current profession. He was actually at his core a very sweet person. He had a lot of good under that facade. I had told him several times he was in the wrong game and had tried to convince him to stay with his passion for cars. "Why don't you just fix and repaint cars to sell?" "There is no used car lot around here and I think you would be doing a pretty good service for this area, by doing that." Especially opposed to the other.

We would have lengthy conversations, and he would refer to me as Mom. He would willingly seek my advice. He really was a good kid, but you knew he grew up with absolute trash, with no direction. He was way too good-hearted to be doing what he was doing. He, with every "trauma and misdirection" of his crazy chaotic profession would just medicate himself more with drugs to numb himself to it. It was self-sabotage at its greatest. He couldn't see that though, we often can't see our own shit, only others.

Every time that Sam messed up on basic human decency, Fetters was always there trying to make it up. I would have gift baskets on the counter with shampoo and body sprays, little stuffed animals, or some funny shaped pen. Fetters excitedly would proclaim that they went shopping that day because Sam felt bad for what he had done. Always saying that Sam wanted to try to make it up to me.

I would smile at Fetters and then glare at Sam. Sam knew that I already knew it wasn't him. He made no attempt at hiding his sheer lack of motivation towards understanding women. He would admit within moments that it wasn't him but instead Fetters. Fetters would seem very disappointed. He would loudly exclaim, "Sam God damn it, when are you going to get this right? It was like living with dumb and dumber, except I couldn't figure out if I was dumb or the dumber?

Fetters' sheer inability to take advice or to try to take the steps to straighten his life out, made me just learn to evolve my perception of Mitchell even more. Maybe this chance encounter wasn't for my happily ever after with an old high school best friend. Maybe it wasn't to be with someone that would have loved me and done right by me. I could see that wasn't the case. Maybe it was for me to meet Fetters?

Maybe it was to be able to understand more of Mitchell's mindset. His mindset through a guy that actually had respect enough for me to engage me in non-combative communication. Maybe Fetters was my key to Mitchell's craziness and God was sending me a new appreciation and tolerance for his behavior. A different insight. My 1212's were back as I had looked at the clock. This kid was a mixture of just a crazy array of chaos and dysfunction with a flair for what I could appreciate as amusing humor.

His father had forced him to sell to expand his business when Fetters was just an adolescent. Although he had a massive number of half and step siblings, he managed to seem to have some sort of love for them all. He would buy presents for his biological children but had no interest in seeing them. He believed his presence in their lives was not good enough or needed, as he would just fuck them up more. Unlike Mitchell when presented with this scenario, Fetters was not shaking or shamed with this decision. No anxiety passed his mindset when knowing he didn't deserve a place in their lives. Mitchell shared the same perspective, but his mother made sure to be a huge perpetrator of shame with that though. Something she could dangle over his head, with no intention of helping him with.

Fetters had dual citizenship just across the water. Canada where his children resided, but he preferred the United States much of the time. His only interest towards the small inlet of water that separated the two countries at this latitude was the time he would have to allot himself to inconspicuously run illegal products across. Especially now that the border was closed due to Covid.

So, let me get this straight? You are contemplating crossing the border via the waterway? Inconspicuously? You are thinking about dropping guns and exchanging payment for these said weapons with drugs? I couldn't contain the pure look of morbid curiosity but with a massive flare of sarcasm. "So, your pasty white ass is going to inconspicuously float on a huge bright purple popsicle raft across open waters?" "Let me guess, the guns are going on the pizza?" "Are you not worried the guns will be too heavy and sink the pizza?" "No?" "No, they won't sink, Sam is going on the pizza to help me, we will split them." Oh, so just in case the guns were going to be too heavy for the pizza, Sam could be on it too, to make sure they weren't?"

"Oh my God, you two absolute morons!" "I can't even believe what I am hearing." "You two are not going anywhere, on anything, so get the "great plan" right out of your fucking heads." "You are both grounded until you grow a brain cell between you." "Matter of fact take these rafts with you; they are taking up room in an already cramped space."" What you do in your own time, away from me is on you, but I can't be responsible for allowing you to try something so fucking stupid." Not just because of the illegal nature behind it, but because their plan was so stupid, I would be highly embarrassed to even pretend I knew either one of them.

This notion just flashed me back to all the simple people I had met in my life, and it made me think of two people more than anyone. My short friend and Chicken wing. Ahh, I told you I would tell you about Chicken wing. Chicken Wing was a name I had given to a fiery red headed man that my short friend dated and lived with for a small time, under a year.

I remember the night she gathered us all via text wanting to introduce her newly acquired prize. This was a common thing us women did to introduce the man we were with to all the others and break the ice, but with short friend we had to do this more often. We would all put on our curious faces and wonder what spectacle we were about to see.

The bar we gathered at typically had an open outside fenced area. We preferred to congregate there, so we could lounge in chairs and get some air, away from the noise. I was late for meetings of this nature because I was always busy with my company before, and I had pushed these back on the priority list.

As I crested the sidewalk all alone, there appeared to be no signs of life outside in our normal sitting area, so I proceeded on. Just then I heard a familiar voice. I looked back to see my short friend standing beside a red headed man, sitting at a table, tucked in the corner. I approached and the closer I got the more of this specimen I could see.

There on this red headed man's face, a trail of hot sauce from one corner of his ear to the other, as my short friend grinned. Oh my God, my inner voice stated. Just pretend you don't see it, don't say a word. This will be a two-drink minimum kind of night. Just politely say Hi, make eye contact and go about your way. Make conversation later when he has cleaned his face, and you're drunk. Don't say it don't say it, but bang, I had to.

I stood in front of this plate of chicken wings, as I peered down at this man's face. All I could muster the energy to say was "Wow, you're eating those chicken wings like she paid for them." I smirked with the tolerance of a mother and was greeted back with a half foolish childish grin. Oh, wow short friend you have truly outdone yourself in the prize category this time. I already knew the dynamic, could see it all, and dear God, I just want a drink.

Anyway, the customary greetings of my friend's newest additions didn't deter us from having girls' night and we carried on anyway. Short friend was drunk and per usual her trailer trash came out at the slightest bit of disloyalty towards her from a man. Little woman complex. She never tried this bullshit with me, because I think she knew better. I never got embarrassed for her though. I would just distance myself and pretend I didn't know her, until it was time to scoop her four-foot ass up and bring her home.

They fought all night and from the gist of it, I believe he may have looked at another woman. I don't know why she would care. I could clearly look from two hundred feet away and see that he still had not taken the time to wipe the chicken grease and hot sauce off his face. If that was me, I would have taken the opportunity to buy whatever inbred slut that flirted with him a plate of chicken wings too.

There, a match made in heaven. Common goals and ambitions. Now leave me alone and all my friends can pretend for my sake that I didn't just have a momentary lapse in my self-esteem and my judgment. I mean what else are friends for. Nope, not short friend though, she lived in a perpetual state of no self-esteem and bad judgment. That was her normal ideal for a man.

Although I never checked in with her or kept up with the saga of short friend and chicken wing, I did know he had sole custody of his fiery red headed child. He was extremely quiet and withdrawn. Short friend would try to include him with our children, but you knew he wasn't impressed. I mean I was feeling bad, how bad must his mother have been?

It was probably two years after short friend and chicken wing had broken up and she had been on through her next several, when the rumor mill was fired up. Chicken wing was being hunted by the county's sheriff department for murder. It had been a two-day manhunt. The media was on the scene, the camera men scanning the layout around his house. The female reporter talked about the frustration in the eyes of law enforcement and the sheer exhaustion of all their resources and man power. The camera man panned out to show the massive numbers of police cruisers, blue lights whirling and the mounting number of police officers on the scene. They all stood leaning on the police cruisers from sheer exhaustion.

The panic in the reporter's voice as she questioned his whereabouts and where the chicken wing could have run to. If you have any information on his whereabouts and so on and so on, the police are exhausted, and they need your help. OMG, I thought. Was my perception of Chicken Wing wrong? Was I so misled when meeting him that I thought he was a simpleton fool? Apparently, I didn't know the charming witty ways of a cold blooded coy and ruthless manipulating killer. Oh No. I almost started second guessing myself, but thankfully stupidity from all angles showed up to save me from self-doubt.

I watched as the reporter rambled on in pure desperation and the camera man scanned the horizon littered with several police officers. There in the corner of the camera's view, like a windblown trash bag, appeared a sleepy man with no shoes. As the chicken wing in a stupor was caught off guard, he walked up and asked the reporter what was going on. She stepped back aghast and replied Oh my God chicken? Chicken Wing? He affirmed his identity and then she said "the police have been looking for you. Where have you been?" He pointed to a house two doors down and said he had just woken up from a nap.

The reporter was in outright amazement that this ferocious, brutal murderer had just indirectly turned himself into her on camera. The cameraman and reporter then both looked down at the hardened criminals' dirty feet. Suddenly these once truly exhausted and completely perplexed police officers were appointed with new life. They ran like military recruits to apprehend him. Many thanks giving to the local police. Their efforts have taken another hardened criminal off the streets. I believe it would probably be the media headline chosen for this one.

He was held without bail in the county jail before Mitchell originally arrived the first time his mother threw him in. They were both in time held together for a small stint on what we lovingly referred to as meth row. Matter of factly, I got to speak to the chicken wing one last time. He was the one appointed to do the honors on behalf of Mitchell. He had to call me to tell me Mitchell had been stabbed. Anyway, this scenario danced me to the fifty dollars I unanimously sent him once he pled out. I figured although he couldn't buy chicken wings anymore, seventeen years would be a long time to go without a radio or a pair of shoes. Thanks for giving me the solid information and for the funny memories, they are priceless to me.

There was just an endless amount of jaw dropping stories of stupidity when dealing with my short friend. This woman was an absolute doll baby whom I had massive love for. Her energy was always upbeat, and I cherished my time with her. However, I am beginning to think I only indulged my best friend's interest in wanting to hang out with her, because on a twisted level it amused me. Before chicken wing came on to the scene, it was a man she married and had two children with. Equally and if not remarkably resembling Chicken Wing, reddish hair and all.

They had apparently met during the moving of short friend's mother from the tiny trailer she lived in with her husband to an even tinier one after his death. It was love at first sight and she knew he was the one, again. They snuck off amidst the moving, for an incredibly romantic interlude and picnic lunch at the sewer treatment plant.

While she really wanted to have sexual relations with him, she couldn't because she was cursed with her monthly friend. However, although she was doing her best to be a lady and hold back, he couldn't contain his lust any longer. He was so sweet and understanding and compromised with her so well. She just knew he was the one. I made up the romantic picnic lunch part, I had to, just to be able to fathom the irony in this whole situation. What better place to get some good old anal from a stranger, than the sewer treatment plant? Anyway, because she was in the friend circle, we had to accommodate her new man, and I guess the one she had just married six months before was out?

I was confused at first, but just with anything in life, go with the flow. You will either learn to have expectations or learn to let them all go. I can sincerely say even short simpleton friends still have expectations. This is not to say that she didn't do plenty to highlight days in my life, but for the most part I really did just stand there amazed with some people's behavior. Anyway, this sewer man became her husband directly after the divorce from her existing husband. We tried to urge her to wait for the wedding. We thought it would be confusing come tax time to have been married to two different men in the same year. She wasn't waiting though and once again tax season was way above her head.

Sewer man already had three grown children and a long-time wife. Let me just reiterate the damn simplicity with people just can't be stopped. It was worse, his wife before the short friend was at least twenty baskets shorter on the intelligence scale. Trust me I don't say that in any kind of allegiance or alliance with short friend. The few outings that I had the fortune to attend around these two were always eye opening even when they were never meant to be. I never really heard about much of the buzz the first year. I am sure she was just smitten with the honeymoon phase of this man and the drama from his ex-wife and their children. The real insights to this doozy didn't happen until our second official meet up. She was nine months pregnant with her very first child, but with his fourth.

Short friend's husband had a granddaughter, and she turned one today. This grandchild was birthed by his oldest daughter. Although we could never figure out exactly what ethnicity this child was, we knew the list of possibilities would be endless with this one. My best friend begged me to come over to the birthday party and bring my children. "Oh Please, we have to do this for her. She will feel better knowing we are including her new husband and his children." "Why me and my kids?" "Can I just include them verbally when we meet up for drinks?"

At the persistent begging of my best friend and her favorite maneuver that only she can pull, "Pretty please with a cherry on top, I will owe you." "Fine, Kids, let's go, we are going to a birthday party." My oldest was such a good sport, she climbed right in. More than likely for the free cake but being nine at a one-year-old birthday party was something that allowed her to feel more adult-like. She liked helping with the younger kids. This day would be a day like no other and a day that went down in history. Not only because of the events of this day, but because it gave me a great insight into what I was dealing with for future reference.

I know I typed the address in to the gps but let me check it one more time. I was supposed to be meeting my best friend here and she wasn't answering her phone. I am sure she is already at the party and has left her phone in her car. Distracted with socializing, and I can't find this place. I knew if I could spot her car, I would know I was in the right place.

I drove past the series of open meadows up a dirt path. Two trailers with sheets in the windows and a half of front porch. The brick houses up back didn't have her car either, I must have been lost. Damn GPS. Let me just turn around and head back home. I can get the kids ice cream to make up for this. I can play this off like I couldn't find the place and she wouldn't answer her phone. Which is all the truth, but admittedly I didn't want to put any more effort into this.

Oh, just one more time, as I made a recurring loop back up the dirt path just in case I missed it. Nope, nothing, I can go now and not feel bad. I ventured down the road and just as I was about to break the news to the kids with a lesser offer of ice cream, my best friend zoomed past me. She looked me square in the eyes, so I knew I couldn't ignore her call. "I'm sorry, I was running late, turn around I will wait for you, and you can follow me." "Ahh shit!" It was already in motion. "Alright kids, the parties back on."

As I followed her up the same dirt path I had just come down from, I was puzzled and thought, now I know I didn't miss this place. Guess what, I hadn't. It was the first trailer in, with the broken porch and the sheet hanging in the window. There were two Hispanic men in the front yard, and they stood huddled over a ten-dollar clearance charcoal grill. This grill was positioned perfectly at the bottom of the stairs of this half-dilapidated porch.

Where are the kids? Where are the balloons? Where are the people? The jumpy house, or more importantly where is this child's mother? The ten minutes that I had stood outside on the lawn with my best friend and our five accumulated children felt odd to me. Then like the floodgates of trash city had opened, it all began. I hoisted my two-year-old onto my hip and clutched the hand of my oldest. I followed my best friend over to a red car that had just hastily pulled in. Dust settling.

I wanted to remark on driving so fast up on to a lawn at a children's birthday party, I didn't though. I usually just silently think about most things. When the door flung open, the newly manicured fingernails of a young girl extended out. I hadn't seen her face yet, but I followed her fake nails to their tips. I couldn't help but be absolutely floored with the little fun sized bag of chips that dangled from them. Now the party begins.

Thank you, God, for my ten minutes of peace on the lawn beforehand, I know what that was for now. This baby's mother jumped from the car. Hair done to perfection fresh out of a salon, and the fingernails to match. She rambled on quickly about how she didn't have enough money on her food stamp card to get chips for all the kids, but they could share. She then quickly threw the little bag of chips over the car's hood, to whom I later found out was her brother.

She then never missed a step, as she unscrewed the license plate from the back of the car she had just driven. Hastily returning it to another car across the lawn. I looked towards my best friend and the look on my face said it all. "But you promised, pretty please with a cherry?" I reluctantly followed her closer to the porch to join in on the outskirts of a conversation she was having with this child's mother. Shortly followed by an attempt to conversate with the Hispanic men hovering over the charcoal grill.

I stood there more out of my element than in it, as the brother with the chips previously sauntered on over. Placing himself directly beside me and my children. I didn't know this kid or the stench that exuded his essence at first. I glanced over to the picture of a big green pot leaf on his shirt and hat and started moving my kids further away. Not in time for them to miss the slew of racial ignorance that fell from his trashy unintelligent mouth. "Excuse me, my kids are here." I was trying to be nice, so as not to offend, but hell look at this mess I was in, she was going to owe me big time!

"Kids if you want to play over there away from the grill you can." I could not figure out for the life of me why a hot grill would have been so ignorantly lined up at the bottom of the stairs. People are going in and out and children are trying to play. To avoid body burns to the kids I have with me, you can go over there and play. I never let my youngest down though. I can't trust nine- and ten-year old children to watch her while I go in and pretend to socialize with these people.

The very turn of my hips and the maneuvering of the hot grill strategically was an accomplishment within itself. It was the rechecking of my baby's feet to make sure she made the hip ride safely that reassured me. I then stood just inches from the grill and inches from the first bottom step of these dilapidated stairs. I was stuck. There was no going backwards. I had to go forward behind my best friend. It was then that I glanced up.

Only to be met by the voice of the holiest of holy. The pinnacle of future stories to come. The poster child for no other than state aid itself. The youngest daughter, Kelly. An excited shriek rang through the air as she loudly expressed the need to hold my cute baby. Startled by such a request all I could do was keep moving closer to her. I stared down at the stairs to watch my footing. "Give me your baby, I need to hold her."

I, in a split second, had to think of an excuse as to why she couldn't hold my child that wouldn't insult her. Yet make it appear that I was not disgusted at the same time. I looked up to lightly grin and say, "She doesn't do well with strangers, I am sorry." To be met with the fresh round face of a young twenties something with thickened eyebrows, protruding cheeks from obesity and no front teeth. As I maneuvered around her, I darkened the threshold to the palace. I had completed only 1/16th of the maze so far and like a haunted ghost ride at an amusement park, I gripped my daughter tighter to keep her feet inside the ride.

Once inside I could see the delectable spread of burnt hotdogs, coleslaw and the hordes of flies touching down for a little taste too. Lined along the kitchen table, a fun sized bag of chips. I greeted the birthday girl and a few older grandmother-like friends. "Do you all want a hotdog?" "No, thank you, we are good." Polite enough. Next obstacle?

I stood quietly beside my best friend as she politely engaged in surface conversation with the elders. I couldn't help but to look at this child's mother. You don't know who the father of your child is, not even a guess? You were late for your own child's birthday party. The whole three minutes I have been standing here, I have loudly overheard your drama about your man. How your mad that he only came back after you got your tax return. You are dressed to the nines, nails and hair done to perfection, but you couldn't use any of that money to buy your child a curtain for her bedroom? Or fuck, for that matter a whole bag of chips for her birthday?

It made me reflect on the fact that I had not bought myself a new article of clothing in years. I had not gotten my hair done since my oldest was three. Maybe I sacrificed too much? Then again this is when I was with their father. I had grown very accustomed to putting myself dead last. The all-too-familiar apprehension of every mother when her kids get to a certain age. An age where she realizes she can actually buy herself something new. It is a challenging process and apparently it was never going to hit this girl.

I was done with the house tour, and I wanted to get my baby and I back outside to check on my oldest. I needed to be able to lay eyes on her and make sure she was alright. I know it had only been four minutes, but a lot can happen to kids in four minutes, and I had to check. I politely dismissed myself to check and hoped that I wouldn't have to see Kelly again. I slowly descended the stairs so as not to gain too much momentum. I didn't want them collapsing and I didn't want us to end up in the clearance grill.

I could see her with the other kids and my oldest was fine. I went over and stood closer to them and waited for my best friend to come outside to join me. With that, the very person I agreed to come to this for showed up. Late but she was here, short friend and sewer husband.

She clambered out of the car, moving slower due to nine months of pregnancy and her husband climbed on out too. I stood there beside them both as they engaged with my youngest daughter, then like a streak of cat piss, his middle child, Mr. Stench himself, Green Pot Leaf Boy appeared. "Daddy, Daddy, I need some money." "I am needing a new tattoo gun," and just like that short friend rolled her eyes. "He doesn't have the money; the baby is due this week and we had to stock up on diapers and last-minute supplies." He mumbled about the new baby, knowing that he felt displaced and displeased and continued trying to convince his father of the urgency of this tattoo gun.

I glanced over to make eye contact with short friend to let her know I felt bad for her and could feel her pain. She was bending over in the car at this point grabbing her newly acquired granddaughter's present. While short friend was bent down, this was just enough clearance for Kelly to see that her father was in fact standing with us as well.

"Daddy, Daddy, I need a favor?" "What Kelly, what do you need?" Mind you all these children were grown already and this man, aside from jokes, was probably done with supporting grown children with failure to launch issues. I shit you not I can't make this up if I tried, or any of this for that matter, but she approached with marked enthusiasm to sell her pitch.

"Daddy, I need a ride this weekend, and I need you to pay for a hotel room, and then I will need a ride back Sunday afternoon." "What, what for? "Well, I met this great guy online from Virginia and he is going to come down and meet me." "I told him I would get a hotel room for the weekend."

"Well, why doesn't he pick you up then?" Simple enough questions when dealing with normalcy, but low and behold that was lacking greatly. "His parents are bringing him down to meet me and staying down with him until Sunday, but they can't drive me home." Oh, my good Lord above, if either of my girls grow up with such low expectations, I will slap them both. Don't explain to her she is worth a little more, instead we will just say "No, Kelly, I don't have any money." Short friend then proceeded to ask sewer man to bring in the cake. The cake that they had to purchase with their more endowed food stamp card for this baby.

This was the point where I placed my youngest in her car seat. I turned on the AC and I hollered for my oldest. She was enjoying playing with the other kids, so she was a harder sell. It was getting so bad that my best friend was rounding up her children too. This day would go down in history for my oldest as "Remember that birthday party you brought us to and made us sit in the car?" She is twenty-three and will still tease me about this. "I am sorry baby girl." "You will understand when you have your own children someday." She says I made her sit in the car because although I had the intention of leaving shortly after, I was still overextended by thirty minutes. My best friend needed my help as I found out that she was using this occasion to peddle her Avon sales. Yes, even to this day, you still owe me for that one.

Turkey Burger
XII

My best friend absolutely swells my heart. She had always been my rock and my mini therapist in the years before. She is a strong person. I always admired her and to this day still do. She always made me laugh and she kept things interesting.

She had opened a bar around the same time as this occurrence. I never drank in those days apart from possibly once a year. My children's father drank plenty, so I never could. I loved the fact that my best friend had opened this bar, and I was so excited for her. Her bar was located just one mile down the street from her home and the church our children had begun going to.

My oldest daughter and her youngest son attended this little youth group. She felt it was best for her son to have a little religious structure. My oldest loved the chocolate snacks she got from attending, so this became my one hour a week to myself, outside of the house. This was my new ritual.

I attended this church the first night our children wanted to join. I had to get a feel for the people and any messages they were trying to convey. I hadn't been to church in years at this point. Maybe it would be something we could all attend? I found my answer out quickly though. I decided the preacher was way too good looking for me to listen to his sermons with pure intent. I would drop the kids off at church and go sit at my best friend's bar for an hour. I know, how bad does that sound?

I knew people in the area, but obviously after she opened this bar, I met far more people. I would sit at the end of her bar every Wednesday night for almost an hour with my sweet tea. I would chat with her in between her customers. I remember one night as I sat at the far end of her bar, my best friend greeted me with a drink. I refused as I had to pick up the kids shortly, and she giggled. "There is no alcohol in it, just drink it. "I'm good, I have my sweet tea, to which she replied, "Pretty Please with a cherry on top, I will owe you." Fine damnit, give me the drink. As I drank down the fruit juice concoction, I looked up to thank her, she was already down the other end of the bar with a group of her regulars. Middle aged women, from the area that I knew very little about.

Time was cutting close to pick the kids up, so I slid off the barstool and waved to her still standing with the same group of women. "Thanks babe, that was good, I will talk to you later, going to grab the kids." She hollered back "Love Ya," and I went on my way. Like I said, a Wednesday night ritual.

It was probably three more Wednesdays of my best friend bringing me fruit juice and giving me the pretty please line, before I questioned what she was doing. As she went to pass me yet another fruit juice concoction, she exclaimed, "O.K if I tell you don't get mad." "What?" "Why would I be mad?" "They are good drinks, are you experimenting with a new drink base?" "Well, you see that group of women down there?" "Yes," I replied as I looked on their way.

The group sat smiling at me and gesturing a wave, so I waved back just as friendly. "Well don't be mad, but they think you are hot, so they have been buying you drinks." As her eyes shuttered slightly, she ducked a little. "What?" "God damn it." "You have been letting lesbians buy me drinks for over a month now?" "Yeah, but I take the alcohol out and charge them for it anyway." Oh my God, at this point, you do owe me! It was my Wednesday night ritual though and I enjoyed the time from the house. Shit, if you want to kind of pimp me out for a drink profit, go ahead, who cares?

The week after the infamous birthday party, my short friend had her first child. We went to visit them at the hospital and meet the new addition. It was with this very event and moment in time that I met not sewers ex-wife but instead his ex-wife's sister. I guess from the buzz of my best friend, this woman had taken up with our short friend. She didn't like her own sister and felt perfectly fine aligning with her sister's ex-husband's new wife. As crazy as that sounded, they were all perfectly happy with the arrangement so all the power to you. The ex-wife's sister had called short friend to ask if the new momma needed anything before, she stopped over to visit. Short friend excitedly answered with her request for a cheeseburger and fries.

I shit you not. As soon as this woman darkened the door of the hospital room, she hollered out the total of the meal purchase. Short friend then drug herself out of bed to get her the money in exact change. As this newly acquired kind of, sort of sister-in-law once removed stood there she extended her hand out to gather short friends pocket change. There on her arm in all its infinite glory in worn ink resembling a prison tat, the word "Mooses" sprawled the width of her arm. "What?" What the fuck is this? Maybe I should have hollered out the cost of the present we brought for her too? Utter disbelief took over my face and I thought. Well welcome to the family, or old family, or whatever who cares anymore.

Even with numerous stories that I have just purely enjoyed looking back on through the years, I believe it was with this that I literally peed a little. Our bladders get weaker after we have children, but I think a normal bladder would have peed to this one. Our short friend after the birth of her first child was an extremely great and very attentive mother. We had often joked and told her that once she had an actual child that her obese dachshund with the skin tags wouldn't hold the same priority. However, of course before you have children you can't imagine why no one cares to have lengthy conversations about your dog's skin boils.

Anyhow, great mother or not, we all get tired. Just adjusting to a new life with a baby is emotionally exhausting let alone physically. Strapped for money and having quit her job to be a full-time mother, she was reliant on her new husband financially. The first set of failures to launch kids would call her husband constantly for money and the stress was mounting. He was having a difficult time trying to provide for both families and I know he was stressed.

As short friend describes it, he became angry, and she convinced him to turn his phone off one night. His other children were grown up and if there was an emergency, they could call her phone. They were not going to get money from her. He heeded her advice and shut his phone down. Short friend had several calls to her phone between the two youngest children and she had answered them both earlier in the evening and knew they were fine. The youngest girl, Kelly wouldn't stop calling and she just stopped answering her too. The baby was sleeping so they decided to get some sleep while they could.

To do this story any justice, I must back up to a few weeks before this and remind you Kelly was the girl with no front teeth that wanted to hold my daughter. Apparently, she did get to her hotel weekend with this strange internet man. They didn't hit it off so well and a month had passed since then. Kelly had already been off with a different internet man the previous weekend and apparently, they had bonded.

The day before Kelly went to meet this new internet man, she felt that she should get her hair done at the salon. A perfectly normal thing for a younger girl or woman to do before a "weekend." Once arriving for this "weekend" with this new internet man, he got to enjoy her new hair. Apparently, they both decided that they did not truly like her new hairstyle. They took the next logical step of course and used this opportunity to bond. A bond like no other as they excitedly gushed over the solution they had pooled together in their minds. They confidently decided just to shave her head bald. (Yep, bald, you read that right.) Kelly and the new internet man were beaming with her new look, and they spent the rest of the weekend in pure bliss. All good things must come to an end though.

The next morning, my short friend and sewer husband woke to several missed calls. However, it was the voice messages that Kelly had left that caused concern. "Daddy? Daddy, are you there? I need you to call me." "Daddy, quick it's an emergency, call me back" "Daddy, I need you to do me a favor." "Daddy, Daddy, please they said if I don't come up with the money in the next twenty minutes, they are calling the cops." "Daddy, Daddy please, they are going to arrest me." "Daddy, are you there? The cops are here, I need you." "Daddy, Daddy, I need twenty dollars now."

The voice mail stopped after that. Short friend and her husband rolled their eyes and proceeded to call around to check on her. Of course, he was the biggest piece of shit on the planet. According to the ex-wife he was too busy supporting his new child to bother helping with the old. "She only needed twenty dollars, and this wouldn't have happened." You know the typical shaming technique. Apparently neither parent had twenty dollars that night, or her bail money, but perhaps a lesson learned? I bet she won't try to steal pieces of hair from a wig shop again.

My best friend and I couldn't stop laughing. Short friend, you not only reeled in a prize this time, but his family is your karma. Keep fucking with married men. I know it is so wrong, because anyone can look and see that the family is not all there. Jesus, sometimes we just have to relax enough to only look at the surface of a situation. Let this be a lesson to all you little girls, when you look at a married man and think, I am hot. I can get him, look at his wife. I am way better looking. Yeah baby, his wife was more than likely hot and sane once, too. How much is that married man and all his baggage worth to you?

I laughed to think about how I used to use these people as punishment for Mitchell. This one week, I remembered short friend inviting us for a cookout. Honestly, I would not have made the time to do this if not for having caught Mitchell in another huge lie. I figured why not? You lie to me and make me suffer, now you can sit here with this excellence and suck it up for punishment. Mitchell sat looking on, as sewer man tended the grill. Swatting all the flies away with the spatula, he was using to flip the burgers.

I smiled and socialized while I watched Mitchell twist in his chair. After thirty minutes or so of this, I got up and left him there with the ex-sister-in-law and sewer husband. I had grown intrigued with a glass vase topped with gray duct tape just inside on the windowsill. I could hear them arguing and I chuckled to think Mitchell had to sit out there with that.

Ducking down to meet this vase eye level, I could see it was full of rocks and sand. I half smirked and then I read the side of it. There in a see-through glass vase a little card hanging from its side with the word Dawis adorned in black lettering. "Umm short friend what's this? ""Oh, that's Davis".

"Your stepfather?" "Yep." "Why are his remains in a see-through glass vase, on your windowsill? Who misspelled his name?" "Momma wanted me to keep him, I have more room over here." I looked up and out the window to see Mitchell trying to appear like part of the crowd. His leg was shaking from anxiety, but he was still smiling. "So, what's the "Mooses" about on your arm," he asked. "Well, my ex-boyfriend's nickname was "Moses", but they didn't spell it right." "Do you want a turkey burger?" I figured that I had heard and seen enough, so I knew he had. "Keep lying to me Mitchell, they have cookouts all the time."

So, let's recap the present day so far. I still don't have any correspondence from Mitchell's attorney on a date. Something I can make plans around. I am going thirty miles out of my way in shitty weather just to have the quiet enough to complete my classes. I am tolerating drama and childish shit just for this opportunity. Living with my best guy friend from high school. A directive that I had to talk myself truly and undoubtedly into against my will. All for a stitch of stability.

I followed the direction of God and his Universe during this tumultuous and very unstable time. I trusted God and his Universe to help me make the right decisions and this is the lesser of two evils? Is this what I get? Was this a punishment? All of this because I fell in love with Mitchell. A man that I thought about every day for eight months and talked to you about God, before I ever made a move.

Why did you allow me to fall in love with Mitchell at first sight? Why when I asked you every day for eight months, did you OK, my advance ahead? You sent me signs to be with him, so is this my punishment? All I ever wanted was to have a life with a man that loved me and a little house with a functioning roof. I never wanted any of this. I didn't sign up for any of this forsaken shit! My intolerance grew more and more every day. I couldn't even move away and start over if I wanted to, fucking covid got me stuck here.

Fetters always cracked me up with his complete and utter ignorance to most things. His chaotic external and inner world kept him propelled towards drama. He was truthful beyond fault with me though and I had to appreciate him for that. Mitchell never was.

He would even be able to have his own little insights when looking towards Sam and our very loosely strung together "relationship." "Well, why is he giving other women money for their drugs when he wants to go South with you?" "I would think that if he really wanted to go with you, he would help save money with you, not give it to other women." "You are right Fetters, that is why he is not going South with me, ever, "Oh, I see, I won't tell him." "Thank you, I appreciate that." I would throw bits and pieces of incorrect information towards Fetters sometimes that only Fetters knew. I do this with everyone. That assures me that I always have my source. It never made it back around, and I knew that he was trustworthy on that front. He could keep a secret, and because of that, I have a lot of respect for him.

I remember Fetters showing up one night while Sam was on shift, inebriated and out of his mind. He wanted to show me his newest vehicle and talk to me about paint colors and his plans with it. I would always encourage this passion of his, in hopes that he would put his effort into more productive activities. He wouldn't give me his keys and refused to let me drive him. He admittedly insisted that he was going to his sisters for the night just down the road. I made a deal with him, if he didn't want to crash on the couch, he had to wait for me to grab my pocketbook. I would follow him over. He was in no shape to drive in my opinion, but of course that's just my opinion. I told him to make sure the needle didn't exceed the fifteen on his speedometer and I followed him over.

When we safely arrived in the subzero temperature, he shut off his truck and laid across his seats. He assured me he would be going inside in just a little bit, so I ventured to pick up Sam. When he arrived to get Sam, I told him about Fetters, and he began to fill me in on a little of the current drama. "What" Sam replied, "I spoke to his sister earlier, she is gone for the weekend." He chuckled and then remarked on how cold it was going to be when he woke up.

He wanted nothing to do with him due to a recent escapade and they were having a slight falling out, which I didn't know anything about. Apparently, his family was sick of him, all his "normal" circle was pissed with him and Sam himself didn't seem to give much of a shit. He was more annoyed than anything when I instructed him to get back in the car. I was going to need his help getting Fetters out of his truck and back to the apartment.

"I can't leave him like that, he will freeze to death." I just wanted to check on him. "It is five below for God's sake." There huddled up in his truck, but still passed out was Fetters, and the struggle began. He wouldn't wake up to open his truck at first, and I got worried. I couldn't tell if he was breathing. He eventually woke up with enough noise and allowed us entry to his vehicle. We took him by the arms and pushed him into my warm car and away we went to Sam's apartment. We managed to finesse him enough to walk a good portion of the stairs himself. Staying right beside him, until we could get him to the couch. "I don't care what he has done, or what people think, I cannot allow him to freeze to death in his truck." This kid had grown on me, and for all the times he had called me Mom, I was starting to see why.

Maybe that is what I had been for Mitchell all those years, a mother? A woman that he could not love and cherish and idolize like Fetters did. Instead, one that he could hate for all the wrongs she had done to him.

I stood peering through the window one night enjoying the quiet. Sam was at work, no Fetters. Sam's son had gone with his grandparents. It was perfect, just silence. I smiled to think we had a new neighbor that had just moved in that day. I looked down at the newest vehicle in the parking lot and thought maybe someone normal? Maybe someone I could talk to occasionally? Sam didn't know who he was. Someone from out of town was all he knew. Strange, this area was so small, everyone knew everyone. Anyway, someone new for me to meet eventually.

I looked up from the new black SUV vehicle in our driveway, to the bushes directly ahead. A light in the bushes had caught my eye. The cops. Why are the cops out in the bushes parked in a truck? The vehicle wasn't aimed at our apartment, but instead almost in stake out fashion for a home across the street. That didn't surprise me. I knew the kid that lived there was supposedly a dealer. He was in the highly expansive friend group of Sam. I zoned out for a minute wondering if this kid knew he was being watched? Not my problem, do the crime, do the time. I felt bad for his unsuspecting girlfriend and their newborn baby though.

I could hear the footsteps of our new neighbors for four nights straight. Coming up the porch and into their apartment. They got home late, so I knew I couldn't pop over and just introduce myself. I never heard them talking though, which I thought was weird. The walls were paper thin. Hadn't moved furniture in or anything.

I just sat with Sam's son and played board games for the second and third nights. It was the fourth night that I instructed Sam's son to sit nearest to the wall that divided the two apartments. "Turn your volume up buddy, so I can hear your song over here in the kitchen." A never-ending loop of a song highlighting all the countries in the world. He sang loudly and laughed, as he played one after another. He would excitedly holler at me about the newly adopted currency of certain countries. While I made his milkshake with the loud blender and boiled his routine pasta.

Sam never believed that there was a stakeout next door for him and Fetters as well. I just smirked knowing they probably had grown just as tired of listening to country information as I had. They left after four nights, but I was still stuck there.

A week later as I sat at the counter eating the supper I had cooked; a knock rattled the door. Sam's son had returned home to his mother, so I was basking in the peace. Sam jumped from the couch to answer the door. It was dark out; I did not get up to check it. Pitch black dark. Believe me, I didn't want anything to do with anyone that may be coming up in the dark of the night that was affiliated with Sam.

I could hear a man's voice, muffled and inaudible to me, but I could hear Sam reply with yep, ok. Where do I sign? Very calm and unshaken, almost like a package delivery. What service is running at 8:00 at night? He returned to the couch, but not before placing a slip of paper on the far corner of the counter. Facial expression unchanged, as he flipped through his selection of anime on the tv.

"What do you mean that was the police? Why what happened?" "Ahh they just explained to me that because of my current criminal record that they had to charge me with a felony, even though it was nothing."" What was nothing?" "A felony charge is nothing?"

I froze for a minute understanding that if I had just been charged with a felony, I would want answers. I would be shaken and afraid of the time and money I would have to spend to fight it. "What do you mean?" "Does this kind of shit happen a lot? "He was completely un-phased by any of it.

"My court date is another two months out because of covid so you don't need to worry about it." He replied. No what I need to worry about is how you can so callously commit a crime and a stupid not well planned one, may I add. You are not disturbed in the least bit that you are about to take another felony? What about your son and your parental time? What about jail time away from him? Oh, dear God. Am I the only one within a thirty-mile radius of people you know that has a level of knowledge concerning consequences?

I awoke to a chime on my social media. I wasn't friends with this girl. I don't know her, nor would I care too honestly. Just by looking at her, you knew she was good for nothing. Not even the humor of stupidity. Just the good for nothing shallow people that exist to create drama. I don't answer people like that. I would rather spend two minutes trying to pick someone else's nose, than be drug into anything more with any more people that he associates with.

I already had a newly adopted son named Fetters because of this whole ordeal. His problems were enough to keep me distracted. She hit me up again a few days later to ask why I hadn't answered her first message. Her tone of entitlement prompted an answer from me. I was like why the hell not, maybe there is something wrong.

First off, I had to correct her when she gave me the title of Sam's girlfriend. "Umm you mean roommate?" I had already evolved mentally from believing we would have any future together, even though he still believed we did. She wanted to ask me if I had taken any of her belongings. Oh my God, I am looking at your picture on this social media platform and knowing I would never want any of your disease infested belongings, but dare I ask "why?"

Apparently while I was at work, Sam had allowed this dirty drug runner bitch to come into our apartment. She had to hide some of her belongings from her abusive boyfriend. This is a typical level one skank activity. All I could do was shake my head. While the drama of this unfolded more and more, I learned that Sam had allowed this while he gave her money for further drugs. He thought he would have the chance with her sexually once her man and her split up. Also, level one man skank shit.

When confronted with why he allowed another strange person in during covid with her disease infested knock off purses of an already knock off brand, I learned that she had stolen his money, and he was pissed. Her boyfriend was threatening his life for hitting on her and had planned on breaking in to beat his ass and to get it all back. So, he and Fetters had to get rid of it.

So, you have once again put my safety in jeopardy, because you are a self-centered prick? I couldn't help with this admittance to just reach out and push him. I wanted him out of my space. The slight push was enough to cause his unprepared body to fumble backwards onto the couch. One person can only take so much, and you are doing nothing to add to me, just take. I am insulted, that yet again, a man stands before me in all his infinite fucked up glory, claiming passionately that he loves me.

Sam was infuriated that I had pushed him backwards. He then stood quickly to his feet and bowed up to me while grunting like a walrus. My lip curled automatically, my eyebrow leapt from its comfortable resting position, and I bowed up too. Taking three very swift steps towards him, I didn't stop until his eye lashes were touching mine. "Go ahead" I urged. "What the fuck are you going to do?" His posture softened but not his eyes, and I walked away silently.

I couldn't get the image of his eye out of my mind though. Not because I was scared, trust me. I had gone enough rounds with Mitchell's abuse that his didn't even fucking register on my scale. It was the same drug-fueled stare down that I had endured with Mitchell. It was the same God damn look. They had the same eyes, and I couldn't get it out of my mind.

"Help me learn, teach me, help me grow." Although those were the very words I would have loved to have heard from Mitchell, I knew Sam pleading with me was a lost cause. "You are highly intelligent, charming, and manipulative. You can work a room and light up a smile. You can socialize with anyone from any walk of life. You can play complicated strategy games for hours and you build computer code in your spare time for the fun of it. I don't need to tell you that the very element needed to succeed in life as a human being is empathy, and honey you have none. I can't teach you empathy, your window is closed.

Mitchell at least had a tiny amount of feigned empathy when he was sober. Unlike Fetters who was actually salvageable, he actually had real empathy. Sam, even completely sober, had none. My attention at that moment was diverted to the television with the mere mention of the name Mitchell. The visual of a pink flam a go was depicted on this cartoon program's lawn.

Was the universe trying to keep me looking towards Mitchell? Don't lose sight of your true love. Don't get bogged down in the insults and ignorance of this man, because you need to keep your eye on the prize? Mitchell had been meth free for over two years now and consistently calling me. Every day he had something to share with me concerning new insights on his journey of self-growth. He had been studying cultures, different religions, and psychology. He would talk to me slightly about childhood dynamics and was learning to piece parts of his past together for a clear understanding of his recent behaviors. He was making so much progress. He seemed like he was almost a grown-up man.

Maybe that recent group of new numbers was to remind me to stay on my Twin Flame Journey, and I took the wrong path? Who knows. The reality of my current situation was this. The love of my life was locked up again for the second time due to his mother. I was trying to fight to keep a tolerable amount of sanity clutching on too little stability.

Nothing I was doing or none of my family's unsolicited advice was working. It would entertain me slightly now to hear remarks from the very family that encouraged me to date Sam. "Oh, why do you stay with that?" "Why would you let him keep using you?" "Don't you think better of yourself?" "You can do so much better." Thank you, I already know this, that's why I didn't want to date him in the first place. You all talked me into it. Entertaining to me, nevertheless. I refuse to believe this is all there is to life for love.

Mitchell was where my heart was forced to lay. With every phrase of don't let the current push you back to the past, I couldn't even help myself looking around at this shit. Mitchells past actions had aided in my insights and knowledge to the drug world and the actions of people in it. I honestly though preferred to never have to indulge in that knowledge ever again.

Why do I always have to be one of those people to see the good in people, despite all of this? Everything that has happened, everything I am aware of and yet I still must believe in the good in people. I am so done. I like to portray the bitch face because I am tired. I am guarded. I am exhausted. I am frustrated. If I look unfriendly, no one will ask anymore of me. The problem is, I am the opposite of that internally. I will help until I have nothing left, and people will use that up. I must put on the bitchface.

It had been snowing outside heavily, so it looked like another few hours' stint in my car. Alone with my thoughts, I will figure this out.

I always do. I will talk to God about my next direction. I can't leave this state, I am stuck here because of Covid. Let me talk about this with the only person that can help me. God and his universe will know what to do. I just need more alone time. I don't want anyone's fucking drama around me, so back outside to my car I go.

I was pissed and I was frustrated not just with Sam but with everything. The past decade of my life had just been a whirlwind of chaos and not one drop of stability. I was my own stability and even that was viciously attacked from every corner. Covertly, and outright overtly. I couldn't help sometimes falling back on past occurrences. I know you can't live there but shit at this point there is no way out, I am stuck. How do you move forward when there is no room on the game board anymore? Just the edge, no more squares. Checkmate bitch. We got you.

"Really?" That sounds like a challenge to me. For the first time ever, my alone in my head time talks made a little room for the angels too. O.K God and the universe speak to me. As a matter of fact, you can all speak to me, because at this point, I will make room for any usable advice.

I knew of the spiritual world; I knew I was of light. I knew that the other side had been vying for my soul. Spiritual warfare shit is no joke. I knew that I was going to listen to God regardless, but maybe just maybe. God may allow something to help me use it as a leg up in this situation. I sat in my car writing for about three hours. I could see Sam peek out the door at me a few times, but guess what? I will sleep in this fucking car before I pretend to be alright with what you do.

I am a very spiritual person at heart. I will try to encourage other people through what I have learned and through the lessons I have been taught. I always try to do unto others as I would have done to me. However, just like anyone when pushed too far, I am going to lash out. Do these people try to provoke me on purpose? Why? I give them plenty of warnings. I communicate quite clearly my expectations, and honey they are bare minimal.

I receive signs. I get numbers and I am humbled and thankful every time. Sam had seen this several times with me and he would just be lost for words. I don't look like the type that would want to start a camp for homeless people or to advocate for inmates. I have perfected my bitch exterior. I have had to through the years, but I really am too nice most times.

I would share advice with Sam when he asked, and he would always remark on how much further evolved I was than him. He would see feathers drop in front of him after my advice or get numbers himself now. Animals would appear unseasonably, and I would tie their presence into something spiritual to help our thought process. Sam was at his rock bottom in life, and I can honestly say I was too. He knew about my dreams and helped me by saying he would protect me.

I remember sitting there one night as we spoke about past events. Sam asked me if I could own any animal in the world, what would it be? I threw some insanity back at him, because I wasn't an animal owner anymore. I laughed and said a mountain lion. Not that I would ever own one, but my memories flashed back to working at the vet clinic years prior. That was one of the coolest animals that stuck out to me. "A mountain lion hah?" "Yeah, why not?" To which he replied his would be a fox.

It was the next evening that Mitchell called me and said, "I had the weirdest dream last night." "You and I were walking through the woods with a mountain lion." I laughed, but Sam was slightly freaked out with the constant uncanny closeness of my "Twin Flame." A spot that he knew he would never take from Mitchell and for the first time ever in this man's existence, he started to feel the all-too-common pangs of jealousy.

I sat in my car thinking back. I did so much thinking and writing. Trying so hard to figure it all out. I know what society says, but I also know what God tells me. I know what the universe gives me. I don't doubt it, I just try to figure it out.

I concentrated on Sam, and I concentrated on Mitchell. Mostly I concentrated on the look in Sam's eye just an hour before this and the same position it owned with Mitchells. What the hell is that? It's a different drug. They are different people for Christ Sakes. They can't both have the same eyes. The same look, the same demon. What the hell is that? What demon has them? Sam was barely even using heroin anymore, mostly suboxone, so what demon is that? After a three-hour stint of thinking and writing, I didn't want to get out of my toasty car. I knew it was time to venture back inside though. Take a shower, force myself to eat and with any luck pass the hell out.

Sam and I didn't speak. I had nothing to say to him, I didn't even look in his direction. I took an extra-long time in the bathroom showering and pretending to comb my hair. I wanted limited time around him. It was probably slightly over an hour before I even attempted to make my move out of the bathroom. With a turn of the doorknob and a calm exterior I proceeded on out. One of my favorite activities to ignore him was to look out the front door onto the driveway so I proceeded to do that very thing. Anything so that I could still ignore my reality in this tiny apartment space.

There as I looked out the window towards my car, sprawled across the hood, there were letters. They looked as though they had been done with someone's finger. No footprints were present through the snow though. Well, apart from mine when leaving the car an hour ago. How in the hell did someone sneak up and write across my hood?

Leave my car for an hour and see what happens. Sam? As I tore through his anime concentration. Did you go outside? Hah, no, why? "Just wondering" I knew he had not just by peering at him. Crossed legged, bare feet, pajamas and no snow on or around his shoes at the door. So I went out of the door.

The letters were defined as if someone had snuck up and wrote them on there with their finger from an adult height, no slants. It was all perfectly even, no excess snow on the ground. It was all level and all pristine, apart from my footprints. Freshly fallen snow. I thought for a moment. Maybe where my car had been running while I was sitting in it, the hood coils had caused this. I had sat in this car plenty of times while writing in the snow and never once did I ever see an indication of any kind of design. Plus, these were not melted, they were too perfect for a melt pattern. The depth of the snow peeking down into the letters looked like it had been scooped out, but with no extra snow. By this time Sam was making his way down the stairs to investigate what I was doing.

"What the hell is that? What does that even mean?" Is that even a word? He giggled slightly. "I don't know, I have never seen that word in my life, is it even a word?" I left abruptly to go look up this meaning or to see if it had any significance to anything I would re- motely find useful on my journey. Up the stairs I went to grab my phone.

Sam trailed behind me asking me questions and asking who would write that. "I didn't hear anyone outside." I replied, "there were no footprints, and no one was outside." He looked at me inquisitively and then asked, "well what is it?" "I don't know Sam, but it definitely pertains to you." "Me?" "Why, what did I do? ``"Why would someone come write that on your car about me?" "I don't even know what the fuck it means." I took this opportunity to smile at him and say," Oh it's definitely meant for you, and it's a message to me." He stood wide eyed and nervously said "I don't believe you." I replied with "you don't have to; it's not meant for you to believe anyway."

Now what the hell does this mean? I giggled and thought it probably is the coil in the hood, but I am going to amuse myself anyway. What the fuck else do I have to do today? The great answers from the mystical universe say, JUUG. The act of profiting off illegal or legal activities. Involves scheming, lying, or tricking other parties for a larger financial gain. Well thanks, universe, I already knew they both embodied these traits. Maybe there is a demon named JUUG? No luck finding one though.

We are up North, and this is a southern term. Mitchell is in the South, but he had no idea what the word meant either. From the very limited source of this definition, I knew it was slang. One that seemed mostly to be used by the African American current culture down south. I could only detect from that, that my guardian angel was a black man. One that had to have passed on recently enough to know that term. My heart absolutely beamed. The clarity of knowing that Lee was still with me made everything alright for me. Sorry you had to find out about my drama this way. I tried so hard to hide it from you. Much love to you always angel baby!

It was the next morning that I was leaving for work that I noticed the neighbor's car. Still sitting in the same position as the day before. Had not moved, no tracks or footprints in the snow. Sprawled across the hood were the same symbols that I had seen across Sam's television not too long before this. The same symbols that had made me reflect on my dream. Triangles upside and right side, Circle shapes etc.

Was this another hood coil design? Well, her car hadn't run. She had not been out to it, evident by the lack of footprints. The temperatures had not risen enough to melt anything, they had only declined. I smiled and pointed it out to Sam. He froze as he mumbled out "What the fuck?" I grinned and reminded him to behave and to have a good day. Ahh my next fun thing to do after my shift at this shit hole is through. I never got to truly investigate this or the designs or meanings, like I would have liked to have.

I stayed pretty busy during this time, mostly wondering about my future with Mitchell. He had heard from his attorney shortly after my letter. It only took two years and five months. I say that with pure and utter sarcasm and a great thanks and fuck you to his pitiful court appointed attorney. His court appointed had come back at him offering another plea deal. He told Mitchell that the main witness was going out of the country for a year on military assignment. He now would have to wait another year for the trial. He told Mitchell that if he took this plea, he would be through with time served. Mitchell, being exhausted from waiting, took it verbally before I had my say.

The public defender knew about the reality of the trial more than a year ago. He did not communicate one time with Mitchell or I about a strategy or anything for that matter. No return phone calls, no email, nothing. He vanished in thin air with the whole situation again. Knowing we were adamant about trial he waited for a year for the main witness to have to do a military assignment for a year?

You sir should be ashamed of yourself for such a ridiculous lie! Plus, there are laws to circumvent this and there were other police officers at that home. He wasn't the main witness to shit. You and the DA both knew you had nothing on him. You thought keeping him imprisoned and ignoring all his rights would force a much-needed plea for the DAs record and ego vindication. You both are pitiful and very corrupt. You have severely abused your positions. Likened only to the basic manipulations of little high school girls. The lies don't stop there between the two of you though. The taking of a plea agreement so he could be released with time served, still held him in there for another five months, with two separate prison transfers.

You two rejections from a glory hole, should be ashamed with what you try to pull over on people. Karma will get you both. Please by all means, carry on and enjoy the rest of your lives.

Sam, this time had not changed. He had just become increasingly jealous of just about everyone that tried to strike up a conversation with me. He would throw out his little passive aggressive comments. Honestly, I have never been with a man that didn't display this type of behavior, so I just smirked. I just kept smirking. Through the comments, the insults, the bluntness and even through the bullets. Yep, you heard that correctly, bullets.

I would wake now, most days with a bullet on the counter. The name Mitchell written in permanent marker up its length. Was I supposed to be scared? Was this supposed to be a fear tactic? Did I think he was capable? Yes, beyond a shadow of a doubt, he was capable, but I just smirked. Insult to my God damned intelligence. A bullet? Please, If I cared a little bit more, I would shove it up your ass, but I don't. Fetters had at this point just been sentenced for his previous crimes and had begun his prison stay. I had no more reason to stay now. I don't have time for this anymore and I have learned my lesson.

Although the fear and hysterical panic of covid was still raging, it had been over a year. They were amid pushing the vaccinations with very little information on them. I would shutter at work to watch the employees line up to get these. Under the guise of "keeping everyone else safe." Now I am all about sacrificing my own needs, wants, and desires for other people. I am all about taking on too much until I crash with debilitating anxiety. I am all about being a lamb for God, but no one ever mentioned sheeple. I am not a sheeple. I guess when you wake up and begin looking you can't go back.

No thank you, I will pass. The urgency of my co-workers, "But, you can talk to the doctor out there about it." Yep, I can, and I can also read the same information he has read on it. I can stand out there alongside him after reading the same shit. I can smile and pretend all I want, to get you all to believe and trust in me, if it suits my agenda. However, it doesn't. He has no more fucking information on it then we do. I am not an anti vaxxer by any means, but I also wouldn't sit down and eat a turd knowing it's a turd.

My grown daughter is now a molecular biologist. She was employed with a covid lab straight out of honors college. She refused the vaccine herself. She would tell me what was known about it and how it worked. I had already made up my mind. Plus, after knowing the amounts of samples, they had to mark just in her one lab as positive because of false positives, I was none too impressed with the massive over inflation of cases for this huge fear tactic.

Just like that, all the flu cases were gone. Cancer seemed to drop, heart disease, the millions of other death causing ailments were all gone. Everyone was dying from just covid. I had gotten covid just before this and honestly with the case I got, I would take that before the common cold. Mitchell had contracted it as well before me, in the jail system and wasn't even aware he had it. Everyone around me had contracted it and we had lost two from the community due to complications of it. It seemed like no one was dying of pneumonia anymore. Just covid. Your ass itches? Covid! Does it burn when you pee? Good God, there are no more UTI's or STD's, it's covid.

What I found the most amusing throughout the whole covid scare were the reactions to the people that questioned covid. People that questioned the media's coverage or reported cases. People that wanted actual answers. These people were no longer upstanding citizens within society, they were now mentally ill. Conspiracy Theorists. I do have to applaud them though I can see the effort this time to include everyone, so that is a step in the right direction. This is a disease that came from, well who the hell knows anymore, but not the obvious. It seems like bats get blamed for too much though. How do you think Bats like being the new societal scapegoat?

Forty years ago, it was the gay community. We all had to fear them because of aids. How did it originate? The white man, the black man. The educated, the uneducated. The fat and the thin. Men and women. Drug addicts or non addicts. Cigarette smokers, or nonsmokers. At least with this one there were no teams, it affected everyone. Extrovert or introvert. Mentally ill, mentally sane. It was politically correct to its core. No one to blame but the bat. Poor bat.

Now we have a new category. The vaccinated and the unvaccinated. That isn't calling anyone out on anything that could possibly come close to political incorrectness. Everything must always be divided into teams. The old team mentality that is displayed right in an individual's home that is dominated by a narcissist. Pick me, pick me. Why are there teams? Who owns these teams? And for fuck sakes who the hell keeps score? Why must people's emotions be exploited all the time? There has to be a reason for this occurring, we are all mad about it. It has affected all our lives. Where do we look? Who do we blame? We can't be mad at the poor innocent bats; animal freaks would have a fit. Moving further and further from the initial source and keep adding the layers.

Did these quickly thrown together, more ineffective than effective vaccines, exist two years ago? Did big pharma have a drop in their profits? Who knows? These are all questions that I am sure have been answered that I haven't taken the time to look at. This is not to take away from anyone that lost their life to covid and only covid alone. Broadly it seems like a clear and concise cigarette smoker stamp to me. It's much more convenient to write. Oh, and profitable too. Now that you all had injections of the devil only knows what, and there are no legal repercussions for the labs and pharmaceuticals that create and push it.

Have the vaccination and now you have health issues? Prove it was this quickly thrown together vaccination. A vaccination that was forced on you in order to keep others safe, or in some twisted states, to keep your job. Oh well the medical community will use research backed up from the FDA that quickly and astonishingly approved it. With information from the very labs that created it to tell you it has nothing to do with the vaccination. The doctors will convince you that it must be something else. Common theme.

There can be communities of people online. They can all be suffering with the same side effects from medicine or a procedure. Thousands and thousands of people, yet no research has been done to show any of their concerns as side effects. Well of course not, much like the slimy DA and court appointed attorney, that doesn't fit their agenda. Even if you could prove it, what are you going to do? Sue in a huge class action lawsuit? Are you going to get enough money from this to reverse the damage done to your body or to make up for the inconvenience in your life? Under normal circumstances it's highly unlikely. Under these circumstances it is a great big NO. You can't sue them at all. Yet again they exploited the very human emotion that they lacked, for profit.

Don't worry though, if you do develop health problems from this, big pharma will be right there with possibly the correct medication to combat it. Maybe. If you can afford it. I am sure they will have more than a few different medications to try. Well, we still have health insurance that can help pay for some of that, right? Yeah, but only some medications while they are sliding off the backside of more stringent drug protocols to cushion their profits. The hospitals can still try and treat whatever you have now. No one is going to suffer financially except you, so it is not a problem for them.

How many decades has it been? No vaccine for cancer, Christ they barely have one for hpv. How many decades to develop the flu vaccine? Yet one exists so quickly for covid? If you don't take it with our playing off your empathy, or our bullying tactics from the other team, you are now officially mentally ill. This was hilarious and just getting more and more amusing to me.

You're welcome for our service during this though. Just like we knew from the beginning, we see what all of us "Essential workers' got for supposedly risking our lives. While the opportunistic people collected an extra six hundred a week for "living in fear of their lives." I got a big whooping 281.00 from the state for being an essential worker. Thank you for that, it came in handy with the nonsensical toilet paper shortage.

Halfway
XIII

Mitchells release date was in February. He was essentially forced to take a plea that left him with an inability to proceed easily in life. I was not ready to go back to meet up with him and start our lives together until Mid-April. I had previous responsibilities with my youngest child and my crappy job. He could not legally come to my state as he was on post release. I was instead adamant that he didn't need to ignore restrictions and that I would come meet him. His probation date was extended until November for a nine-month stint. I never pushed for a transfer because honestly, I never wanted to stay there another day.

I could watch in that short span of a couple of months how everything was stacked against him. It was unbelievable to me. I watched him persevere through. I watched him stay on task. He had his probation transferred to a new county, where we had both lightly discussed at one time trying to start over. I never really thought he put any weight to this, it was just a suggestion. Four hours away from our original county of residence. He, however, followed through. He stayed on task.

He immediately upon arriving in this new county was accepted into a sober living home. He became employed in his old profession and was saving money for me to come down. He called me every day; he sent me messages throughout the day and was very thoughtful. Although he was hurt that I had gone off with Sam to stay with him a little, he verbally had forgiven me and understood why. I mean realistically what could he say? His behavior is what put me in that predicament.

The important thing is that I wanted to start over and be with him now. He apologized for all his wrongdoings and wanted to spend the rest of his life proving to me that he was worth my time and investment. We had missed each other horribly and this time of separation was now water under the bridge. He had to spend two weeks upon his initial release at a covid motel. I never knew any of his moves because he didn't have a phone to call me yet. Since the sober living accepted him, he was able to move forward and on track to his future goals with me.

Only two weeks into his sober living stay, he had paid all the bills for the home and had brought the home up out of the red. He contributed to paying for some of the other guys' stays too. His plan was to save all he could while there, so he could get a place before I came down. He had paid for an attorney to take care of all his driving issues and was on track to get his driver's license back within a couple of months. He told me to mark the date on the calendar because he was going to buy me an engagement ring in six months. I giggled because that would have marked the night we originally met. The night when I first saw him across the field, and he had no idea. September 5th.

He had set up with a doctor in the area and was taking all the steps to make sure he could get back on his medication. He was on medicine when originally incarcerated. County jail felt he didn't need it anymore and abruptly took it from him. Replacing it with a totally different medication a few weeks later. One they prescribe to all the inmates, due to extremely cheap cost and having nothing to do with his treatment plan. The nurse at the jail felt it would be perfectly fine to do so. Kind of makes me giggle a little. I wasn't aware that LPNs could regulate and prescribe medications. They must have a special pass in jail though because he never saw or spoke to a doctor. When he asked, they could never provide him with one. Just her.

He was touring parks on the weekend and taking time to himself to be one with nature. He would send me pictures of the local parks and sights in the area. As excited as I was to finally be with the man I loved, sober and matured, in a state with nice weather, I kept my guard up. He promised me due to the job I had to endure while he was locked up and the losses, I incurred that he would financially provide for me. Allowing me some time off from work.

Although I could see that he had stepped up and was becoming the man he should have been from the start, I was still guarded. I knew I would need some solid time to change that perspective. I had told myself that I would move with him, and I would watch him for the first year. I was not going to take any steps towards seriously merging a future with him until that first year was up. He had to unknowingly prove to me that his words and actions aligned. I was not going to jump back in headfirst, naive and hopeful.

I was not going to get a job. Prove to me that you can provide for yourself and me. I did it for you, two children, myself, and most times my ex, for years. Prove it to me Prove you can do it for me. I knew from previous behavior, that if I did become employed, he would have the option of falling back on me. He knows I am going to make sure the bills are paid, and I would have to fight to get a dollar from him. No job, no money, no problem. I just keep enough aside to get back to Maine if it gets bad. I will play a domestic goddess, while you earn money and take care of me.

Prove to me you can provide a living for me. You get a rental, your name goes on the lease, and you work. Things that a normal person would expect someone to do for themselves. The very things I always had to step up and do for Mitchell. My expectations of the dating pool had narrowed significantly through the years, and he was one of the root causes. Honestly, he owed me so much money that I could spend the next three years of my life unemployed. Drawing little pictures of dog shit on post it notes, and he better not say a damn word to me.

I had at this point put in my two weeks' notice at work, and I was excitedly looking forward to my future. Not so much a future with any particulars, but a future of being in better weather. Within three days of me putting in my notice and saying my goodbyes, Mitchell called me. He was leaving the sober living home and relocating to a hotel down the road. He couldn't have roommates anymore. It was too much chaos, and they were all petty and acted like schoolgirls. He had sent me copies of the texts they sent each other at this home, and I agreed with him. I was excited that he had matured to the point that he knew he didn't belong around that kind of behavior.

A few days later I got a call because he needed advice. He had been calling his probation officer all along and doing everything that had been recommended to him upon release. He could never get a hold of his probation officer however and had to continuously leave her messages. She had his phone number as well as mine, and she never attempted to call him back and certainly never tried to contact me. He was nervous about moving to the hotel because they would need his new address. He couldn't just show up at the office as covid was still being used for every government official to not have to do their job. I told him all he could do was call and leave her another message.

It was less than a week later, while I was still working out my two weeks' notice that he called me panicking. Apparently, they had him down as an absconding inmate. They had him under an active arrest warrant for absconding from the original county he was in before he transferred. Mind you they had his phone number. They had his new address. They had his job information, and they had his list of people to contact, me included. None of these avenues were used on the probation officer's end.

The new county that he had transferred to had assigned him to a probation officer that doesn't normally handle that area. They had assigned him to the wrong one. This probation officer never checked any of her messages that were left but decided to show up to his old address and of course he wasn't there anymore. She absolutely did nothing other than transfer the case back to his original county and the original probation officer he had been assigned to.

No follow through on her end. No checking her messages, no calling him, nor myself. She just marked him as absconding and sent it back. Lazy ass bitch! His original probation officer made no attempt either to contact him or myself, nor his job. Nothing, absolutely nothing. Amazing to me, those two are cream of the crop let me tell you.

Mitchell had to, at this point, contact his original probation officer and listen to a barrage of insults, threats, and condescension. It was actually the no good for nothing probation officer that should have had the insight to understand it was his fuck up. Project much? I mean they are in the positions they are in because people expect them to be responsible grown adults as a probation officer. However, my amazement of disappointment and disgust with this whole system and its people just never ends. I guess expectations are too much to have anywhere.

Mitchell walked three miles to the county jail to turn himself in for absconding over Easter weekend and nearly lost his job. How's that for absconding? He didn't get very far if he just turned himself in did he? Pathetic! He panicked, not knowing his fate. He had just gotten out and was doing so well. Now he didn't know if he was going to have to go back to serve his extra nine months of prison time or not. It seemed the universe just didn't want us together or for me to leave this state. Too late now I had already worked out my two weeks' notice and made my excitement about leaving remarkably well known. I had to go now regardless.

His probation officer, in all his arrogance, lied by stating he had tried to call him and I several times with no answer. Although his probation officer tried to back up his stories with lies and no truths to substantiate these, I guess in society's eyes the probation officer is naturally the better of the two? I mean just show us the phone records. No Mitchell was a felon now, there is no way he is telling the truth over a probation officer. Mitchell still had to have a hearing and sit before a parole board. He was narrowly allowed to stay out of jail again by agreeing to pay extra for an ankle monitor and be on curfew. Extortion at its finest.

I had to hand it to his new probation officer though. She was a Godsend, and the type of person that should hold that position. She felt so bad for the wrongs and lies that were placed onto Mitchell. She apologized for the sheer lack of decency displayed by the other two. She assured him that he should have been placed with her from the start, but she never received any paperwork about him. She knew what they had done to Mitchell was so immorally wrong. As a result, she waived his fees and only made him participate on the ankle monitor for a month. Thank you. Although you did nothing to make the other two look like useful members of the title they hold, you did partially restore my faith in half decent people holding those positions. I wish you the best always.

This scenario made me think of stupid people again. So of course, my mind goes right back to short friend and her old horde of the 'gifted." I knew since her divorce from sewer man a few years back, that she kept in contact with Kelly and pot stench boy. The oldest daughter with the one-year-old at the time, had since passed away. She had been hit by a car that same year while walking with her baby and her boyfriend. The sun proved to be too bright, and the driver didn't even see them. Thankfully, the baby and the boyfriend were unharmed, but she had to be removed from life support a day later. As tragic as this was, there was still a lot of unsophisticated humor, believe me. There was not a shortage with this group, even during this.

I would reflect on this event sometimes and all I could ever think was why in the hell would a man be letting his woman walk on the outside of him nearest to the road? If he had of been any kind of real man, that would have been him on the outside. Although not dismissing one's life for another, but dude, she had a job to do. She had a child to raise.

Your selfish and very misguided ignorant ass caused all the drama inflicted on this child in her later years and she has lost her mother. All because you never had a clue how to be a man. Watch it ladies, do better raising your sons. If they are walking on the inside of their girlfriend and expecting her to protect him, be leery of the fact you didn't do your job and correct his ass. He could have at least died with respect, dignity, and honor. Instead, he is shacked up with some other clueless girl that pities him for the tragedy of that day. Pitied for what only he had to endure, while he spends her tax return.

I remember the funeral, and I remember the night she was taking from life support. My best friend and I had the baby. She was tiny then and barely tall enough to peek over the sides of the playpen at us. All I could do was pray to God to help her through. What a tragedy.

This poor baby, no mother, and no hint of a father. She was going to be sentenced to life within the confines of being stuck to the sap on that family tree.

Girls, honor yourselves, your children, and the responsibilities of this massive yet glorious job you have been blessed with. Make sure you know who your children's fathers are. This story doesn't happen to everyone, but please respect your children enough to know this. I am willing to bet even in the worst-case scenario that at least he and his family would have had a better shot at raising this little baby. Or at least being another avenue of family, and a support system for her as she grows up.

I remember at this funeral; the building was packed. It was a small town, and I was used to the small-town vibe. Everyone wanted to show their respect. I wasn't sure how to dress appropriately for this "event" as I had previously met the family. I decided to dress casually, with just a silk blouse and some dress capris with sandals, as I wasn't too sure. I remember second and third guessing myself as to the outfit I had on, on my way over. Not that this tragedy had anything to do with me, or that anyone would even be looking, but I didn't want to appear like she didn't matter. I remember thinking I didn't want to look disrespectful.

I remember the brother walking by the car at this time and stopping to conversate with the friend I was with. He was anxious and sobbing, a bright orange shirt and still adorning his dirty pot hat. Dirty ripped jeans and shoes with the toe worn out. My friend complimented him on his shirt, "Like your shirt, looks good on you." Apparently, this kid was notorious for only wearing a pot leaf shirt. He smiled and nervously clutched at the front of the bright orange material. He looked for a second like he wanted to say something profound as he hung his head lower and then looked up. "Do you think so?" "I was nervous putting this on, because my sister wouldn't have wanted me all dressed up like this" My heart broke for how lost and disconnected he appeared, but my anxiety about my outfit subsided quickly.

As we walked into this girl's wake, the family was all present. I couldn't help but overhear the mother speaking cheerfully. No hint of sadness or disbelief. Not fraught with tears or even disheveled. She spoke excitedly, about how she would have the baby now and something about the social security check. I could only shake my head further as I gazed up to see.

Laid out in an open casket, this poor little girl had suffered all that trauma. They had her in an open casket, for all to see. Not just this baby screaming and wanting to be held by her mommy one last time, but for all to see. There on display, this grown woman, body swollen from trauma was stuffed into her final resting place. She lay in the one and only outfit they could find suitable for her. Her sports uniform from her freshman year of high school? "She loved basketball that year."

I could only blink and pray for that baby. Like I said girls, do your children a favor. No matter how badass you think you are. No matter if you believe you need the father of your baby or not, they need them. Put your little ego aside, it's not about you anymore. Your children need them and their families.

There are always lessons to be learned from anything and tragedies are no different. Not to say that this family would ever learn, but I had met this little girl for a reason. In just the short time of meeting her, I learned it's alright to buy yourself something occasionally. She helped me to understand how thankful I was that my children knew their father. Finally, her death helped me to reevaluate the actions of a true man.

I learned later through the course of the years that Kelly did finally get the opportunity to have and hold her own children. Four of them, all with different internet fathers. Three children had been placed for adoption and the fourth the father took to raise. She was severely underweight. Living now in a run-down trailer with no electricity and a crack addiction. The brother graduated from pot smoking along with his tattoo gun. I did get the opportunity to see some of his work. He is now a frequent flier at the jail, battling a massive meth addiction, and I am sure a whole host of new clients for prison tats.

The baby is now a teenager and is still a permanent fixture in short friends' life. After a few years of tortuous court battles, the grandmother finally got arrested for selling narcotics. Short friend and sewer man finally got custody. Not before the damage was done though. They fought so hard to get that baby from her, but the judge never listened. The judge still didn't want to listen even after the grandmother got arrested for selling drugs. Ego within the criminal justice system, it's a hell of a thing. She is now a "troubled" child with anger issues. I can only hope the stability that has been provided in the past few years by her grandfather and short friend will help her. God bless.

I set out; car packed to the roof with material possessions. I had accumulated items during my Maine living and off I drove into the night. Normally I love driving all alone. It gives me time to clear my mind. Like I said, I had evolved to a world in the past few years where I craved a massive amount of alone time. Driving afforded me this as well. I drove this time excited to be after three years, finally starting over with some direction.

The thoughts of Mitchell and I being able to finally start over. The thoughts of him putting work into himself while imprisoned, undisturbed by parental influence. I was excited to think that after all this time I was going to finally be able to move ahead with a real-life grown-up man. The love of my life, finally clean and sober. I was so proud of everything that we had overcome. In the dark of the night, I drove all alone. As I belted out my half of the old classic nineties' duets on the radio, the sparks began to fly.

I had been struck by the retread of an eighteen-wheeler tire. It took out the whole back of my car. Not drivable at this point, but I managed to safely maneuver across three lanes of traffic to the shoulder. This in itself was quite a little adventure; however, I just viewed it as another moderate inconvenience.

Yeah, I know. I decided at this point that I wasn't supposed to leave Maine, and apparently, we were not supposed to be back together then. The Universe was speaking loud and clear to me. I know I had expressed that I wasn't going to meet him more than halfway again. I know I had said that he needed to meet me on my grounds from now on. I understand all that, but Universe, I meant with maturity. I didn't mean the actual location. What was my alternative?

Great looking out for me though. I could see the point you were trying to prove. You protected me, by allowing the tire to take me out, but it did not actually hurt me. One more foot or one more second and it would have taken out the front of the car and me. Don't think I don't see that and understand it, so I thank you ever so much for your protection. Was it angels protecting me so that I could safely go about my mission? Or was someone trying to deter me and cause me to give up? I meant maturity not location. As the night went on, I grew to understand I was only three miles short of the halfway point between the destinations.

I can take this opportunity now to appreciate this for what it was. I wasn't going to turn around and head back at this point, anywhere had to be better than where I was. I had changed to an unrecognizable place with him as well. Eliminating any shit, he may unsuspectedly throw my way was not going to be an issue. I think Sam had fine-tuned my skills in that area, and honestly, he may have been a slight reminder of how things used to be for me with Mitchell. Maybe the universe didn't want me to forget. I not only felt drawn to stay at Mitchells side, but I was also forced to stay at his side this whole time. I got pink flam a gos constantly to direct my path and there had to be a reason for all of it.

BUTTER KNIVES & BREAD
XIV

I pulled into the great state and area of NC that I needed to be, just in time to align with Mitchell's work schedule. I journeyed on to pick him up. Three years of not seeing him at all. I knew he had grown his hair out. He had sent pictures, but I hadn't seen him in person in three years. I didn't know how our energy would align now. I was slightly nervous, but you could tell he was incredibly nervous. We didn't pick up where we left off, no friendly banter. We almost acted awkwardly like being on a first date. I guess in a sense it would have been.

He was very sweet and accommodating and he proceeded with a goal in mind. He mentioned marriage again and told me he wanted to have a ring for me by November. I smiled slightly and crossed dates in my mind. Remembering that just a month and a half earlier he stated he wanted to have one for me by September. He was already moving the goal post and I hadn't been there for half of a day yet. Mitchell had not returned to his full capacity from his last drug binge and only appeared worse from the trauma he endured during extended incarceration.

As I looked around the hotel he was staying in, it was a typical bachelor pad. I thought if anything, I can look at this like a vacation from my life before, and just head on back. I noticed a pink and blue change purse on the spare bed beside him and knew he had not gone to a covid motel like he had stated. I never let on though. I knew he had gone back to his parents.

I waited a couple of weeks and wrote a letter. I couldn't honestly see myself staying with him at that point. He had already moved the goal post, and I had already caught him in a lie. I decided to leave and go to SC to visit my oldest daughter. I brought the letter with me however, because I yet again guessed if I was being unreasonable. Relationships are work. I must be more understanding of his situation. Yet again I must take the time to look inside myself to see where I am wrong with this.

I do this way too much. Bend myself to accommodate other people. I wonder if anyone has ever done this for me? Quick I already know, wait for it, wait for it, no, they never have. While driving back from an overnight visit with my daughter, that I myself had not laid eyes on in over a year, Mitchell called me. After three weeks of me living in a hotel with him, taking my classes and thinking about leaving every day, he was excited he had found us a place.

It was a massive challenge to find a place during this time due to covid and housing shortages. Not to mention his newly acquired criminal charges. I smiled and thought, Good, maybe this is the transition I need to be ok with everything now. Maybe this will be my new start with stability. I tucked away the letter and followed his lead.

Mitchell at this time was on his ankle monitor. He called and asked permission from the probation officer to leave the county so we could go get our belongings out of storage. Storage that I had been paying for, over the past three years. Three years of storage fees thanks to his mother. Four hours from our new apartment, with just six hours to spare before curfew and with a four-hour ride back. He packed a three-bedroom two-bathroom home's worth of belongings into a moving truck.

This was exciting to me to finally be able to see stability happening. I was still numb to most things and very guarded. I figured the universe would guide me. It will tell me what to do from here on out. I was with a changed man now, he looked to God, and I was to follow him following God.

The apartment was beautiful; however, it was in an old warehouse that had been remodeled. During this time the only apartment available was a two-bedroom two bath, with absolutely no window. One exit with a peak hole and no window. It was like living in a bank vault. I knew we wouldn't have to stay past his probation release. I began to learn how to deal with it. Mitchell and I were so happy for the first two months in our new apartment. It was almost like we had a real relationship.

He was a workaholic, and I love alone time, so this dynamic worked out great. I cleaned obsessively, waited on him hand and foot, and always had big meals cooked every night. Although not without sacrifices from me, he made enough money to support us both and I began relaxing. I knew that I could enjoy the next couple of months before going back to work. We had discussed the fact that I would go back to work in September, after my youngest came down for the summer. I wanted to spend time with her freely. I was content with more pink flam a go signs and continued silently amused.

He was making little jokes now about the other men at the apartment complex. Calling them out of their names, because quite frankly he didn't know them. He would come up with amusing nicknames though. I would giggle at this, because I could see how he was becoming slightly jealous, but honestly, I never knew of anyone he was referring to. I would just joke alongside him.

I hadn't taken the time to meet anyone there, and I only left to go grocery shopping or to sit in my car to get some sunlight. I had no interest in another man, I was just happy to be with him. I know how a man's insecurities work. I made no attempt to add to this for him. That is a childish tactic used by little girls to make someone jealous. I had no intention of making him jealous, nor the desire to do so.

The jealousy had started to become increasingly noticeable after the fourth of July, more towards the end of July actually. We had adopted a dog from the shelter. Mitchell said the dog would keep me company during the day and keep other men away from me. I would giggle about this because I wanted to rescue a dog, but admittedly I would have liked to take more time looking.

The dog had massive behavioral issues, and I spent a huge portion of my day just attending to this dog's needs now. I like things clean, and I ended up having to sweep the floors and vacuum a minimum of four times a day and mop them twice. I have never seen a dog shed so much in my life and I worked at a veterinary facility for five years. He was not housebroken, and we didn't even have a window to open for air. I was starting to become ugly.

Mitchell would laugh about this though, because he would spend his whole day gone into the late hours of night. He would remark that the dog had to stay because he warded off other men. He barked constantly and started attacking me and my children. Mitchell absolutely refused to get rid of him and would try to make me feel bad. Acting like he had a bond with the dog, so much so that he couldn't be bothered to even walk him more than once every other week. Well until I threw a fit. I had to walk him six times a day. I was becoming miserable with my living situation. I knew what was coming.

When he outright accused me of having sex with the man down the hall, I had had enough and decided I should probably take the time to see who this man was. I had been accused of sleeping with him several times and I didn't even know who he was referring to. I was having wild sex orgies next door with the maintenance man, and at night to taunt him, I was upstairs in another man's apartment stomping on the floors. This was to rub it into him, how I could get any man I wanted. Mind you I was sitting in the kitchen, but in his mind, I was upstairs, so that is where I had to have been. When I tried to correct him, he would become enraged and accuse me angrily of lying, dismiss me and then leave.

Fucking meth, here we go again. Try explaining your side of anything to a meth addict. Good luck. That drug is evil! Alone all day in a bank vault, knowing no one, he kept accusing me. Not nicely either. He had told me that he was going to install cameras at the door so he could see who was coming and going. He then decided that would be a waste of time and money, because I would just leave and have sex with all these men in my car out in the parking lot. Just the most disgusting vile accusations and then would top it off with "No one wants you except drug addicts and alcoholics." Does he drink? Who? Does who drink?

You cannot have a rational conversation, or for that matter any conversation with someone under the influence of meth. Mind you none of this started until after my youngest had left. I had my suspicions, but it was in the early stages. While my youngest was down he kept it together and I never mentioned a word, but I knew what it was going to be when she left. One because I knew I was about to give him an ear full, and she didn't need to be there when I did that.

He started making friends with other girls and contacting the same flock he hung with previously in his hometown, except I was the one fucking around on him. It came to its pinnacle in mid-October. I was supposed to have been back to work at this point. My daughter had spent the summer and was back in school and the plan was for me to be back at work. I knew I couldn't go. Having a job means I would need sleep. Sleep every night. Who was going to tend this behaviorally challenged dog? Who was going to clean this place? He wasn't capable of even knowing where he was half the time, he was absolutely no help with anything. Just the opposite. Compounding the mess and stress.

He was withholding money for bills and accusing me of only being with him for that reason. He was working fifteen hours a day and would come back just long enough to start fights over, well who knows. You don't get sleep when you are with a meth addict, because they don't sleep, and they will make sure you don't either. Plus going to work would surely mean I was fucking all my coworkers, so even more fights and no sleep. Torment, that is the best word I can use to describe their behavior. Just torment.

His probation date was October 15th. He had successfully completed this through a series of active addictions and withdrawal, with even worse mood swings. I endured these too. He left that night to go celebrate his release with his meth buddy and a little girl that was equally yoked in that scene. He had looked her up previously on the computer, stalking her in essence. Yet I was the one fucking around. You see how that works? He wasn't answering his phone anymore, well not for me anyway, so why bother calling.

Here I am in an area, living in a bank vault, knowing no one. My man was gone all day and into the night, and we didn't even communicate during the day. I could have been dead for days and no one would have found me. He would have come back to the apartment just long enough to scream at my corpse. The dog would have been gnawing my bones and pissing on me. I was there for one thing and one thing only. To destroy his life. Right back to having no one to rely on, no one to talk to, and no desire to do anything about it.

He was like having a rebellious behaviorally challenged teenager around, with absolutely no respect for me. He would storm out, dog barking constantly at first, trying to defend me, and I would be stuck in the bank vault. His and the dog's behavior were very much aligned, and I could see how the dog fed off his energy. Of course, the dog is going to start attacking me, he loved Mitchell and Mitchell attacked me, so why not. I felt bad for the dog, but at this time, there was nothing more I could do. I began separating myself from Mitchell. I moved to the spare bedroom and in my mind was planning my departure.

This dog was so misbehaved and fed off Mitchell's energy so much that I remember going to hide in the bathroom one day. As I sat there in the dark of the bathroom and peered out, I could see the dog. He came over and sat on the rug in the hallway in front of me. He just quietly and intently stared up and to the left as though he was transfixed. I could never see what he was looking at because of the wall in my way, and I would have surely disturbed him if I moved from behind him. This was so out of character for this dog to be calm and just sit, that I remember after five minutes that I just felt compelled to record it. That is how odd this was.

It was probably a couple of weeks later during one of Mitchells calm moments that I showed him the video. To which I got the reply of "Oh wow, who do you have standing over there keeping his attention?" "Who is dimming the light?" "Pretty funny you didn't go out and record what he was looking at, you didn't dare, because then I would have found out who you have been fucking." To speak to Mitchell about anything was to be assured you would be insulted. I had just learned to live in my own mind and become extremely silent.

I had called him this one day but per usual, no answer. It was probably two hours later when I decided to venture outside from cleaning and get some sunlight. I never knew what I was in for weather wise, I didn't have a window. Upon exiting the building, the very man I had been accused of fucking every day for almost four months was walking the same corridor. His back and arms weighed down with backpacks and bags. I held the door open for him, as I consider this to be common courtesy, and curiosity had got the best of me. It wasn't his fault that I lived with a crazy, delusional, abusive meth addict.

Holding the door for this man felt unworldly to me. I knew nothing of him, other than the nickname that Mitchell had referred to him as. As he departed the door, I felt an indescribable ease in his space. His eyes appeared to light up and his smile was gorgeous.

He thanked me for holding the door and began to ask me about my day. I had no hesitation for the first time in my life, no thought behind it, no unease, no discomfort, no nerves, nothing. Nothing, totally void of any reservations. It felt like something almost guided me.

This guidance aligned me on the inside of him as we walked up the sidewalk together having a mini conversation. I hadn't heard the words thank you in so long. I was wondering what I did so profoundly. Why would someone feel they had to thank me for it. Admittedly, I could fully understand why Mitchell would be jealous of this man. Fuck just the fact that he thanked me for something was more respect than I had received in several months. The fact that he was extremely good-looking and charming was an afterthought. I felt someone's friendliness and warmth for the first time in months, and for a split moment in time enjoyed small talk again.

All good things come to an end though, and in my case a very quick end. As this man, who I will respectfully call John, tried to extend small talk while walking, I could see the top of Mitchells work truck in the driveway by my car. Never returned my phone call from hours ago and had no intention of coming inside to check on me. He just thought he and his little worm looking methy coworker would sneak back to Mitchell's car real quick while on lunch break.

My pace began to increase, and I made a notable attempt to not walk evenly with John's strides. I didn't know if I had been, but I was feeling way too comfortable in this man's energy. Just in the twenty seconds of walking with him. Any move from here on out would be sheer torment for me for the next few months. Either way I was going to be accused of sleeping with him, so I smiled at John and told him to have a great day. I then hastened my steps towards Mitchell. I knew with my one act of good intentions that I would be verbally abused for the next, well who knows how long honestly. No good deed goes un-punished.

It was three days later when I was exiting the apartment to go sit in my car, away from the accusations, the verbal abuse and just sheer torment. Away from Mitchell and all the glorious, beautiful shit he was spewing. My anger was beyond anger, and I had flatlined with disgust. I sat in my car contemplating my next move. I couldn't go back in there tonight, but I knew I had to, maybe I will just get some distance from him in my car.

I also knew that if Mitchell followed me to my car, per usual, that he would try to act a little nicer to me. At least then there is a possibility of witnesses. He would always try to play it like it was me being irrational, by not wanting to speak to him. I could sit outside trying my best to ignore him, while he looked like a saint, and me an unreasonable bitch.

He would even go so far as to get on his knees outside my car door and loudly beg me to tell him why I was upset and cry out that he was just trying to make me happy. The second he knew no one was around watching his act anymore he would spring to his feet. He would smirk wildly and launch himself through the car window, expressing how he was going to kill me.

His voice would deepen as he pressed his face firmly into the side of mine. Teeth grinding to remind me that I wasn't ever leaving him. I could get that thought right out of my fucking head. He always raged that if I ever tried to that he would kill me and the man I tried to leave with. He would taunt me by stating, "Do you think I am fucking lying? Do you? Try me, I dare you." He would then go into how badly I treated him and begin hitting himself violently and crying out "Ouch, look what you just did." Crying out and asking me why I was hurting him?

I suppose that way if we both have scratches and bruises then he can look like a victim of abuse too? He would scream how I never loved him or cared about him. The usual, but when I would question any of his prior behavior even from just an hour beforehand, he would deny it all. He would then ask me why I was bringing up the past. "Why do you keep bringing up all my faults? "You can't move on can you? "Always bringing up my past,"

He projected so much that 90% of the time, I just stood in pure astonished disbelief. He would speak decently of me around others while in public. Cracking jokes with people he knew about my apparent quiet disposition. "Don't mind her she's just autistic." Behind closed doors, however, he had no problem telling me how wrong I had always done him while threatening me with butcher knives, machetes, and even once, grenades.

Anyway, this night in particular happened to be three days after holding the door for John with small talk. Mitchell's fear of me fucking with another man had now been solidly cemented in his mind. I had fled to the car. Mitchell was relentlessly making me recall details of my previous twenty-second conversation with John. The conversation from three days ago, and for the third night in a row. I never gave Mitchell the details he was hoping for, because honestly who needs that added crazy drama?

Christ, how many times can you say the same thing verbatim about a twenty second conversation? He always did whatever he wanted. He spoke to women all day long. He would spend hours at their homes. Collecting phone numbers along the way. Like I said, what was fine for him to do, was always forbidden from me.

I recall him grabbing me this evening in a blind rage, butcher knife in hand and screaming he was going to kill me. I was a fucking liar, and he couldn't trust me. I just stood there back too. Disgusted because he was holding me hostage with a knife again. I could see the knife at his side. All I had the energy to say was "Go ahead." "I won't have to come back and do this shit again, you will!" He became so infuriated that he turned the knife on himself and threatened to stab himself with it.

"Go ahead, I am not going to stop you, but aim lower, those cheap knives are not going to pierce your breadbasket." Nothing more to say, and as he grabbed my arm to pull me back through the door he shouted "cunt," as I pulled away to the safety of the hallway. I had done a lot of healing away for those three years without him and just like that, my bottom-line apathy was back.

Mitchell had for the past four months repeatedly pointed out that John always parked next to my car in the parking lot. "Who gives a shit?" I say. I never noticed that crap in my life. Who the hell cares where the man parks? "If you truly cared, you would park next to me, but you don't. You park on the other side of the building." "You think you are going to sneak in and catch me doing something, so I guess the spot is empty." It was this night as I sat alone, replaying the knife drama from just minutes ago in my mind and talking to God, that the empty parking spot next to me, became full.

John and another tenant that he was apparently friends with pulled up alongside me. Smiling ear to ear and waving his arm off. He leapt from his vehicle and excitedly hollered to his friend about meeting me. I sat there encased in the night sky peeking around to see who was coming up alongside the back of my car. John's excitement at seeing me stopped me in a moment of inquisitiveness and I decided he must be drunk. He was so friendly as he excitedly waved his friend over and then stood outside my car door peeking in.

I peered out at this man who was hunched slightly over to make visual contact with me, and our eyes met. My heart fluttered for a quick second, but I cut that shit off. The last time my heart fluttered, I ended up with Mitchell. Not ever wanting to make that grave mistake again, I stared at him instead and asked, "Can I help you?"

He looked boyish and slightly sheepish as he bowed his head slightly to gaze at his feet and remarked by saying, "I just wanted to see what you were up to." That was so sweet, I thought. I haven't had a sweet friendly gesture in months, well apart from him three days ago. Keep just being normal, and I am going to fall in love with you. Not going to take much at this point. Instead, I answered him with a "Not much, how about you two?"

He, his friend and I conversated, breaking the ice for all of five minutes. If honestly even that, but I remember trying to listen for signs that he may be trying to hit on me. He didn't introduce himself until the end of our conversation, but he did tell me his name and apartment number. I didn't know what to consider since his friend introduced himself first and told me what apartment he lived in too. I could only consider it friendly banter upon meeting someone new, so I guess my John hero fantasy would now be officially short lived.

It was within moments of John and his friend walking away and wishing me a good night, that Mitchell appeared. His face was half solemn and half remorseful walking slowly by my car. He did, however, have his much-bonded dog. The first time he had walked him in a week, but I suppose the dog was a convenient excuse. He began to run his mouth and accused me of hitting on them. Apologizing profusely and begging me not to leave him. This in turn developed into a three-hour conversation of me trying to talk some sense into him. Trying to deescalate whatever he was thinking.

I wanted to say, "Oh my God, a man that is not an alcoholic or drug addict that is taking his time to speak to me, it must be a delusion. I didn't though. Mitchell is a rapid cycler. I knew after the pinnacle of his rage, he always felt remorse and shame. His insecurities would be the highest and I knew when I could assert my authority, and smart ass remarks. It would always make me wonder if others knew how Mitchell acted. Were they trying to rile him up? The slightest bit of hospitality now from a man, makes me question everything. I can't have normalcy anymore.

He was always hollering at me about how I was going to put him in a hospital or call the cops and that he couldn't trust me. He would accuse me of grand schemes to have him locked up and accuse me of being in cahoots with the police. Then tell me that the only plan he had made for our future together was to have me placed in a nut house. I knew he was reliving past trauma from his mommy, but I didn't give a good shit anymore.

I just sunk into my thoughts that I, alone, couldn't take care of him anymore. People like him are in psych wards with around the clock care. I was one woman with no support trying to take care of a delusional mentally ill, meth addict. I talked to God again just like always. Every night in my car, silently in my head. I couldn't openly write and journal anymore like I could for the past three years. Now I had to hide journal entries in my car and make sure I hid both sets of car keys. I also had to take the keyboard stick with me to bed at night, so he couldn't operate my computer. It wasn't quite to the point where I had to sleep with my purse yet, but I did have to hide it.

Meth addicts are extremely delusional and paranoid. You will question paranoid schizophrenia numerous times. Every word I wrote would be dissected and hyper focused on, but not one word I wrote would be understood in the context it was written. He would scream at me about writing and insult me about the fact that I did it. He would rip my notebooks from me and would hold them for ransom. Mitchell had always, through the years, made fun of me for writing. He couldn't understand why I did it, and nothing I wrote made any fucking sense to him, because I was a dumb bitch.

I could have written that I gave the dog a flea bath, and in Mitchell's world, he would read that to say a lot more. I was giving the dog a coconut oil spa bath with another man, because we were getting ready to take the dog away. We would move in together and leave him abandoned without even his precious dog. Do you see the lengths of unreason with this? Try arguing with that? The words on the very paper say one thing, anyone can read it. Mitchell would holler at me for trying to lie to him though and accuse me of erasing the words. There is no basis for it. Pure delusion, plain and simple.

While they are in the delusion you are whatever they say you are. You are doing whatever they say you are doing, and you wrote whatever they think you wrote. He would spend hours staring at pictures on my computer and instead of focusing on the picture itself, he would focus on something in the background. Perhaps a man that may be across the street in the photo, something that would clue him into the man I was seeing behind his back. I could dissect this and say, it's because he knew that's what he deserved to have happen for his actions. Yet God kept giving me the energy from somewhere and I don't know how. I am stuck here now though, so let me rifle through some more videos on BPD. Let me try with all the little that I don't have left to understand how I can make this better for him.

I would make it quite clear to him, that he fucked us up. He overstepped a boundary that he knew I had laid out before I came down here. He chose to take a drug that I told him I would not tolerate anymore. I made it quite fucking clear that if he touched that damned shit again that I would leave. Yet here I was trying to steer him out of one delusion and the next and the next. I can't keep bearing the brunt of his past traumas. I can't keep raising a man that was not raised properly. I can't keep allowing myself to be his focal point of abuse and accusations. Yet I knew I couldn't leave him alone. Although I couldn't rely on him for anything anymore, I knew leaving him to the wolves was not within me.

We didn't even eat dinner together anymore. Any resemblance of normalcy that was exhibited when I first arrived here with us was all gone. Just one week of meth use is noticeable, but five months of it, via needles and huge amounts trying to end their own lives, they are unrecognizable. Needles, disgusting! I am not sleeping in the same room as you and if I go to get in the shower and see a needle tip sticking up out of the drain again, I am going to freak out! They don't give a shit about what they do to others on their path of self-destruction. They wholeheartedly believe their actions only affect themselves. Nothing else exists in his world, other than a strong obsessive belief that something is growing in his ear, and that I am fucking other men

MMM.....MILK

XV

He took out his phone one night and began with his infamous snickering laugh. Not a cute inviting laugh, but a cynical and maniacal one. A laugh that would cause anyone to become curious. I had grown to understand that this laugh from him always meant verbal torture for me. He would always let out this snicker, usually once or twice a night, before revealing to me some huge lie he had caught me telling him. This one night as he snickered, I rolled my eyes and said "What, what is so funny now?"

"Oh, you already know." as he glared at me. "You think you are so smart, always lying to me, but not now." "I knew it, how do you try to explain this one to me?" I had no idea what the hell he was talking about, but with Mitchell anything was possible. He came at me with his phone screen to reveal to me the contents. As I looked down, I saw several people in a group photo. It was a sunny day, and it appeared as though they may have been employees at some company. A group's photo. I looked closer at the picture trying to scan the photo for what he was talking about. It was a group photo at an airport. "What Mitchell?" "I don't know anyone at a damn airport."

He snickered again as he said "Oh yes you do, and it says here you have known him since 2014. That's when the picture was taken." "You have been fucking him for all these years." "Is that why we ended up here?" "Why would you bring me here, so you could keep fucking him?" "Who Mitchell?" "What in the hell are you talking about?" "Oh, you know, and I can't believe you are doing this to me." "Doing what Mitchell?"

His anger would burst. He would be full of rage at his discovery and continually accuse me. "What Mitchell, show me what you are mad about." Swooping in angrily for the second time shouting about how he was sick of me playing dumb, he forcefully dropped his finger down on a person standing in the group photo. "Him, right there and you are standing right beside him." "I have caught you, there is no denying it now." Mitchell, move your finger so I can see." As he moved his finger away from the people's faces, I zoomed in closer. There in this group photo was John, standing alongside a couple of different women.

The obsession with this man sent shivers up my spine as I tried to zone out to align more with his world. "Mitchell, that is John, and none of those women are me." "Yes, right there" as he pointed to a woman on the right side of John. "Mitchell that is not me, I didn't even know this guy's name until recently or where he worked, until right now." "That woman is not me, and I am insulted that after all these years you can't tell me apart from other women." With that remark, he decided to take a closer look.

"It's not you." his facial expression dropped. He realized at that moment that he had not caught me doing anything and he looked disheartened. "You knew that I was going to find that picture, so you got online and took the old one down and replaced it with this." "You were scared you were going to get caught." "You know the other

picture was you, now where is it?" "How can you do this to me?"
"You are a sneaky lying bitch."

Pure delusion, you can't argue with it. You can't apply logic to
it. You can either sit and be tormented and abused by it, or you can
leave to your car. That way when he follows you out, he will be a lot
nicer with an audience around. He could then drop down on one knee
outside of the car and loudly plead. He could state that he was just
trying to make me happy. Then he could beg me to look at him, as I
stared off. Then he could plead and cry that he doesn't understand
why I am always mad at him and beg me to forgive him for the audience. I can sit looking like the unreasonable bitch that demands I be
treated like a queen, and he can look like the truly devoted martyr that
just wants my attention. See how that works?

He would actually be so delusional that he would stand in the
mirror with a utility knife. Picking away at the botched, bloody skin
hanging from his ear for three to four hours a night. I would try to talk
reason into him, by trying to get him to go see a doctor about it. Of
course, I didn't know, I was too busy with other men to care about his
ear and didn't want him to get better anyway. I was lying to him trying
to make him look crazy. There was something in his ear, and I didn't
care at all. I was just there to make fun of him.

The best I could ever manage was to talk him into the tweezers
instead of the utility knife. Simply amazing to me that he could throw
a hat on his head the next morning to hide his ears and that no one
found this odd. He lived in the outside world like he was just a workaholic with a crusty ear cyst, and no one questioned his behavior? I
suppose if you have never been exposed to this world, it wouldn't enter your mind as an option, but I had been immersed in it.

I would go outside some nights to retrieve him from his car. I
knew he was stuck. They hyperfocus and he was either going to be
picking in his ear or watching porn. Neither that I need him to be

caught doing. I tried so hard myself to hide this from the outside world. It was more than embarrassing to me.

Who the hell wants to wake up the next morning to find out a whole apartment complex of people have seen your man passed out in his vehicle? Calling the ambulance on him because he has picked at his ear so much that when the blood pools in his collar bone it looks like his throat has been sliced. Bonus of me being blamed for the ambulance call and a loop back to the paranoia of me being in cahoots with everyone. He would fight me so much with just disgusting obscenities. At least I knew if I could get him inside, I could just take the brunt of his abuse privately. He could go about his night inside and I could go sit in my car.

The first winter in the mountains and my first encounter with snow beyond dusting in North Carolina. I giggled because it had snowed about three inches. I could see people in the apartment complex gearing up their sleds and their snowman faces. Yet my face didn't reflect the same excitement. For one I am not a fan of the snow, I had enough thanks. Two I was a little envious that other people could just get excited about wanting to do something and actually be able to do it. Free no restraints.

While the other tenants frolicked in the snow and giggled with their partners, I was headed out to throw salt behind Mitchells tires. He had the night before tried to drive in the storm and I had advised him not to, but what do I know? He got his car stuck in the middle of the parking lot and decided it was fine to just leave it there in everyone's way. Of course, he screamed at me and berated me for this. I tried every day, salt in hand, to move this car for three days, while Mitchell lay inside recovering from an overdose.

He couldn't get out of bed and refused to allow me to call the ambulance. I didn't care about him anyway, and I just wanted to send him away, he shouted. I figured he had sustained kidney damage from the amount of pills he digested while I wasn't looking, directly after he scratched Mitchell is a fucking loser in our apartment floors.

I am sure he did this to try to make it look like it was me, because the letters he carved were extra fancy and loopy. Almost like he was trying to make it appear that someone else had done it. Namely me, I suppose. He recorded the floor carvings and the mess I had begun making from packing up my belongings. He continued with his video button on his phone, pleading that he didn't know why I was behaving like this.

I packed and moved around my belongings because I was leaving. Don't try to play victim to what you have caused. That chapped my ass! Who are you going to show that to? Some poor woman you have marked as your next target? You want people to feel bad for you and take your side? What type of woman is going to believe your shit? Well, let me rephrase that, I know exactly what type that is. The low level and desperate, and while on meth binges, just his type.

Mitchell lay inside in the dry warmth, recovering from an overdose, still delusional, still verbally demanding, and abusive. While I was once again, cleaning up his mess so as not to inconvenience others. Admittedly more so because his car was directly in front of Johns, and I didn't want it still there when John returned. He was a pilot apparently and would leave for a week or so at a time. I had grown to understand through Mitchell's obsession and stalking more than I cared to admit. John never knew he was the center of an argument every night in our apartment. I suppose Mitchell had to be ready for whatever this man and I were going to throw his way.

Having to suffer out cleaning up Mitchells messes in front of John and be nice about it was a feat that would prove to be too hard to accomplish for me. I knew I would say something out of sheer frustration. Possibly that would indicate that I knew entirely too much about him. Abnormal to the extreme.

Sheer frustration, hah it happens. I remember walking quickly down the hall one night to get away from Mitchell. I knew if I could just make it outside and into my car, the abuse would be less. He was following me and as I rounded the corner to the outside door, I could hear his threats quieting. He knew even in his delusion to quiet down because people would be around.

Now he wasn't threatening to kill me or accusing me of fucking other men. I silently walked ignoring him. He caught up to me and walked out the door right alongside me. I never looked up, my mind was aimed at the prize sanctuary of my car, one track mind. He spoke in a loud whisper taunting at my side. "Oh, don't want to walk with me? You think you are too good for me? Oh, I see, do you want me to leave? Do you? Do you? Embarrassed to be seen with me? Don't want to spend time with me, would you rather be in your car? You never want to spend time with me, you think you are better than me. You don't like to hear the truth, do you? You don't want me to tell you how it is," and with all the accusations and the loud taunting, his demeanor changed.

"Oh, I see why you are always in such a hurry to leave me and get outside." I looked up and there walking in front of us was John. Mind you I have no window, I can't foresee this, but admittedly in that moment I had been noticing him outside more now. Quite possibly because I noticed everyone more; I damn near lived in my car.

Mitchell continued to taunt me as we walked only twenty feet behind John. "Meeting up with old John there to suck his dick? Is this what you do at night, pretending to sit in your car, so you can sneak off and fuck John? I love you; how could you do this to me? How long have you been doing this to me? I knew it, I knew you were fucking him behind my back." I just continued hastily to get to my car.

As I crossed over the sidewalk that marked a halfway point to my car from the front door, John popped out from behind a truck. "Hey man," huge smile and all. "What happened to your car?" Mitchell had been backed into a week or so before that at a side job and his headlight was smashed out. Reasonable friendly question. With that I kept walking, but Mitchell smiled from ear to ear and stopped to have a polite conversation with John about his headlight.

Unfuckingbelievable. You have accused me of fucking this man for five months, on a daily basis. You were just walking only feet behind him for the past twenty seconds. Loudly taunting me about being out there to fuck him, and suddenly you are going to stop and sweetly talk to him like you two are best friends? What the hell, and with that my annoyance bubbled over. I looked back with a glare, and it fell from my lips. "You fucking piece of shit!" Sheer frustration, it must come out sometimes. Yes, I know that I probably looked like a classless unreasonable bitch, but at that moment I didn't care.

On my birthday morning, I awoke from a dead sleep to Mitchell excitedly panicking. He had barged into my room demanding the bags of clothes I had for the homeless. I had packed a few bags of clothes and blankets to bring to the homeless when moving in. I had reminded him of these bags for about a month when they were first packed. I kept them in the closet, waiting for him to tell me where we could bring them. I had got sick of looking at them months prior to this. My youngest daughter and I had decided to drop them off in clothing boxes over three months ago. I had told him this already, but he was just remembering them now.

He had been speaking to some people at the convenience store a few minutes before that and he felt they could use them. Apparently, they were outside waiting for the bags. "Mitchell, I have nothing to give them right now." I will have more stuff, but right now I don't, we dropped those off months ago. He was panicking and scrambling around the blankets in the closet looking for something to bring them. His intolerance with me grew quickly. "Well, you are the one that keeps telling me to help people, now that I am, you say we can't. "Do you want me to help people or not? Make up your mind." I rolled from bed to help him look for something he could bring outside to them, because now this was somehow my fault.

It was starting to get cold out and I told him to grab a couple of blankets from the top of the closet. He swooped his arm down and took the blanket I was sleeping with right off my bed. He threw it on top of the other comforter he had taken and made his way out the door, as quickly as he came in. I guess I am up now, happy birthday to me.

The next morning, as I ventured outside, I could feel the chill in the air. As I made my way to my car, I could reflect on the day prior. Although Mitchell was obnoxiously unorganized and he had started my birthday off and ended it with his typical behavior, I had to feel thankful that at least those people had blankets now. Mitchell always put so much effort into appearing to the outside world to be everything he never was at his core.

It was cold and it made me feel better to know that they could at least be warmer. As I scanned the parking lot, I looked down to the parking lot across the street. There in all its purple and pink sequined distinction lay my youngest baby's comforter. An adorable comforter that my baby's nana gave to her before she passed. A comforter that had sentimental value to all involved. A comforter that froze my baby's childhood to me that I would have never given away. He had snuck it under the other blankets. I just looked up and looked the other way.

I wanted to cry, but I couldn't. I would somehow be at fault for being sad and be berated further. I had honed my ability to appear emotionless. How much does that bite? How much does that hurt? How many times can he repeatedly keep getting this wrong? How much more do I tolerate? When is he ever going to learn? When? When? When? I could feel the rush of anger, sadness and disgust just radiating all at once. Laying abandoned, tattered, filthy and torn was my baby girl's blanket.

Could I feel good about sacrificing this to help someone else to stay warm? No, because it wasn't being used to warm someone. Was this blanket wrapped around another child that needed it? No, instead, it was left in a parking lot. Was it on the bed of another little girl that loved make believe and fairy princesses? No, instead it was left abandoned with only one purpose. Draped over a half gallon of milk to make sure the milk stayed warm.

After everything. After every abuse and every insult. I could feel my insides start to boil and, in that moment, I never wanted to rip the flesh off someone's face as badly as I did his. Saying something about it wouldn't have done me any good. He would have just answered me back with intolerance. Some sarcasm about how he can never do anything good enough for me. How he isn't going to try to help anyone else ever again, because I obviously don't want him too. Out of every remark. Out of every insult, every sarcasm and demand that ever fell from his sped-up meth manic mouth. All the stealing, lying, verbal and physical abuse. Constant chaos on every level imaginable. I had overcome and forgave them all, but this one, I still have not forgiven for.

Valentine's day, a day for lovers? Or so I have always heard, just never experienced. Single or not, I had never had a valentine's day. It flashed me back to my children's father and the two valentine's days we celebrated in our 16 years together. The first year of course per usual while they are trying to draw you in, but not the second. By then

I wasn't allowed to drive into town to get him a flower anyway. Someone may look at me, and valentines was just some stupid fucking holiday anyway. I didn't need any flowers. They were just going to die, and it was a waste of money. I admittedly erased this celebration out of my mind years ago, but still, I guess one could hope for Prince Charming.

I left my children's father for a short time about seven years into our relationship. So, our second valentine's day celebration consisted of us being split up and him putting in an effort. He got me a card with twenty dollars in it and a box of q tips. We had discussed how I needed to go buy a box, I was all out. A simpleton Gary's wife, or a girl that had to go back for the sake of the games he played with our child. The stalking and harassment were just as typical from him. Anyway, Valentine's Day up to this point with Mitchell was never anything extraordinary.

Honestly, I can remember one year he brought me home a cute bag full of things he had collected during a meth binge around his parents' home. A card was laid out in front of it. Happy Valentine's Day Bitch! Underlined and everything. He wasn't there when I opened it, but I am guessing it was for me. It was on my counter with my loving pet name, so I took it.

This year, he was coming down on the backside of one of his delusions. I didn't hope for anything and never expected a goddamned thing. I wasn't in the mood to like him, let alone be in love with him. Here is where the expectations come in. I wasn't expecting a gift or even an acknowledgement of the day. I wasn't even expecting a phone call that day to say Happy Valentine's Day. Not even a text actually. We had stopped talking pretty much and I still had his number blocked. I didn't want to listen to his delusions and demands and I had blocked him a few days before that. Not like he called me to say anything nice anyway. Continue making my day a little less stressful and just deal with his shit if he comes home. Like I said, absolutely no expectations.

It was about 7:30 at night, I was sitting in my car, and he approached. Out of breath, smelling like six days of no shower and his ears encased with dried blood. "Hey babe, can you give me a ride to the gas station?" "I was headed home from work earlier, but I fell asleep in my car in the parking lot at work." "I have run out of gas." To which I replied, "Do you have a gas can?" "No, but we can go buy one though." I replied with "So we need to go to the store first, right?" I always had to double check, because a meth addict's delusional plans will change from one moment to the next, no kidding.

In the two-mile journey to the store to get a gas can, his plans changed twice and then he started a fight. Disrespectful, hollering at me, kicking the frame out of my door. Chipping my shift column and repeatedly punching my dashboard. Physically ripping my pocketbook to pieces and stabbing my car seats. I was a fucking bitch for not agreeing with a statement he made about his coworker, and he wanted me to just bring him back to his car, NOW.

With this I turned around and drove him back to his work parking lot. I had every intention of just dropping him off with his out of gas car like he demanded. You can figure it the hell out. You don't need me anyway; you have it all figured out. I mean if I needed someone's help, I wouldn't beat the shit out of the interior of their car and call them a fucking bitch. What do I know though?

Now I had the expectation that I would drop him and all his rage off and drive home. Like I said though, expectations can't have any. He wouldn't get out of my car and insisted he made the past five payments so he could do whatever he wanted to it. "I am not getting out; you NEED to bring me to get a gas can. With that, I shut off the car, took my keys and tried to fake him out, so he would get out of the car to follow me.

Normally when he pulled this I could jump back in and lock him out. I knew this night I didn't have that kind of time, or the desire to try to maneuver around him with my car. He would have just jumped onto my hood per usual, and it would have marked my official fourth time of hitting him with my car. As soon as his raging ass stood from the car and shut the door behind him, I locked the doors with my key fob and started walking. Two miles along the side of a busy highway in a pair of high heeled boots.

I could hear his rage behind me as he hollered "I hope you get hit by a car you fucking cunt, I hope you die." I walked two miles back to the apartment, no phone because it was locked in the car. Thinking, Wow, no expectations, not one for Valentine's Day. Yet I still did have the expectancy of basic human decency. Like I said, no expectations! Go into everything with absolutely no expectation? I bet everyone still does anyway!

He did, however, remember to call the gutter trash that helped him shoot up for the very first time, to wish her a Happy Valentine's Day. They say to help bond with a man, to be his first with something new to him. I guess twelve years of me being beside him was nothing compared to the beauty that shot him up though. Not to exclude anyone though, the other meth girl he had visited in October, he wished her and her son a Happy Valentine's Day too. I wasn't allowed to exist in his world as a decent person, yet he was the one trying to line up gutter trash to feel bad for him.

I often told him when he would try to triangulate me with women he knew, to please up his game. It was an insult to me. If you are trying to make me jealous, could you at least start with someone I would consider in the same league as me? My God, if you want to run off with common street trash, go ahead. I am not going to stop you. Oh wait, I lied, before you go. Here is some money, so you can both fight over a crack rock. Now don't come back.

I know to the outside world, if they ever heard my genuine answer to his pure and utter disrespect, they would probably feel bad for him. Let's trade spots, honey. He can maliciously insult you and threaten to kill you every other day. He can harass and torment you, and you can watch him roll out the front door with a smile plastered on his face. You can stand there while he conversates with other people that you are accused of fucking, and you can keep it all quiet and smile. Best of luck to you. He provokes in me the answer he deserves.

Provoke, provoke, provoke. He wasn't happy with the fact he had a woman that stayed at home. Cooked gourmet meals, cleaned to perfection and treated him like the king of his castle. I stopped cooking, I stopped cleaning and honestly just stopped caring about what happened to him in general. I was trapped though. I knew I couldn't go to work because the harassment would be tenfold.

I am not going to try to immerse myself in a new community dealing with that. Insistent phone calls at my new job. Harassment, no sleep. Having to be cold to my co-workers because if I smiled and said good morning, it's because I wanted to bed them and their whole family. Watching who I parked beside at work, not being able to wear makeup or comb my hair. The whole extreme gamut that comes with it all. I had no desire to start a new chapter in my life with him.

He demanded that I drive over to help him with a side job. He insisted that I didn't want to work, which forced him to have to work around the clock. Of course, this caused him to develop a meth habit to keep up. Of course, his actions were my fault. I mean what was his excuse for these behaviors before? I had worked a hundred hours a week at my own company and financially supported him for years. I was just a lazy no good for nothing bitch now though.

He couldn't relax and unwind anymore because he had to work to take care of me. It was my fault he was still at someone's house at ten o'clock at night hyper focusing. It was my fault he had to sleep in his car at a side job overnight. It was all my fault because he had to support me. I would go help him with side jobs when he asked. I have no problem working, he didn't want me to. I had mentioned several times going back to work in the middle of his rage and he would calm down immediately and tell me that he didn't want me to have to work. Yet accuse me of only using him for his money, because I didn't want to get a job.

This particular job was for his office manager. His mom's replacement. She was much older, and not too bright, but he could manipulate her and use her to take his side. You know, develop a relationship with her, where he would be able to complain about me, when I was done taking his abuse. Maybe his backup plan, who knows and who cares. If he can't understand that he is the one being used by these people, then why bother explaining to him anymore? I was the evil tyrant sent to destroy his life. Everyone else was a gift of God.

Anyway, this woman had a lot of work done in her home, for practically nothing. I suffered the ramifications, emotionally, financially, and physically per usual. He ignorantly demanded that night that I stop what I was doing and come to help him. I had nothing going on in my life, and he was sick of being expected to work to support me. I had to come pick him up anyway so he couldn't see why I didn't just stay and help him in the first place. Normally I would always stay to help him when asked, however, my oldest daughter was visiting, it was her birthday weekend.

My daughter and I had put on makeup earlier in the evening for something to do together and when I left the house, I still had it on. Of course, while I stood at this side job, amongst the normal loud chaos of electric tools being operated and flung, he stopped berating his tools long enough to tell me I looked pretty. "Well Thank You." I replied. Which immediately enraged him. He leaned into me to assure being out of the earshot of the homeowner. I only looked pretty tonight, because I was trying to fuck the homeowners mentally regressed grandson that lived with her.

You stand tall. You swallow hard, and you stand tall. Trying to smile at a homeowner while in their home and trying to not remark in someone else's house. I just carried on through the tension and helped the best I could. He assigned me to clean up duty. The acid wash wore through my gloves, and I ended up scrubbing all the skin off the end of my fingertips that night. The pain was so bad I couldn't use my fingertips for anything for five days. Just touching something to pick it up was too much to bear.

I didn't get a thank you, as usual, or an inquisition into how my fingers were, no sign of concern from him at all. I did get a "Thanks for Nothing" Acting like you want to help me, and Now I have to go back and do it for you. You don't want to help me, so why are you trying to act like you do? You don't care about me, or you would help me more.

Through it all, I was still there to talk logic and reason. I still approached his self-induced situation with empathy and kindness. I would take the time to care for him. Not only physically but mentally as well. I would talk him down from every ledge and talk to him about how to treat himself. How to treat other people, especially the woman he says he loves. I could see all his moves before he dealt them, and quite frankly I was just disgusted.

A woman should never ever have to explain to a grown man that professes to love her, how to treat her. They know better. I am not by any means saying I need to be treated like a queen or a princess. I don't need to be showered with materialism, I don't need jewelry or vacations. Fuck I never had gone on a vacation with a man. I wasn't unreasonable. I drove an inexpensive car that I had always paid for before and I wore the same shoes until the soles fell off. That is what I have always been used to, even when I owned my company and made way better money. I still carried on with this lifestyle. I didn't care about anything different, and I certainly never expected someone to do something for me that I couldn't do for myself.

Just give me what I give to you. You can start with basic human decency. It's a good start, I don't expect more than that to start. Do unto others as you would have done to you. I wouldn't walk in and spit on your floor, so don't spit on mine. That simple really, but no, this man made sure to spit on every floor and then push my face in it.

I could stand in the middle of the kitchen floor some nights and if he had just the right amount of meth in his system it would mostly act to calm him. His Bi-polar and adhd typically were just off the charts. Occasionally during this I could spend a moment or two of calmness with him, but never very often.

I remember on this one night he had decided for my sake, he was going to try to get clean. Per usual, he said this about three times a week, while he was actively using it. He had convinced himself this night that DMT would help cure him. Along with the Meth in his system, his prescribed antipsychotics that I force fed him and now DMT, he decided that he could talk to me. He had an eye-opening awakening this night and began to tell me about the life lessons he had been learning. They were all the things I had been repeatedly telling him all along, but he would not have allowed me credit or acknowledge that.

Per usual what I felt about anything had to be pushed aside, while I acted as though I was just happy, he would converse with me. Bare minimal. No expectations. If I had shown any kind of unhappiness or sarcasm with this knowledge he would have said, "See that's why I don't talk to you because you are a fucking bitch." He would have left the apartment and took off in his car with all those drugs in his system, to just go find more. Stating that I just wanted him to go use drugs and that I was the reason he had to get high. Suppress my own feelings for his betterment, always, always, was the theme.

Who wants to defend themselves from an onslaught of insults for something they could easily just ignore and tuck away. Like I said, my feelings were never a consideration in this relationship anyway. Even though he thought he was putting an effort into be nice, he was still miles from the mark. I guess I could be thankful that he had listened enough throughout our time that he could repeat them. Even if he thought all my efforts had been his own.

His beliefs were so unreasonable and so far-fetched, so ignorant, disrespectful, and counterproductive to happiness. He would never be able to sustain a healthy relationship with anyone, he doesn't even have one with himself. The love I held for him was immeasurable, but I was left on the outside to observe. I didn't want him to fail, but he wanted to and there was nothing more I could do for him. No more hours long pep talks I could give. I will never have a love this power-ful, this transformative and enlightening for the remainder of my phys-ical life. The humorous part of it all was he never had a clue how to love back. You can't stay in the cycle of being "in love" when the cycle isn't fed back. The irony lied in this, the one person on this planet, the man I loved, the one I would want to share knowledge with, will never comprehend a chapter in his own life, let alone a book I wrote, thanks to him.

It's odd really. Everyone has a story. Everyone has a path to walk. We all have a story. I don't care who you are. You have a story. I believe this while I am walking quietly alone, minding my own business; dressed in my hoodie and worn-out sneakers. I believe that no one would think, hey, that's the woman that lives with an abusive, mentally disordered, meth addict. That's the woman who dates a three-time felon with a now six-page rap sheet. The woman who will never have anything if she stays with him. That is the woman that has allowed her very life to spiral down a rabbit hole, in the name of love. That is the woman that has taken so much for so long that now she wants to be alone. No, no one thinks that. No one knows that. They see my face, they see my body, they don't see my mind.

I don't suppress it and pretend it didn't happen; I deal with it. I process it all. I alone in my car, by myself, with just God, process it all. I have to. It gives me the strength to do another round. Even when I don't want to do another round. I know God will let me know when I can go. He will move me to my next assignment when he is ready, not me.

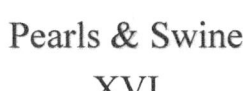

Pearls & Swine
XVI

Twin Flames, it has quietly kept me in this hold for twelve years. There could be no other explanation. Spirituality is more than definitely a God Send. I have always been spiritual opposed to religious. This man, if nothing else, helped me gravely on my path to evolving higher spiritually. Yet again, another great argument for the Twin Flame Journey.

Twin Flame Journey? I have had enough, fuck this journey! I want to get off this roller coaster. I am done with this mystical, magical thinking of these separations and these reunions. The good and the bad, the runner and the chaser. Why does God keep me here? Why won't he just let me go? It had been played out way too fucking long in my life. Don't I get a stand in when my twin flame is an utter and complete moron? Don't I get a replacement? Why do I have to suffer just because he couldn't take the heat of life and decided to fuck up all his brain cells on drugs? Why in the hell is this my prize? Fuck this, it sucks!

Don't throw your pearls before swine. He loved to answer my questions with that. A regurgitated remnant of something somewhere he had picked up in years gone by. I know this phrase all too well myself now. I had been doing it my whole life and the whole time I had been with him. Maybe every time he spoke these words to me during a psychotic break, it was God speaking to me through him.

A warning that I was throwing pearls of wisdom before swine. My patience, my compassion, my empathy, my desire to help and learn. It was rewarded with an answer from Mitchell of "I will not throw my pearls before swine." A direct insult to me with a sense of superiority? Or God trying to talk to me through Mitchell, and I was too caught up in my external self to notice? It enraged me to think he would insult me like that when I was trying to help, but maybe it wasn't Mitchell, maybe it was God.

My oldest daughter and her boyfriend of three years were splitting. She had decided to stay with Mitchell and I for a short while, while she looked for a home in the area to purchase. I was thankful that I would have her company now and with any luck she would be all the motivation that I would need. She was aware of Mitchells condition and as an adult she had the opportunity to see. She came in the height of his paranoia, and although disgusted with his behavior, she still treated him with patience. She considered him more as a troubled stepbrother and would converse with him as such.

My daughter had a few pairs of sunglasses when she moved back in with me. She gave me a pair because Mitchell had purposely stomped on mine during one of his physical attacks. Of course, the ones she gave me from her stash were aviator glasses. That assured him that I was messing around with John down the hall, knowing he was a pilot and all.

Mitchell poured on the charm inviting her to stay rent free. He reiterated the fact that he just wanted to help. He felt he owed it to her now because he was trying to make up for all his failures with her of the past. A great gesture as a family man. I knew what this meant for me though. Mitchell was financially irresponsible and spent money hand over fist on whatever he wanted. Sometimes I had to wrestle enough from him to pay the bills on time. Other times he would be responsible and pay them without being prompted. I was never sure. She knows his game though. He could look to the outside world like he is doing all this to help her out, but nothing is ever free. I would be paying for his gesture of kindness mentally.

My youngest would be down in a few weeks for Christmas with their father and I had no desire to even celebrate Christmas again. My oldest daughter and I didn't even decorate and honestly had no plans of celebrating.

The week they were down, shit would have melted in Mitchell's mouth. Hugging them and welcoming them in, while he ran around buying me presents in excess. He, for the first time in eight months, even cleaned up after himself. He put his very first dirty plate in the sink, it was monumental. I spent three days cooking, but it almost felt like I could be slightly at ease. He invited over a helper from work that I had met before. He was a good little boy. Very polite and helpful. Mitchell figured that way my oldest would know someone in the area, and I could be thankful for that.

This little boy who I had met a couple of times before carried with him a pink flamingo phone screen on this night. He had caught my attention just for that. I had laughed at this, because I had told God I would follow the pink flamingo to my happiness. It had been my symbol for almost two years now, my symbol to my supposed happiness. I had in essence followed the pink flamingo back down here. I had followed this pink flamingo for my own happiness, and my daughters were with me now.

Afterall our children are our true happiness. Following the Pink Flam, a gos, brought me here, and my oldest wouldn't have been here with me otherwise. This awoke me to the fact that anytime I prayed now as an adult woman outside of the strength to endure, it was for the safety, happiness, health and beauty of my daughters. I hadn't seen a pink flamingo since initially moving down and it had been several months. Considering the number of times I had seen these before, I had to feel solid in that fact.

This notion made me consider my prayers from my youth. Dear Lord, please fix my mom. Please let them find a cure. Please help her. I never prayed for the strength to endure then, because I had no idea I was enduring. Every night while I lay in bed I would pray, and it was the same. I know as an adult now that my childhood centered around my mother's illness and that I had to take on adult responsibilities at a young age to help. Like I said I developed a fascination for the mentally ill, abnormal psychology and phobias due to this.

I was always told there wasn't a cure and her intermittent trips to mental health hospitals would only seem to alleviate this slightly. I just wanted her to be happy. I wanted God to show me what I could do to help. The adage of God answers your prayers in divine timing definitely rang through.

I could see that God was showing me now, a world I couldn't have comprehended as a child. I had grown to understand that God was granting me my insistent prayer as a child through Mitchell. I had grown to understand through the course of all this time that is why God allowed this love at first sight.

You can hear people saying that you will couple up with someone that is familiar to your childhood, comfort. God knew I never would have willingly dated someone displaying any of Mitchell's behavior. The disturbingly undeniable and unshakeable feelings I received. So strong across a field without even seeing his face. God did zap me with the knowledge Mitchell was the one. He knew this man would help me live out the cycle that bothered me so much as a child. He knew

this man would help heal my childhood wounds that I had long forgotten and suppressed.

God knows! Mitchell had been given to me by God to help teach
me. He was a lesson and in a lot of ways a blessing to me, and Mitchell
never had a clue. I began to understand my mother's "mental disorder"
was never her fault. It was induced by her expectations as a woman,
for a man. The emotional and physical abandonment. The cruelty that
she endured from my father and his mother. She was emotionally
wrecked and had numbed herself out and put herself last. She saw no
way out due to societal expectations and having to raise her children.

My father in his younger, unhealed days had driven her there and
rode off into the sunset fancy free. He came from a very toxic environment and had severe mother enmeshment issues. He was mired in
an emotionally incestuous relationship with his own mother. She was
the woman he craved validation from. He was still in love with his
mommy's approval. Men still in love with their own mothers can't
possibly be in love with another. They are groomed to protect the
woman they love. Never being able to achieve healthy validation from
their own mothers leaves them resentful and lost. They take out their
anger and rage on the next best thing, their spouses.

My father was confused because he couldn't understand my
mother's behavior. Blaming her for not being who he married and being mentally ill. He was mired in the manipulations and could never
see or admit his own fault. I had been living with the same emotional
neglect my mother had lived, and I had been clueless to it all. Nothing
had been keeping me with Mitchell though. Nothing other than the
strange, indescribable push from God.

After the current months of endlessly exiling myself to my car to
remove myself from his toxicity and abuse, I just sat staring off and
began to cry. I had no control over any of my emotions anymore and

I just gave way. The endless frustration that I had pent up over not being able to help him see that he wasn't cursed. God didn't hate him, like he screamed while deeply carving those very words into our kitchen table with a knife.

The endless hopelessness I felt for being trapped with a man that kept up an incredible facade for everyone else. The sheer exhaustion from having to keep up a lie and to help nurture a two-year-old child, trapped in a grown man's body. I couldn't do it anymore. I cried alone before. I prayed to God before for strength to endure an endless number of times. I had begged him to release me from this shitty assignment, I didn't want this anymore.

I had prayed for him to give me someone else. I had done everything I could to beg him, negotiate with him. I had received signs to keep enduring. I would consider the understanding in the downloads of information that I would receive from certain situations. Although I always found myself thankful after the fact about what lessons I had learned, this time it was different.

I was mad this time. Not mad at Mitchell per usual, but with God. I had never been mad with God before, but I couldn't pretend I wasn't. Then on that day, in that moment, I was infuriated. You think this is a fucking joke? You want to keep using me? You think this is funny, I know that you do! You like watching me depleted and absolutely disgusted.

I don't know what the fuck I did so wrong, so against the flow of human nature, so atrocious and egregious that would warrant you to treat me this way. I will not do this anymore, I fucking quit. I will stand in it if you want, but I am not emotionally taking part in this shit anymore. My daughter is here witnessing this and trying to live harmoniously, while suffering her own heartbreak.

I have lost more weight, can't eat, can't hold down food. Mitchell constantly insults my appearance and reminds me daily of how he is not attracted to me anymore. He even tells other women. I am 5'7 and I only weigh 110 pounds for fuck's sake. You either release me emotionally or I am fucking done! I had been praying for a few months for God to release me emotionally because I couldn't take the torment anymore, but he never answered.

I was so disappointed, but not with Mitchell this time, now I was disappointed with God. I never cursed him. I never said he couldn't use me, but I demanded I be put on autopilot. I cannot accomplish what I need when I am being thrown distraction after distraction, and I am sick and tired of having to put myself last for everyone. I mean everyone. No one has ever put me first. Not even myself and although I try to do it now, there is always something. There is always something to keep me off track mentally. I am fucking done! You allowed this.

You forced me to be with this man, this is not what I wanted twelve years ago, and I am done. I don't want to be around anyone, and I don't fucking need anybody. I will take off through the woods and stay in a tent. I am abandoning this post. I was so fucking mad, as the tears of just pure frustration ran from my face.

Twelve years of just pure trials and tribulations. No bliss, barely moments of peace. This has been a twelve-year walk-through hell, and I am done! I have been emotionally tested beyond anywhere I ever planned on going, and I was done. This wasn't frustration over one incident of me not getting my way. Or for that matter a thousand incidents of not getting my way.

This wasn't about being some sniveling little girl that believed Mitchell had wronged me because he didn't do something I asked. This wasn't about me prematurely saying he was personality disordered because someone hurt my feelings, or didn't see things my way. Like it appears in today's trends. This wasn't about miring myself in the narcissistic/empath dynamic that distracts so many. My limits had been tested and stretched on too many levels, and I couldn't possibly fathom what else I could learn. No more routes of compassion or empathy I could display for him anymore.

My past twelve years with him not only ran rampant with disappointments but with pure and utter turmoil, instability, and disgust. I had all the other happenings in the past twelve years that I couldn't foresee or control either. I was just depleted, disgusted, horrified and drained of everything. If I had to do everything alone even with a supposed partner, then why have the partner? He was just stress I didn't need. I can do bad all by myself, thank you.

Actually, it had been thirteen years. I thought about him for almost a year before I reached out. Choked and twisted on thoughts of him with God for several months before I ever made a move. I waited for signs from God. Thirteen years of trials and tribulations. Thirteen years of the deep plunge of psychological and spiritual warfare. Searching for an answer, navigating societal norms and what they say, "We should do." Thirteen years was as far as I was willing to go, I guess, I never thought about it till now.

Thirteen years of anemia and profuse bleeding was all I could physically take. Now thirteen years was all I could mentally take. Thirteen, made me think of the odd house of S. Winchester, some of the strangest shit I had ever heard of. There were thirteens placed all through there. Why thirteen? It seemed to relate to so many things.

My efforts all felt like broken records now. I wasn't looking to learn anymore about anything. I wasn't looking to teach him either. All my advice, love, patience, and compassion just kept falling on deaf ears. I was dead last for everyone including God. I felt abandoned and used. I am done with this shit. You throw me a bone. Something just for me. I don't care about signs pertaining to Mitchell or some whispered wisdom. I need something to know I am not fucking crazy, because this shit, this anal leakage that you have allowed and encouraged for me as a partner. This shit is crazy!

I blame you for this and I need a sign. I need you to tell me what to do. I refuse to do this anymore. I was so angry, replaying everything over the years. Everything I had sacrificed of myself. Every moment that I poured into him. Every nice and encouraging thing I said to him. I relived conversations in my head of encouragement and hope I would spread to him, while he was cursing me every step of the way. Fucking waste of time.

In reality I can get as mad as I want, and I can have all the realizations I can muster. I can look at him and know that he is nowhere near my level. I was done working to try to rescue someone. I was going to join the ranks of the animalistic and jump ship. I threatened it, but we all know that God is just chuckling with the amusement of us believing we have any control over that. We can't ever make the mistake of demanding from God, he demands from us. He will force our path. He will release us when he knows we are ready, and not a second before. We can have all the temper tantrums we want.

All the good men, that you have made me pass up for this fucking lunatic. This imbecile. I can't in this moment pretend to be thankful, I am pissed! I can't look at the positive and learn anymore lessons. I can't turn water into wine, that is your job. I can't turn a frog into prince charming, that is a fairy tale. He is pure evil, and I am not going to be looked upon in society as a mean, controlling, or pathetic bitch for staying in this shit anymore, I am done!

I knew Mitchell and his triggers so well that I could stand and know when he himself said something that was going to trigger a certain behavior from him. I would be quiet and just listen. Not that you could ever get in a word around him in public anyway. His charming display of boisterous confidence around others made it impossible. I would have to sternly interject with a different topic just to stop his thought process in front of people. I knew if I didn't that his triggered thoughts would be more hell for me behind closed doors.

I thought, if you ever cared about me God, you would have him arrested again or simply kill me off. I cannot take his mouth, his abuse, his manipulation or lies anymore. I want a man, I need a man for a partner, not a small child.

I knew Mitchell was retaining the information and advice that I would throw his way, because he would regurgitate the things I had told him in conversations with other people. Never giving me credit but instead acting as though it was genuine advice for other people that he was throwing off from the hip. He never used the advice himself, but it sounded good for others.

He would then turn around and attack me by saying things like, you moved me down here to isolate me from everyone. You are gaslighting me, you are a narcissist because you give me the silent treatment. Yes, I admit, I did try my very best to ignore him and block him out during his extreme verbal abuse and insults. I was exhausted. Who wants to try to explain their perspective to someone to help grow together in a relationship? He wasn't growing, I was wasting my breath.

I couldn't see any other symptom that would fit me with that. Him however, all of them, when abusing meth. His words were projections, all I could do was turn away. Ever annoyed, I wanted to argue. Mitchell, we chose this place, I moved here with you. I am isolated, you're gaslighting me and you are diagnosed with Bi-polar with psychosis and BPD. He would have turned it all around on me. Saving myself the energy of an argument was a priority, so I just stayed quiet. He would then go on smugly for weeks believing he had something else to hang over my head.

If I brought up a concern of mine, he would just tell me he wasn't going to argue with me, because he believed he was taking the higher road. He already knew that a concern of mine would trigger him into an argument. The fact that I had a concern and wanted to be a part of our "relationship" was already too much attention being taken from him.

He threw Sam up in my face constantly, never being able to see it was his and his family's actions that caused the past few years of our lives in the first place. He would scream at me to get the hell out and go back to Sam where I wanted to be, almost daily. When I grew tired and would agree with O.K, he would then say, "I knew you still loved him, get the hell out." "Why would you come down here if you still wanted to be there with him?" I love you, why would you go back to him?" "If you leave, I will never talk to you again." Nothing he ever said made any sense and living with him was more than impossible. His insecurities were impossible and so was he.

He believed what he believed, and, in his mind, he had to "get me" before I got him. I would point out what he was doing and tell him I wasn't going to participate in his unhealthy cycles anymore. Do the work on yourself Mitchell and figure it out. He said he feared failure, but I corrected him and said, "You have no problem failing Mitchell, it 'is what you believe people expect." "You fear success."

I would encourage him still to use his talents to start his own little business. He would pretend to be thankful for our conversations and then less than one hour later he would be hollering and accusing me of trying to sabotage and undermine him and his thoughts of success. Like I said, only small moments of peace.

Mitchell was so arrogant that catching him in the middle of one of his numerous daily lies would surely garnish his unbridled wrath. He would still rage at me that I was wrong and then somehow blame me for his lie. I could ask him what he had for lunch that day as small talk and somehow that would warrant a very angry reaction of hollering "Nothing "You don't care if I eat anyway, why are you pretending that you care? You probably ate lunch with John, so you are all set, thanks for nothing. With that he would disappear into the mirror for hours to pick away at his ear.

He would always blame me hours later, when he was done, for not wanting to spend time with him. That is on the nights when he decided to stop picking at his ear of course. Some nights he would just stay up all night locked in the bathroom, either not sleeping or depending on his meth cycle, passing out on the bathroom floor. Who the hell wants to be around that? What was he possibly offering as a man let alone as a relationship option? Dear Lord, above, I am sick of being in charge of the romper room. I deserve better. I had said this a million times, begging and pleading, but apparently God still felt this a fitting assignment for me.

Pure neglect, isolation, abuse, and dismissal. The porn stars on his phone were all he needed, as he joined online dating sites. Always accusing me of being on them, so of course he had to join them looking for me. When I would confront him and call him out about the fact that he wasn't going to find me on any of them, especially BBB Woman, he would still try to keep up his lies. Insult to my intelligence.

Now any woman in the same circumstances would have found herself wandering through the halls to flirt with this "John" but I was instructed to stand down by God. I would sometimes pace at the anticipation of the possibility of walking down the hall, but I knew I had to be the bigger person. He was never going to learn what he was supposed to learn if I moseyed off to get my freak on with the gorgeous man down the hallway.

Porn, another hot button issue created only from the love of money and lust. Another tool in the devil's arsenal of distraction. I must laugh at the hypocrisy of its creation in all forms. Men today are crying out. They want traditional women. They want a woman that loves them, supports them and their dreams. Encourages them while we cater to them and care for them and the home. A woman they can confide in and seek safety and refuge in. They want a woman that puts their relationship first. One they can trust to be alone during the day and still be there when they get home at night. They want a woman that is all their own. One that hasn't been viewed by millions or been a cum dumpster for hundreds. I don't blame them at all. They are asking the same basics a woman would ask for.

A woman will need to feel appreciated, loved and desired. She will require safety and to know that she is protected, not only physically but emotionally as well. She will need to feel that her man is proud of her and the family and home they have created. A woman needs reassurance from her man, and then she will give to him everything within her abilities.

Men will fall in love with a woman that he desires above all others. If he is successful at making her feel the most desired in his life, she will usually follow his lead from there. She will observe his behavior. If he silently reassures her, she is the most desired through dating, then marriage is a real possibility. It will be at this point that she will need a provider.

If a man wants a woman that can provide him with his basic needs of refuge, attention, adoration, and encouragement, while running a home, you men become a full-time job. When she gives birth to your children, your legacy, she will need to know that she can do that job fully and to the best of her ability. You as men will need to be able to provide financial support. She is giving up her individuality and independence to merge with you. You and your children are now, her full-time job. She has given that up solely because you made her feel the most stable and desired. She followed your lead, and she is relying on you for that. Vulnerability, feminine energy at its finest.

Men what do an overwhelming amount of you do once you have achieved the woman of your dreams? The woman you desire more than any other? You betray her inner sanctity, her beliefs and her security, by cheating on her with other women. She feels this, she sees this, and she will respond as an individual. Men, you can either decide to honor her wishes and her viewpoints on this subject, or you can disregard her and continue in your own self-serving needs.

Don't be upset if she puts her guard up and goes cold. Don't be upset if she tunes you out. Don't be upset if she becomes passive aggressive and decides to disregard your needs as well. She is only following your lead. As a man you need to fix what you broke. Accept accountability and follow through or don't. It's your roller coaster; she's along for the ride.

I can see the prevalence in porn viewing by men. They are visual creatures. I understand. I understand their need to visually be aroused. I found myself asking why men find it okay to fulfill what they need sexually, but when concerning their partner, they would become insecure. They would equate it to nowhere near the same. If my man chooses to spend one hour in the bathroom viewing porn and reaching a sexual climax without me, is that cheating?

Most men will always respond with No, it's not cheating. Always having varying excuses. Two of my favorites being that viewing this is a coping mechanism for stress and the other excuse of "Men are genetically made to spread their seed.

Yes, men have the capability of spreading their seed, but can they consider themselves a whole man without the title of provider and protector? Men love to preach that they are the provider and protector and that women are supposed to be submissive due to this. Can men provide for and protect one woman and his children? Hell yes, they are more than capable. That is their job and they do it to the best of their ability and capability of resources. We women honor men for this.

Can men then decide to go spread their seed with another woman? If they choose to yes, they are capable. Are they capable of providing the newest woman with a home and protection also? Can they be in both places to protect at once? Can they afford to provide homes for both women and sets of children? More than likely not. They instead have to decide and believe that the one that is less desirable to them should just go without. While forcing her to shoulder all the responsibility of what he left behind. Self-centeredness at its finest. Is being self-centered a masculine energy? How about a masculine trait? No, it's a sense of entitlement and what modern women are trying to convey as toxic masculinity.

Kings and royalty could afford to "spread their seed." They had the resources to make sure all were provided for and protected. The average man took a wife and spread his seed several times with her and had huge families. He could afford to protect "his" when they were all in one spot. It makes you look at the welfare system a lot differently. Are our taxes going to aid low-income mothers or are our taxes going to pay for a man's sense of entitlement.

Coping mechanism for stress? My woman is not fulfilling my needs. I don't feel needed or wanted blah blah blah. Maybe if you hadn't cheated on her with porn in the first place, she would still feel desired enough by you to fulfill your needs. You disregarded her like she didn't matter to you by continuing, but you are going to play the victim when she disregards you? She is just following your lead.

I found myself wondering why men believed this way. In their minds they were not touching another woman, so it wasn't cheating. So, if a man spends an hour away from his woman being turned on in the presence of another woman, why is it not ok for a woman to do the same? Men would say, if she wants to watch porn for an hour, I think that's hot, she can if she wants, wouldn't bother me a bit.

There you guys go again from your self-centered state. Like I said, a woman doesn't get turned on visually, she requires emotional connection by design. What I meant was tit for tat. The hour you spend being visually turned on away from her, should be the hour she spends from you being emotionally turned on, correct? That would be even in the sexual arousal process for both sexes. Fair?

So, while you are beating off in the bathroom to porn for an hour, why is it not alright in your minds for her to be spending an hour with another man and connecting emotionally? She isn't touching him, so it's even. No touching from either side. Why can't she go home after and fantasize about the man that turned her on emotionally? You masturbated, she masturbated. Neither one of you touched another person, so where is the problem?

So, for all you men with your self-centered, defensive and adamant porn stance, I want you to think about your woman hanging out with and feeling desired by another man, while you are busy. If the thoughts of that don't bother you, then congratulations you already know you shouldn't be with her. Or that you are not emotionally capable of a relationship. If the thoughts of that does bother, you, if you feel threatened by that at all, then congratulations now you know how your woman feels.

I don't want to hear about how it's not the same. I am watching them on a screen, it's not a threat to her, she is with him, that is a possible threat to me. Me, Me, Me. Still not acknowledging her. It's a possible threat because he is there in person and could steal her away? Her time away? Porn actresses are not going to steal your time away for that hour are they though? He could steal her away physically all together. Why because he is putting the time into her that you should have? I mean you were content with visuals; she is content with emotions. You are the types that would whine about how good you were to your woman though, and how you did everything for her, and she cheated on you. Just think about what you could have built with your woman emotionally in that hour, you chose to spend desiring other woman.

Just basic decency. Mitchell thought he could watch it for hours, but when faced with this same scenario, berated me for months about this posed question. Accusing me weekly of sneaking off to eat lunch with the neighbors during the day and orgies at night. I could never just warn him, or appeal to his senses, I was just attacked more. Conversations of any extent were just futile, but silence was met with a hateful disdain. I would be immediately berated when speaking to him and verbally attacked for not speaking to him. When asked how to address him, I was met with even more anger.

Why wouldn't a woman leave a man that treated her like that? Yet its men like this out in society crying on the shoulder of some random woman at a bar. Wanting to elicit her pity. "I did everything for her, and she left me." So, explain to me what exactly that you did for her? I bet you were not ever going to mention the fact that these women had the patience of Job with you. That they supported you for years. How about telling the woman at the bar how your woman left you because of the truth? For the first time ever, you had to prove you were a man and take your momma's titty out of your mouth. Was it too much for you to handle? She is the bad one for not eating your lies, neglect and abuse and now pity you, all alone.

Now I know that I have refused before to continue in this, but like I said, disgusted, pissed, angry and just sheer apathetic. God is in charge, not us, and if he commands, we stay, we stay!

Men, there are still a lot of us women out here that see you as the leaders. We look to you and follow your direction; we allow you to take the lead. I know that you may feel this isn't true, but I will tell you this. A new generation of little girls. Millions of them. You shame them for displaying their bodies and participating in disgusting acts of pornography. You shame them by stating no man will ever want them. Laughing at them for attention seeking behavior that you feel confident is from daddy issues.

The whole-time you men are completely oblivious. These little girls are taking your lead. They are trying to be for you what you desire. You say you want traditional women, but the staggering porn numbers prove you desire otherwise. Pick a side man, you can't have your cake and eat it too.

The Most High
XVII

I couldn't even muster up any hope for new meds helping. I just didn't even care to go to the doctors with him. To me this was just a ploy to try to reel me back in to him by having me believe he was wanting to get better. Like all the hundreds of other times. Another round of lies, new medications, more side effects, more money, more fights when I had to force him to take them, and a big No thank you. I wanted a grown man, not a child, so why did God keep insisting I stay with this child as a partner. He must have known if I was putting all this effort into "helping" him grow, that I wasn't going to find any of this sexy or masculine.

He must have known I wouldn't be able to find any of this appealing, so why have I been elected to help this one for reciprocity's sake? Why couldn't I have had a way easier one? Maybe one without Bi-polar and BPD? Maybe one that wasn't addicted to porn and meth? All together though, come on. Plus, with Mitchell, I could put all this effort into making him understand and helping him grow. It's not like I was ever going to get credit or even a thank you from him. Why do I have to do this? What kind of grand reward was I going to get for releasing this prize back out into the world?

I know that some people may believe that being upset with God is a fragment of oneself being upset with their own actions and not wanting to take responsibility. Hence blaming God for the bad in their lives. It's easy to be dismissive and label so you feel better about what you don't understand. I guess in a way this would make the ones that don't understand feel better anyway. The rest of us know.

I walked around the next couple of days trying to ignore God. When saying this, I mean by not talking to him. I had tried in my mind to be dismissive of him and to detach. Detach like I had with any other man that wronged me, apart from Mitchell. God knows I tried with that one! When I found myself wanting to talk to him through the day like normal, I would cut off my conversations with him. Almost like a spoiled child that didn't get my way. I figured I was pissed; I am not happy. I don't want to be here. I can't stand Mitchell or the fact that I am even back in this mess.

Honestly Mitchell could have died, and I probably wouldn't have blinked. It would have taken every ounce of energy within my body to pretend that I cared. Cared even enough to give the police his name. I was so jaded from enduring his abuse, that sometimes I would catch myself in nanoseconds of daydreaming about this exact possibility. It actually made me feel better. Like I said, I had no more lessons to learn. I couldn't fathom the possibility of any "bright side" that would come from this.

They say if you love someone you can't stay mad at them for more than three days. I guess that reigns true, well for me anyway when concerning God. I, all alone per usual, sat on the floor of my bathroom and began to talk to him again. I clasped my hands together and let the weight of my head just fall onto them, I couldn't stop crying.

All the hopelessness and frustration from everything just began to fall again. I had been trying so hard for the past twelve years to just have normalcy. I can't have that if you keep me here with him. Please, Dear Lord, please, I am so sorry. I don't know what I did, but I am sorry. Just give me the strength to endure what it is you have for me, because I can't do this anymore. I am one human. I do not hold a candle to you. I am breaking and I have broken.

I will not question you anymore, but I am going to be of no use to my children if I spend the rest of my days in a mental institution. I know my mother's words of you don't leave the mentally ill, have always stuck with me, but how long before I am the mentally ill? How much longer in my sane mind can I bear this. Use me as you will, teach me, restore new life in me. I need to go on and I can't like this. I am giving it all up to you. I will not worry anymore. You know what you have for me, and I am letting it all go. Keep me and my children, keep us, keep me. Please, I will do what you want, but I can't keep living like this. Please God Please!

I had been seeing so many 444's again as of the past couple of months. So many fours that I had taken notice. I had taken notice of all the others too. I had been seeing so many numbers that I actually took the initiative to carry a paper with me to write them down when I noticed them. I had always seen numbers in excess, but this round was alarming to me. I could stand and feel something happening, almost like the energy of something wanting to come together. Something trying to manifest, it was alarmingly disturbing.

They were not just always random acts of looking at the clock or seeing them on license plates or addresses. These were deeper mishaps. Sitting alone in my car watching my phone and a horn would honk. I would receive a text notification, or a certain song would come on the radio. A heart palpitation, or a quick ringing in the ear. Noises to take me from my bubble. I would look up to see a number.

I had been seeing numbers and understanding synchronicities for about six years now. I had learned to dismiss a good majority of these. Didn't mean I didn't see them, but I would always look to the "Angel numbers' ' that were so popular with this seemingly growing phenomenon. Let's face it, all the angel number meanings seemed to just repeat themselves with "change, transformation and balance, blah blah blah."

Not to take away from the fact that during some really low moments in my life, these numbers were reassuring and very much kept me going. I always thought angels were sending these to me to let me know they were there. Encouragement. Seeing all the numbers that I saw, kept my mind occupied in the mundane and helped occupy my time, so I thought. I could have easily looked back on this and compared it to the infamous apophenia that professionals use to explain this.

It seemed to me that when I was bored, I saw numbers. Almost like I had more time to notice them perhaps. When dealing with Mitchell and all his crazy drama, I would see them a lot less. Maybe I didn't have the time to notice. They came to me in times of worry, anxiety, or complacency. Times of slight happiness or when things may have seemed to be going alright. The numbers didn't discriminate, and they always had an uplifting message. No matter how vague, they were still uplifting. Trust that I was cynical and skeptical. I used to look for reasons to discredit most things that occurred. You can only discredit for so long though. The numbers I began getting now, were horrifyingly alarming.

They were so glaringly obvious that I couldn't have dismissed them if I wanted to. These number combinations were coming at me now every day. So much and so often that it no longer mattered to me what Mitchell had to say. Go do your meth, leave me alone. I had no interest in helping him get clean again and again. I didn't beg, lecture, or even attempt to encourage him to quit. No more talks about how he was better and deserved better. No more trying to get him to realize what he had. No more extending my help or being worried.

I had numbers to figure out. Just go away from me. The police will get you and I don't care anymore. If you don't like my detached attitude, you can go live back with your parents. Maybe they could actually do their job and raise you this time. I have something else to do. You are no longer my problem; God will take care of you.

For the first time in years, I just didn't care. No worry no unease, this was about me. After all these years and after all the torment and abuse, I had stopped feeling I had to explain myself and make it better. All the thoughts of closure or wanting to encourage him to strive for better. You are not going to get better. I must accept that and just move on with me.

I am sick of sitting in massive chaos, confusion, and neglect. One hour I am sneaking off to fuck the neighbor. The next hour I am not, and he is sorry. The next hour he cries and begs me to stay. The next hour he wants to start a business again. The next hour he tells me that if I leave him, he understands.

One hour he knows I love him, and then the next hour he screams at me, because I never loved him. This pretty much encapsulated our nights. Like I said, meth addicts don't sleep, and you won't either.

I had been trying to help him for years and it's been the same pattern for all twelve. No wonder I felt closer to him in jail. No wonder I thought he was stabilizing out. I couldn't talk to him every hour in jail. Now I was just left with an ease of not caring and numbers. I was left with God's strength to heal myself all over again.

I just want a man who is stable. Emotionally stable. The money never mattered to me. I can help you achieve any plan you have. I can't grab on to emotional instability. It is like a riled-up bull, you can only grab on and enjoy the ride for moments. Knowing in a short time you are going to be bucked off. No stability, not a drop.

You never know where you stand with someone like that. You cannot even begin to imagine how to build a future. You are locked into surviving the present moment every day. Amongst your role as a favorite person, one minute you are their everything and the next moment you are scum and for the streets.

You must comfort every one of those moods. You must reassure them through all of them. You don't matter, only they do. One wrong word will assure rage, so tread carefully. Be cheerful, be polite, but most of all act hopeful that they will get it right. It is depleting, thankless and mentally exhausting. The attention is on them and what they need, constantly. You do not matter, ever.

No man to tell you it is going to be alright. You need to be the one to tell him everything is alright. You need to have a plan. You must lead them. You must be the one to pull him to safety. If you don't align with the vision, he has for himself in that hour, you are evil, wicked, and out to destroy his life. The amount of deep damage that had been done to him by his upbringing was more and more obvious every day.

My children come to me for advice and guidance now. They can choose whether to use it or not. They are grown. My children don't rage at me. We sit and have open discussions, and they can tell me anything they feel they need. None of us were perfect mothers. It is never going to happen. Life gets us too. My children learn and they grow. People learn and they grow. Mitchell does not. My children I tell once. Mitchell, I must tell five hundred times. He can understand if I am upset, he doesn't know how to or even care to fix it. He doesn't seem to comprehend his actions and the effects they have on others.

My children understand that all too well. He has no idea how to approach a situation that he has caused. He uses emotional manipulation and anger, to turn it all around. He must feel like he is in control by minimizing his actions and placing the blame on me. I have somehow caused his actions. My children know better. They accept responsibility with people. They try to make their wrongs, right again. Smoke and mirrors. He believes if he gets angry enough, that I will back down. I will dismiss what he has originally done, and he can walk away like he has outmaneuvered me. It's a game to him. I know it's a coping mechanism. I officially knew what the old ladies were talking about around my mother's table years ago. I have raised my children, and I am done raising him.

He would beg me to talk to him, like I always had. He would insult me or do anything to try to infuriate me. I would smile and say have a great day. When he locked me out of the apartment, I would just sleep in my car. He would tell me he was getting clean and needed my help, like usual to try to pull the attention back to himself. I would tell him to talk to God about it and that I had been reassigned. He would grow so mad with insults and rage because he wanted to fight. It was the only cycle he knew from childhood, to validate that someone cared.

I am done. If you don't want to look to God for help, then call up one of your "old" acquaintances and cry to them. I am sure they would love to help you out now. I could see him reeling and twisting inside about how to approach me. I didn't care. I didn't look at him in disgust or as a burden, an acquaintance, or even a friend. I was just indifferent. Wished him no harm, but he meant no more to me than another man I would pass by on the street.

I could see that God was helping me to emotionally detach with these numbers. I would thank him and talk to him about the irony of what he was doing for me every day. I knew what the numbers were for in that respect, but what was he trying to say to me? I had given everything to God. He was in control, not me. He would make Mitchell what he wanted him to be. Mitchell's observation year with me wasn't quite up, but I had observed all I wanted to see.

I must admire my father for a moment. His move was iconic. He laid around in his spare time and never socialized and said, "if I am meant to have someone, she will come to me." I used to giggle at this but couldn't help to admire his magical manifesting abilities. She did go to him. She sent him a letter from the hospital where he attended swimming classes, and the rest is history. I love the fact that they get to enjoy their lives together now.

I can't pull the same because we both know the dating world is different for men and women. Men usually come to women. Most times in excess, this wasn't going to help me sort anything out at all. I like to focus on one man. I just happened to focus on one, unannounced to me that would help me free myself from my own childhood trauma. I had to relive it with him. I don't have a focus anymore, and I am surprisingly ok with that. I know that if I want to date, there will be someone meant for me and I think when that time comes, I will embrace it. My cycle is complete now, I have been released.

The abuse I have endured at the side of this man is indescribable, and no one would ever believe. He puts on one face for the world and three more for me. People see him as charismatic, charming, helpful, talkative, and friendly. I see him now as unstable, volatile, self-destructive, manipulative, angry, abusive, and unkind.

Personality B clusters are designed that way. They are great if you don't get too close. They will be very charming and helpful for people that they don't give two shits about. Their guard is only let down around the one favorite person they care about. It's sad for them and it breaks my heart. Defense and coping mechanisms from childhood. They vary between wanting love and rejecting love. There is no in between. Black and white. They cannot even begin to comprehend the gray.

No one will ever know this until a couple of years in. They don't display abusive behavior right off instead they love bomb. These are never as cut and dry as women who have never endured will have you believe. Is he, or isn't he? That drug makes him evil every time. Have I helped heal him, or have I just made it worse for the next person? Only time will tell this for me.

I am desensitized to it all. What most would consider abuse, I don't even blink about. I quietly know who I am at my core, I haven't lost that yet. They fear abandonment above all else but strive to push the envelope on their fear every day. Is it a game? Do they push just to pull you back? Is it a challenge? Maybe it's an adrenaline rush on their end? They are in their very fear, and it's a rush. I can't abandon my daughter, yet I can't stay. Did God send her to me now, to prolong my stay with Mitchell? I think he did. I know he did.

They say in life you get three great loves. One that you believe you are supposed to stay with for the rest of your life. You believe that's what society expects. That would be my children's father for sixteen years. The second tends to be abusive, hurtful, manipulative, and narcissistic. They show you everything you don't want. Which I would agree would be Mitchell on and off for twelve years. I guess I was hoping he would have changed and leveled up enough while incarcerated to fill the role of number three. I could see that was lazy and wishful thinking on my part.

The third is one that you don't see coming and never consider your type. One that just "falls" into your lap in essence. It feels right unlike the other two. Opposite of my type, I was either waiting for cupid to shoot me with the arrow of an unattractive, emotionally balanced, billionaire, or I had outrun cupid years ago. Plus, I don't know how willing I am to give a man love anymore.

God knows if someone is going to catch my attention, it has to be fucking fireworks. Otherwise, I am going to slam you in the old acquaintance category. I am not now, nor have I ever been the type to slowly fall in love with someone through friendship or acts of kindness. Not the kind of "in love" I need to sustain a sexual interest for a relationship anyway. Look at Sam for Christ sakes. I tried it the way society believes it should be. Must be friends first. Fuck that, there was a reason I fought so hard against that. Women put men in a friend category for a reason. I knew we had no sexual chemistry, and you are not going to build that overtime.

If there is no big hoopla of sexual energy how the hell are you going to overlook the glaringly obvious red flags in the beginning? The sexual charge needed to get you in a relationship to start with. Otherwise, I am going to sit there day by day and just look straight on at your red flags. Knowing I have no interest in getting involved with you. If I must put effort into fixing them, I am going to automatically understand that he isn't desirable in a masculine way to me. Let's face it, we all have red flags to a degree if we want to pick enough. Mitchell's and my past were going to force me to pick away at red flags like Mitchell picked at his ear. If you are going to captivate me, it has to be done in a matter of seconds, on a first impression, heavenly sent, and I don't get intrigued by people much anymore.

I was doomed to be one of those women that spent the rest of her life alone. Although I didn't want a real cat to rock in my lap as I envisioned this scenario in my old age, I could always get a fake one. Yeah, maybe one that meows too, like I saw at the old age home. This thought sat alright with me, but I also thought, it's too bad. There are some men that would love to date me. I can't date anymore. I see and know too much and the thoughts of having to pretend that I am getting to know someone was already exhausting for me.

The remainder of the week, I could feel a renewal of some sorts. I was happier and more content with ignoring my external distractions. The bank vault of an apartment, an abusive meth addict, with the demands of a toddler on a mother. Not having the desire to care about cleaning, cooking, or taking care of anything. I had seemingly been renewed with the energy to suddenly not worry about anything else and just focus on me.

The fact that I could focus on myself now was revitalizing my ability to take care of others, only when I felt like it though. I would sing in the kitchen. I would clean the counters I didn't mess with, and wash dishes I never ate from. Just like all us women feel we have to do. I didn't mind though, because I worked it in when I felt like it, not when others needed it. I figured if they needed it done quicker, they would do it for themselves. Which all us women know never happens.

This wasn't the prevailing and overwhelming thoughts like per usual. I didn't have to get it done because no one else would do it. It didn't all fall on me. I wasn't overwhelmed. This wasn't done out of spite to prove a point. I am sure many other women have found themselves falling party to the spite thing. There was no spite, no regrets and no sense of being overwhelmed. I was held in the energy of doing my part. Not all of it, just my part. I had given up all control of my current situation to God. He had renewed my energy and beliefs with the current situation, and I was truly happy. Happy not knowing what God had in store for me. I knew he had me though, and I can't explain it any other way.

The numbers were hitting me from every angle. Every day never failed for three months straight the 444. Unimaginable amounts of numbers. It kept me looking at the positives of a twin flame journey.

This time though it had me looking for a way out of it too. It was helping me look at all angles and a new possibility.

I have watched psychologists lecture on "Twin Flames" and the supposed delusion that people are in when under its "spell." I have listened to them lecture on the fact that they worry that abuse is being romanticized under this title. I can see that myself with some of these people's stories. I can understand the "professional" perspective. It is their job in their minds to be able to break down people and tie their behaviors into something. They need to feel the need to break down all behaviors to tie them into something of the mind. That is their addiction. However, anyone on this journey will tell you there is not one damn romantic thing about it. This part of the journey isn't about meeting the love of your life and frolicking off into the sunset. It isn't about holding someone's hand, finishing their sentences and lovingly gazing into one another's eyes. That is puppy love, this shit has nothing to do with the cuteness of puppies.

This is a journey of egos clashing. Fine tuning and perfecting patience. Compassion for what most would consider the enemy. Teaching and tolerance. Many disappointments and letting go of any thoughts of control, or how you think it should be. Empathy, unconditional love of not only another but of yourself. Saving another of God's children while God saves you. Not everyone is fit for this journey, and if you haven't been blessed with this opportunity, consider this fact. God already knows you couldn't handle it or develop awareness enough to learn the lessons needed to "level" up.

I know with this the possibilities and scores of diagnoses that people would love to place upon this. Chomping at the bit to be dismissive and label. Like I said, don't attack something you don't understand. Don't try to make others' lives play to your narrative. You are no more in charge of your own life than I am of mine. Don't try to persuade me of something that makes you feel better about what you don't understand. Don't be dismissive and place a label on those that do not comply with your perspective. It's not your journey, it's someone else's. I implore you to put that time into understanding yourselves and do your own self growth. Make the effort to align with God, to have your own veil lifted.

Slightly amuses me for a moment, to hear someone say, you can't save another. Are you trying to be a hero? Have you heard of the savior role? Save yourself. All I can do is laugh. In its very essence that is the role that they have delegated themselves to. Pertaining to anyone else, there is something wrong with it though. Are you essentially advising someone to revert to animalistic basic behavior? Are you advising women to minimalize who they are at their core? I agree that you can't save them all, wholeheartedly agree to that. However, who are the ones that say you can't save another? The ones trying to save another?

If that is the consensus then why do we have police, fire or rescue? Why do we have child protective services, shelters, or for that matter, laws at all? Why do we have any of that, if we are supposed to believe we can't save another? The savior role? The very role you have put yourself in while you are selling your advice to another. Trying to make them believe its abnormal. Jesus, the hypocrisy just doesn't stop, does it? Neither does the profiting from people's emotions and misguided beliefs.

I am not a religious nut job. I don't attend church on a weekly basis, a yearly basis, or for that matter at all. I don't walk around believing I can heal people with my touch. I don't lecture people on the streets, and I don't believe I have a made-up babble that only the holy and I understand. I don't even bring up religion to people.

My father always told me, the quickest way to make an enemy is to bring up politics or religion, and to this day it reigns true. I smoke nasty cigarettes; I swear a lot and occasionally I feel the need for a drink. I don't live the eradicated "sin" lifestyle. We all have addictions and coping mechanisms, every one of us. If you for some reason believe you don't, do the work on yourself below the surface, you will quickly find out that you do.

There were so many new numbers. Everyday. My 1111 started again. I remember a scheduled blackout. The electricity had been out most of the afternoon. 1111 flashing big and blue across my microwave. The time never advanced, it just flashed for more than thirty minutes before I fixed it. I got this number three to four times a day for over a week. After that it came to me sporadically.

1212's and 1222's from a couple of years ago were back. Those had come to me a lot before meeting up with Sam. I got this combination everyday as well for over a month and a half. My 222's were always followed by 777's. I found it strange that I always received these two together in that order. The last time I had that number combination was when I had gone back to N.C before Mitchell was arrested again. I got this combination every day for about two weeks and then it stopped.

I would get 555's often too. Although these had always signified change to me, I remembered back on those as well. I had received the fives in excess upon closing my company. Then I got them a lot before my second mother and Lee's death. Never knowing what these meant beforehand. They were back though.

The four was the most prevalent, however. These were every day. Most times upwards of ten times a day. Seeing all the number patterns again made me nervous and slightly apprehensive. Why so many numbers? What is God trying to do? So many numbers. What is happening here? 1010. These were every day too for over two weeks, and then sporadically four to five times a week.

I would get the 333 sporadically, but not to the extreme that they frightened me. My 333's had probably run their course a few years back. I saw them everywhere then. I got 111 now. Only three ones now opposed to four.

I had stopped caring about Mitchell and I being together. I had spoken to God. I was done. I would stand there if needed, but I wouldn't put another drop of effort into him. I didn't care if he stayed sober. I didn't care if he took his meds. I didn't care if he ate. I didn't care if he had showered. I just didn't even care to talk to him anymore. I knew God was sending me down a new path. Every drop of effort I exerted with Mitchell had just assured me an extra drop of piss hitting me in the mouth. Who wants to drink piss? Well, some I suppose, but it's not my thing. At this point, I was throwing my pearls of wisdom before swine. I was done. I would exist with him, but I wasn't going to exist to help him at all. I was done.

I was in the kitchen, doing the dishes. A song came to my mind that I had not heard in a few years. I began to hum this. Humming, like I said, has been a long-held distraction method of mine since my toddler years. According to my mother I spent close to two years humming as a child. I wouldn't speak. I just stayed locked in my own world. I began talking and then I just stopped. I stopped talking and just started humming like a bumblebee constantly for two years instead. I never broke character, not even once. My poor mother, having to listen to that.

Weird, random songs would sometimes just come to me. I couldn't remember the whole song, and this piqued my curiosity. I decided instead to take the lazy way out and just listen to it on my phone while I finished up the dishes. Taking three steps to my right to retrieve my phone, I brought the song up and began listening to the words. I smiled as I hummed the lyrics. I looked up to see the numbers 444 sprawled across the microwave. I smiled again at the numbers knowing that everything was going to be alright.

I then turned, to position myself in front of the dishes to finish my task at hand. It was with this first step back to the sink that I stopped. I just stood still, almost held. I couldn't look up because the light above the sink was too bright. The light was so bright that it caused me to squint and look towards the floor. The warmth from the light above me just seemed to radiate. I quickly wondered if the light bulb was about to blow but couldn't even worry about it. I was just enveloped in warmth, peace and not one thought beyond how perfect I felt. It was incredible.

I hit one knee, never being able to look up. It felt almost like your children hugging your head when you're playing with them. All I could keep repeating was thank you, oh my God thank you. This presence spoke to me. It wasn't words out loud; it was almost telepathic. We spoke to each other without saying a word out loud. It promised me many great things, and I cried. I just kept crying as it kept promising me.

All that I could ever compare this to was how I believed it would feel to win the Powerball. Amazing, the more it spoke, the more tears of happiness just uncontrollably flew out. I became weaker and weaker under its presence. I didn't have the strength to even sit before it on one knee anymore and down I went. I still could never look up. I sat in a blubbering pile of my own tears. I just kept sobbing and could barely catch my breath. Sitting on both of my legs, all I could manage to say was "How do I tell people how great you are?" The one word that I clearly remember it speaking to me was, "Write." I let out a loud wail and just collapsed to my side.

I lay on my side sobbing and crying in the fetal position for upwards of five minutes trying to compose myself. I knew that everything that I had endured was for a reason. I knew that the information had to be given to me in stages, to learn it all at once would make someone lose their mind. I knew that I had passed my test and I just deeply exhaled as I silently thought, Fuck that was the hardest one ever.

I can't remember anything that it promised me at all. I just know to this day that has been the most amazing occurrence of my life. Even more amazing than giving birth to my children. I have never felt anything even remotely close to this in my life. The highest of highs. I will gladly accept his orders just to be able to keep living in the memories and feelings of that light.

I questioned mania as I lay on the floor. Was I going crazy? Was I just inflicted with some kind of five-minute mania? Was this how manic people were? I had never had that happen, and I never had a pattern of mania. I remember in all my life having two moments of euphoria. Both of those were the happiest I had ever been. The most at peace and just truly happy and comfortable, and both of those were after the birth of my children. One moment after my oldest was born and once after my youngest. Not right after, however, this was months after their births. This light was those feelings of euphoria combined, times I don't even know what number. It was just incredible.

I placed my hand solid on the floor to boost myself to a standing position and looked intently at my hand. I could see my writers callous. I grip a pen differently from most people I know of, applying pressure to a different finger. I could remember decades back to kindergarten. I could remember the weather that day and how I quietly stood in the recess line. I was never a talker; I was unbelievably quiet. I could feel the sting from the bee that day all over again. A sting directly to my finger. I never made a noise that day as I shook it off, but I remembered the welt it left. A welt that had long since healed and been replaced throughout my school years with a pretty sizable writers' bump.

This small moment in my life has propelled me forward. I don't question it, and I use it as motivation every day. I could feel something happening. I knew there was definitely going to be a change. I could feel it in the air. I can't fill in the blanks on what it promised me, I just know it did. Just like always though, don't assume you know God's plan.

Dr. Jekyll and
XVIII

It was two and a half weeks after this miraculous event that I had awoken to the sound of Mitchell leaving out the front door. I hadn't mentioned a word to him about anything. He would have just berated me. I looked at the clock and realized that it was much later in the morning than Mitchell normally leaves. He had quit his job at this point though. He had officially been unemployed for over a week, so I supposed he was probably trying to keep himself on a schedule. He knew that my daughter was there, so I wasn't going to leave. He knew that I would pay the bills with my savings just for that fact alone. My daughter being there and needing a place in that area was the only thing keeping me there.

I got up and began to venture outside to my car. It was gone. Mitchell had left me home with no phone and had taken my car. As I stood there absolutely disgusted, and staring off, John walked by me. He was entering the building but stopped long enough to have a mini conversation about the greatness of the day. Regardless of what was going on in my world, I had to agree.

Normally my daughter didn't stroll in from work until after seven at night, sometimes later. I contacted her on social media from my laptop and asked her if she could come directly home that night. My daughter knew his games, and I simply stated that he had taken my car and my phone. She arrived home that night earlier than normal. We sat in the parking lot talking about reporting the car stolen for all three minutes when Mitchell arrived back. He knew that normally she wouldn't be home for another hour or so.

He figured normally, he could just pull in and play it off as though I was upset and misunderstood him from the night before. He knew that I would be upset and accuse him of stealing my car and my phone. Just like every time before. He knew that I would be enraged with his behavior and my disgust would have been escalated by the time she arrived home. He knew he could play that off to her like I was being unreasonable and a crazy bitch when she arrived. Except she was already there.

He tried to tell me that he asked me to use the car. Yet we had not even spoken the night before. Mitchell loved to come up with erratic thoughts in his own mind and then tell me we spoke about it, but I just couldn't remember. Always with the excuse that I don't love him because I don't remember. He tried to pretend he had been at a side job all day. When I knew he was out scoring meth in my car. He had every intention of making me worry that whole day. Otherwise, he would have woken me or at least left a note. His games were many and daily, and I always was made to look like the unreasonable one.

I discussed going out that night with my daughter. She frequented the bars, being in the younger scene. Mitchell had been to the bars a couple of times. I had not been out of the house at all at night. Not even once. He never invited me out but would stay out himself and turn off his phone. As his phone chimed with responses from all the women, he had text the night before in a delusion, I just smiled. He never got a reaction from me about stealing my car. He never got it from me about the other women. I was done. I finished straightening my hair and I smiled. "Have a great night." He was infuriated that I was going out.

As he screamed at me from across the room, I just smiled. I raised my voice to match his and shouted. "Mitchell, do whatever you want, with whomever you want. I don't care anymore. This is how you wanted us, so you got what you wished for. Go hang out with so and so, I am sure she is lovely." "I don't want her nasty ass." He raged back. I simply said, "Well, I guess be careful what you wish for." "You have women lined up for some reason, so apparently I need to have some men lined up too?" "The difference with you and me Mitchell is you know I will have a line by the end of the night. Don't wait up, I won't be home." He screamed at me and chased me to my car.

He knew damn well out of the both of us who would have a line. He had just grown complacent in his beliefs that I was going to keep enduring his abuse. He then proceeded to bulldoze his way into my car and dump a whole pint of hard liquor onto my floorboards. "There I hope you get arrested for drunk driving, and I am going to laugh at you." he taunted loudly. I calmly stared straight ahead until my daughter beeped her horn for me to follow her, and he snuck in another angry threat before he jumped out of my car.

Repetitive cantor, provoking me. He wants to get me riled up, he enjoys the chaos, he loves it. That is the only thing he is capable of loving. Surely if he can get me angry it puts the attention back on to him, he needs to try to remain in control. Only he doesn't understand control is not exercised through shame, guilt and accusations. Like mother, like son? Why didn't he take the initiative to break free? He enjoys it, he knows no other way. He is destined to keep riding the ride, he doesn't want to get off from it. The only certainty I could bank on was the certainty that he would keep abusing me. Way too much self-hatred.

Nothing is ever a question with him; it is an accusation. I was held on a path by The Most High to come back here to start over with him. I knew he always needed help. I guess not having my attention divided anywhere near like before, I could see the gravity of exactly how much help he needed. I'm tired with this full-time job God. Nothing I do or say is going to matter and me staying is only hurting me and my children for me.

I hate the bar scene. I'm old and can't be bothered with the noise and the little kid jargon. There is nothing more painful to me than going out with people half my age to a bar. Drunk men hitting on you that were probably the same as Mitchell. Who the hell wants it? Not me. I left two hours later. I didn't even take a sip off a drink. The smell permeating my vehicle was reason enough for a cop to think I was drunk. The only thing that would have saved me in that situation was a breathalyzer. I arrived home to Mitchell curled up in a chair watching his phone screen. He stared at me, and I closed my bedroom door and went to sleep.

Mitchell had taken that time to talk to God. He begged God to bring me back. He pleaded with him and even negotiated. Mitchell felt he had no options left other than to talk to God in those last couple hours. He bonded with God again like when he was in prison. He had lost sight of God and knew he needed him back. He had spent the last eight months treating me like a loathed afterthought and he had never put me first. My light had stopped shining for Mitchell and my indifference was highly noted. If God brought me back to him physically and emotionally that night, he would quit drugs.

Although he went through the regular withdrawals, he would distance himself from me with his rage. Not to say he still didn't rage around me, but I would just leave and go sit in my car to write. He wouldn't follow me anymore. I didn't care to listen or throw in any advice. I didn't care to try to calm him. I didn't care about any of our physical property. Break it all, I don't need any of it. I would hide the knives and out to my car I would go. I just didn't want to be trapped in the thickness of his rage. You could eat the tension in the apartment, and I didn't want any more of it. I was full. This is on you buddy you're going to make it, or you're not. I didn't care anymore.

Unemployed and now having to stare down the reality of losing me too. These were the consequences for his own choices and Mitchell did it every time. He would fight his ass off to get where he was, only to sabotage himself. I was not going to be there to help pick him up this time. "Use the strength God gave you." "I am not going to help you rebuild this time." "I am sick of going without." "I am sick and tired of being expected to just deal with your aftermath of self-hatred." "I don't hate myself and I am not going to keep trying to help someone that does." "I have had enough." Through it all though, God still allowed me forgiveness and compassion.

Mitchell, being unemployed, would start talking to me about his own business again. Just like I had tried to encourage him to do for years. All through his prison stay and all before he started meth again. He was excited in spurts while awake. Mitchell was excited when sober because his mania and ADHD was uncontrollable. Mitchell becoming sober was only one layer to the onion. It helped greatly with his psychotic episodes though.

Mitchell did nothing but sleep for hours upon hours every day. No desire to get a job. No desire to get off the couch, he was severely depressed. No help to me physically or emotionally high or sober. He was just a blimp. A messy lump I was supporting with my savings, because I had to keep a roof over me and my daughter's head. No concerns or worries on his behalf, and no talks of business plans anymore. He was just in full sleep mode. He would get up for tiny bursts and could never manage to murmur out anything nice. No motivation, no desire. No purpose and no drive.

I was starting to see that Mitchell had no other way to relate to sobriety other than what he had learned in between drug deliveries in the jails. Being sober mostly during his prison stays had taught him to cope with sobriety through long endless bouts of sleep. This was not a quality I found sexy or masculine even though it had a sober tag with it. Sober or high, he still personally was doing nothing to keep me there. He could have cried out "Well I am sober now." Yeah, and you're still nowhere near the mark I need. Through it all, God held me there quietly.

It was my youngest daughter's school vacation, and my aunt lay on her death bed with cancer. During our trip to Maine to visit with them both, mile marker 409 to my right and then to my left the exact make and model of the car John drove passed me by. I looked up gas 4.09 and another vehicle exactly as John's passed by. Two 409's and two vehicles within five seconds. I had been getting 1122 as well.

I reflected on a night when I sat in my car with my daughter. She was playing a puzzle game on her phone as I watched. Lights entered my eyeline and I looked up to see John was pulling in the parking lot. I looked back down towards my daughter, and 1122 was her score.

The appearance of 409 and two vehicles drew me back to a dream from a few weeks past. I don't usually remember my dreams. The night paralysis' while staying in Maine, however, were unforgettable. I had remembered this dream the morning I woke, because it seemed odd to me that I even remembered it.

I was walking through a restaurant with my oldest daughter. We had eaten already and were getting ready to leave. Hanging on the doorknob of the exit, I turned to my daughter behind me to ask if she wanted to go to the beach. Before she answered me in this dream, a man sitting directly behind us at a table got up to leave. I didn't know this man, but I did know the man sitting behind him. John spoke up from his table to tell me "He wouldn't be able to see me anymore." He looked slightly sad, but I asked him why? "I am moving soon." I remember he looked sad, and just his facial expression made me sad for him.

One of the short stints that Mitchell managed to stay awake, he had ventured outside. Quiet but muttering. He fought to initiate a conversation with me, while I sat in my car writing. I sat in my car so much at this point, I might as well just say I lived in it. I craved alone time so badly that one half of my body was tanned from the car's window. Evenly split right at the neckline. One side of my neck was tan, the other side white. I would laugh at this sometimes and switch my ass over into the passenger side seat. He had been sobered for two months at that point and still had no job. My savings were dwindling drastically. I had discussed with my daughter previously the reality of me having to move back to Maine once again. He was taking no action towards even wanting to engage, let alone man up. He was like a sober preteen now.

As Mitchell stood alongside my car staring in, I saw him lift his arm and cheerfully holler across the parking lot. "Hey there, how have you been man?" As I peered in my rearview mirror, there walking over to the car was John. I knew not to make eye contact or to even blink at his presence. This would all be misconstrued as an affair previously and I would be berated for hours. I was still left reeling in the aftereffects of Mitchells delusions, two months into his sobriety.

I never said a word, as John stood talking to Mitchell, I didn't even acknowledge his presence or look his way. John seemed sad though. That was odd to me. John's energy never felt sad to me. He was always happy, smiling and so friendly. His energy just felt glum. Normally I would ask anyone if they were alright but with him in that situation, I had to ignore it.

Mitchell asked me at that moment if I could pass him a business card. We had managed to order business cards earlier in the month for Mitchell's desire of self-employment. I passed him one and kept on with my writing. John bid him a good day and then left. I felt so bad for him right then. I wanted nothing more than to reach out and make sure he was going to be O.K., but I had to fight it, for peace with Mitchell.

"Hey John just said he was sick of it here." "I gave him a business card because he said he had been looking at a foreclosure in the next town over." "He is going to be moving away." Although I was happy Mitchell was starting to take the initiative, my heart sank slightly, and I recalled my dream.

Too many signs pointing at John. It made me nauseas to think that God and his universe were pointing me to him. I hadn't known much about him other than the stalking that Mitchell had done, but he was very friendly to me. The Mercedes guy, internet men and my old acquaintances were friendly too. They made their advances noticeable, but the universe wasn't sending me anything their way.

John always took the time to stop his truck and wave at me. He would sometimes attempt to get my attention. "Hey girl" How have you been?" He would stop to pet my daughter's dog and make small talk with me. He had walked by my door one day, as I was heading out. I was in the middle of an eye roll exiting my door at something Mitchell had said. John stopped walking through the hall to turn and ask if everything was, O.K.

I wanted to cry to think someone cared enough to ask if I was ok. I answered, "Oh yeah, same Ol same Ol." He laughed slightly because he had not one idea of my same old same old. I know that men and women are different, but I had to try and dismiss this behavior before. I know if I wasn't interested in someone, I would still take the time to be nice anyway, but maybe men were different. Who knows, he, much like Mitchell when outside, was very friendly with everyone.

Maybe Mitchells insane accusations did have a basis for them? Maybe he was insanely and erratically jealous because he could pick up some kind of "man vibe" that I couldn't. Maybe in Mitchells delusional, disgusting, misaligned world, he had unknowingly manifested this? He would often ask me why we were here, or why we ended up here? "This isn't us; this isn't how we are." "There has to be a reason." "I am not comfortable here." "Did it ever make you wonder how we got here so easily?" Mitchell would constantly question the apartment complex we resided in.

He had known about the manifestation of jealousy. Accusing someone of behavior and of bringing it on themselves. It's the excuse he used with my children's father. "Well, if you were not accusing her, she wouldn't have noticed me in the first place." Logical enough explanation, and Mitchell knew it all along.

Maybe God was trying to throw me hints all along. Mitchell's jealous accusations. Normally that would cause any woman to look elsewhere for comfort. Especially at the man he was accusing. All the numbers pointing to John. All the synchronicities. All the friendliness towards me on John's behalf. Maybe I was supposed to be with John, and I was so caught up in all my external, that I didn't see it.

Maybe me being forced to stay on Mitchell's path through all his senseless drama was because I was supposed to follow Mitchell to meet John? What was I doing? Why was I wasting more time? Mitchell and I had barely spoken in months. His barely noticeable half attempts at muttering a sentence here and there were all basic cave person communication. Still no semblance of any type of attempt to heal the damage he had caused. Still no concept that he had even caused any. He simply thought I would make everything all right, and he wouldn't have to put an effort into anything. We would just wake up the next day and pretend that he didn't try to kill me the night before. He was too busy sleeping on the couch now to even try to pretend. Small heavenly breaks for my peace. Why would I stay with Mitchell and all his abuses?

I had ignored the signs being thrown at me. Maybe I was too late? Who knows, but I also know it is not my job as a woman to approach a man. I learned that the hard way with Mitchell. If a man wants you, he will come to you. John was not chasing; he was just simply a nice man.

Three days. Three long days. I sat everyday contemplating. Maybe he isn't chasing because he is normal? I was used to possessive, obsessive psychopaths all these years. Maybe he felt he came on to me once, and he was going to leave me alone. Balls in my court. Maybe he thought I was happy with Mitchell and didn't want to interfere? Or maybe because of all the abuse I had endured and all the accusations I fought, I felt strangely bonded to John?

Maybe I was imagining it and it was all in my head? Maybe because he asked me if I was O.K? Maybe because he had thanked me for holding the door. The Mercedes guy thanked me for holding the door, I did not think twice about him. The universe wasn't pointing me to him, it was forcing me to think twice about John. Maybe my daughter moving in was to force me to stay. Force me to notice John. Mitchell was in an odd way right, there had to be a reason we were here.

Three days I sat, playing the conversation in my head. The line I might throw. A line to let him know I was interested. Would he bite? Would I find out for sure? I had to know. I couldn't leave this unanswered; everything had been pointing to him.   Mitchell's manifestations. The numbers, the synchronicities. I had worked up the courage. I had the perfect line.

An open-ended statement that would allow me to gauge his response. His response would tell me all I would need to know. Do I stay here and spend time with him in between flights, or do I just go back to Maine? One option sounded fun and invigorating. The other sounded, well I already know how that sounded. The thoughts of this were exciting, but then again, I try not to get excited about much anymore. Mitchell wasn't even an option to me. I had already told God I was through. I told him I was done.

I could lie in bed at night and know I had no man. I had no one to hold me or comfort me. The person I would need in my life to help me through my down times, was the cause of my down times. I had learned through all his abuse and abandonment, how to live alone without him. I had learned throughout my life how to live without a man. I could hear him snoring on the couch, and I would lay there and think about how it used to be. I would try to remember the magic I felt when we first met. The same thoughts that I would reflect on through the years to renew my faith in us. It felt like I did not even know him anymore.

I would sometimes lay there and think about how it used to feel. I could not anymore, that felt like lifetimes ago. I would instead think about seeing Mitchell in my future and just waving to him in passing. He had made no effort to stay in my future and waving to him as friends was fine with me. I had finally learned to let go of Mitchell after thirteen years. This is all we have become. I got more attention from the birds that shit on my car.

He had muttered to me a couple of times over those past few weeks about marriage. He had stated, "Well we've been together forever we might as well just get married." I chuckled and remarked on his romantic sentiment. "Aww that was so romantic, maybe if you had asked me ten years ago, now I know better." He threw out a line of sarcasm, but I wasn't kidding anymore.

Dr. Jekyll and Mr. Hyde is the closest to describing this. Mind numbing on a whole different level. I just spent eight months with an abusive, delusional, disgustingly jealous meth addict. Now I was faced with a docile, humble, easy-going man of sobriety. He didn't care about forcibly checking my phone anymore. I didn't have to sleep with my car keys or my keyboard stick for my computer. I could write and he never bothered to read it for clues on my latest affair or my newest death plot against him.

John could say Hi, and he would say what a nice guy he was. I could tell him about a man hitting on me and he would say "Hah, well maybe he likes you." Absolutely mind blowing. Right back to how he was twelve years ago. Right back to the man I originally stayed in love with. Could I trust it? No. Could I wait for him to relapse in another month or so? Yes. So of course, to the outside world I again look like an unreasonable uptight bitch. I realized this was the cycle he had me in all the years before. Except before I had emotions for him, and I loved him deeply. He had the ability to emotionally manipulate me then.

Why stay and do another round? A lowered mental capacity every time he came out of his drug binges and the inability to control emotions worse than before. The damage had already been done to me, and I had been taking the time to heal. I could look at him sometimes from across the room snoring away and think about how odd we were together. We just don't belong anymore. I loved that man so much. If he had loved me back, I know I would have stayed in the delusion of love with him the rest of my life.

My God, I endured his abuse for twelve years before I stepped away. I would have been in love with him until the day I died. He did everything in his power to push me away. He didn't trust that I ever loved him, and I didn't have the energy to just throw any more of my love away. This is always what he wanted. This is how he wanted us to be.

I could stand there then in his energy and just know that passionless, dried up and existing is not how I wanted to be. We all have our own definitions of happiness and that isn't mine. My children's father and I existed together, passionless and dried up, but we were at least friends. I could trust him and his depressive stability. This man most times didn't even try to bother to talk to me. What am I doing? What was I trying to make work? Why was I here? Everything felt at a distance and outer body to me. It was like a spell had completely been lifted. I would spend all day in my car writing while he spent all day sleeping. Never accusing me or asking me what I had done. Absolutely no interest in me.

I had been looking cute that week with half of my face and neck tan. I was feeling more confident, probably because of my sun overdose. I don't know what it was, but I was ready. No more nerves. It was down to the wire. I couldn't move on without knowing, but with knowing I could move on. I went to bed that night, excited for the next day. I would be able to see John's face and throw him my line. The sun had been shining all week, and he was getting ready to move apparently, and I had to as well, in whatever direction.

The next morning, I woke up alone as usual. I was on a mission. I knew what had to be accomplished that day. I walked lighter to the bathroom. I looked to the mirror to brazenly apply my eyeliner. Makeup now that he was in a docile state may not be questioned. Even if it was, I no longer cared. "What in the fidgety fuck is this?" I could feel it burning a little when I first woke up. The whole entire left side of my face was swollen out, and I looked to have a chin double my original size. "Oh my God." Facial cellulitis? Really? Today was supposed to be my day. Really? Really God? Why? Why are you keeping me here with him like this? What did I do?

I told you I didn't want him anymore. I had forgiven him, but I can't carry on into my future with a man that didn't care. I was not going to do it anymore. I had put too much effort into him already. I thought we were on the same page God. You spoke to me. You gave me my purpose. That moment was momentous to me. It is irreplaceable. Anytime I feel discouraged, I think back on that moment between us, and I push ahead.

That was the most magical moment of my life. No other can even hold a candle. I don't know what you promised me, but it was exceptional. I laid like a baby crying and just relishing the good things to come. I don't think I would have cried with happiness if Mitchell, being in my future, had been part of it. So, what the hell is this? Why do I look like Jay Leno?

Just like the dead had risen, suddenly Mitchell was up. He had just lived ninety-five percent of the past two months on the couch but now he had things to do. Invigorated with new life and all the things he had been putting off. They needed to be tended to right then. No time like the present. That's right, no time like the present Mitchell. Yet again, the way you nurture me and take care of me doesn't go unnoticed by any means. Just like always, anything was more important than me. Anything was more important than taking care of or showing concern for me.

My mind flashed back to all the hours I spent waiting on him, especially when he was sick. All the time I spent making him meals. All the withdrawals, all the cleaning, all the pep talks of encouragement. All of it. Wasted on Mitchell, because not an ounce of it was going to be thrown back towards me.

I knew God was holding me. Was he allowing me to view Mitchell's actions now from the outside? Completely unattached? Was I going to be able to see him now like I should have thirteen years ago? Save me the trouble God, I already know. Was this yet another test I had to pass, while he walked off clueless and carefree? I am sick of observing. I have been doing it for years. I don't want another test, I told you I was done. I am pissed. I had a plan for today. I wanted to be able to move on with my life, in whatever direction.

I want a man I can sit on the front porch with, peacefully. I want to be able to have a drink and talk about the weather. Talk about the children. A man that communicates nicely with me. Maybe about something that isn't always centered around him or his drugs. A man that comes to bed at night and sometimes cuddles me. A man that makes plans and sometimes invites me. A man that just wants peace. I know, even through all of this, I still have expectations. What an unreasonable bitch.

Expectations of what I want my future with a man to be. I could sit there on that day with my swollen face and know I must be thankful. I knew God was behind the scenes protecting me. Possibly from drama or from embarrassment. Maybe from further emotional or physical abuse. Either way from rejection or from happiness right now, no one truly knows other than God? Honestly, John wasn't around enough to protect me from Mitchell anyway. All I know is apparently throwing John a line wasn't in the cards for me. I guess I will sit here and wait for my next direction.

Numb ..... bers
XIX

My massive number of numbers had stopped. I would receive maybe a few numbers a day. No more bombardment of numbers and synchronicities. They kept me sane for three months, they accomplished what they needed too, I guess. I could feel something changing that whole time. As far as I could see the changes were only me, and Mitchell's newfound sobriety.

Was I supposed to stay and start a business with him? Christ he would get mad at me when I asked him for a receipt. He couldn't keep track of or organize anything because of his ADHD. He would take my keys to unlock my car and then lock my keys in my car. Then he would become upset with me, because my credit card that he needed to buy something to unlock my car with was locked in the car. Yes, yet again another bill on his behalf that I could take care of. This was constant childish behavior. Occasionally, shit happens, but with Mitchell this shit was daily.

He caused all this stress for me but would berate me until I calmed him down. I would have to tell him that everything was going to be o.k. Fuck, I am sick of having to be Mother Teresa. I am not. There were times when I could envision punching him right in the mouth. Wrestling him to the ground and kicking him down the hillside into the traffic. Did Mother Teresa think like that? I don't think so.

All the twin flame meanings of the numbers I had seen throughout the years were beautiful and sentimental. The angel numbers were
great as well, like I said kept me going through some hard and stressful
times. I do believe we are protected by angels, and I know that Lee is
one of mine. I don't know how many we have, but I know mine get
tired. When you have been seeing numbers as long as I have, you must
stop and question the validity. They will make you stop and look.

The four were the most abundant. 444 being the most prevalent
in scary amounts. The numbers had been mind-boggling. My daughter would remark on the odd combination of numbers she had received
most days, and Mitchell would join in sometimes too. I had to begin
to look somewhere besides just the angel and twin flame numbers.

My conversation had been with something other worldly. I believed I had conversated with possibly an angel sent from God? The
only next logical step I could conclude was numbers from the bible. I
know people could argue all day about inappropriate numbers due to
a lot of original text being removed. I had to believe that God knew I
knew this already. I also had to believe he knew I would look to the
bible eventually. I also had to believe he knew what bible I had. The
same one that I have had in my possession since I was nine. I hadn't
opened it in thirty years. He knew I would look there.

*Genesis 111 Now the whole world had one language and a com-
mon speech.* People were instructed to be fruitful, multiply and fill the
earth after the flood. People disobeyed by building a tower and trying
to reach the heavens without God. God knew the tower was about convenience for the people, not obedience to him. He knew that people
were attempting to glorify themselves. God then stated "if as one people speaking the same language, they have begun to do this, then nothing they plan to do will be impossible for them. God is very aware of

the power of people when they unite. He wants us to unite for the right reasons.

Daniel 222: He reveals deep and secret things. He knows what is in the darkness and light dwells with him. The bible was just letting me know that I had been blessed and instilled with knowledge and clarity. A gift of a different perspective from God. I laughed and understood that apparently God was telling me Mitchell was an old wineskin. One that was going to burst if I shared any of my knowledge with him. Which was weird since I never had an urgency to share much knowledge with Mitchell in the first place. My twos were always followed by 777 though.

I couldn't find a verse to match but even with no known biblical verse, these numbers were mostly aligned with belief in perfection with creation and balance. One day Peter came to Jesus and said Lord how many times will I forgive my brother who sins against me? Up to seven? For Peter forgiving up to seven times was already reaching the maximum of his spirituality. Our lord surprised him with the answer "I do not tell you until seven, but even seventy x seven. Ahh, I had done that with Mitchell as well, and from all of my accounts, I had exceeded the forgiveness the lord called upon from Peter.

Jeremiah 333 Call to me and I will answer you and show you great and unsearchable things, which you do not know. John 333 Whoever receives his testimony sets his seal to this, that God is true. Revelation 333 Remember then what you have received and heard, keep it and repent. If you will not wake up, I will come like a thief, and you have no idea at what hour I will come to you. These all made sense to me when pertaining to my timeline. The understanding of the simplicity soothed me. The fear of the complexity that could be dealt by the hand of God had me looking back.

I couldn't find any resolution with my fives, and they were a pretty pertinent part of this search. It seemed I got these before big changes, and they were not necessarily good changes on the surface at all. *Isiah 555, Surely you will summon nations you know not and nations you do not know will come running to you, because of the Lord your God, the Holy one of Israel, for he has endowed you with splendor.* It didn't pertain to me at all, but I found it slightly comforting anyhow.

1010 John 1010. The thief comes only to steal and kill and destroy. I come that they may have life and have it in abundance. (Referring to failed leaders of Israel) I am the good shepherd. The good shepherd lays down his life for the sheep. The hired hand is not the shepherd, and the sheep are not his own. When he sees the wolf coming, he abandons the sheep and runs away, then the wolf pounces on them and scatters the flock. I could relate this with my own actions and sacrifices I had made for Mitchell. The coldness of professions with actually helping those that need it and with the structure of our own government. Control and Greed the two worst addictions of them all.

1122 John 1122 But even now I know that God will give you whatever you ask. Romans 1122 Note then the kindness and the severity of God, severity toward those who have fallen but God's kindness to you, provided you continue in his kindness. Otherwise, you too will be cut off. Mark 1122 Have faith in God, Jesus answered. The verses in this bible mesmerized me.

The two numbers I saw mostly during my despair. *1212 'Romans Rejoice in hope, be patient in tribulation, be constant in prayer. (Expectation of fulfillment.) 1222 Luke, Then Jesus said to his disciples, "Therefore I tell you, do not worry about your life, what you will eat, or about your body and what you will wear.* I just shook my head in astonishment. These meanings hit me deeply. More deeply than I could ever describe.

My fours. Ahh my trusty fours. They had been outlandishly present for three months, while I stood in anguish and despair. As I stood hopeless in only the strength of God to get me through the days. *John 444 For Jesus himself had testified that a prophet has no honor in his own hometown. Ezekiel 444 Falling down before God. Then the man brought me by way of the North Gate to the front of the temple. I looked and saw the glory of the lord filling the temple of the Lord and I fell facedown.*

I had too, on that day in my kitchen before the light, I fell facedown. I have no choice but to wait.

This is the path that I choose to walk. There is no going back now. I wanted to walk in the light, I wanted God to be able to use me as a tool for light. Do unto others as you would have done to you. I wanted to believe in something outside myself. A higher existence. Did the delusion that I was walking in the light and doing good for God, get so bad, that I was caught off guard by an abnormal presence that appeared? I couldn't see a shape, just felt a presence. I couldn't retain the words; I just began crying and thanking God. The all-encompassing warmth of this light crippled me and brought me to my knees. I couldn't tell you what it said, it was just a straight beam of comfort that I couldn't even raise my head to see. I, as a grown woman, laid blubbering in a pile of endless joyful tears. Under the same light the dog had been transfixed on just a few months before in my video.

Does the crippling, crashing and all-encompassing understanding that trauma will push upon you the greatest of delusions apply? The greatest lie ever told. Hope will push, it will dilute, it will disillusion. Trauma will cause the most intelligent of people to look for a reason. It will force someone of good intentions to look for a reason. A reason why this has happened, a reason that we should still be able to go on and thrive. Just give me a reason.

In our darkest of times and our lowest of days we will look to any direction to grasp on in belief. This is when we will look back to God. We will align with God; we want someone to notice that we are good. We want validation for just being burnt, mentally destroyed, and invalidated. We want someone to acknowledge the good intentions we had in our hearts. We want to know that in our days of social isolation and our core beliefs being rocked, that someone has our back. So, we turn to God.

We want so desperately to believe that we are not alone. We want so desperately to achieve validation for doing the right thing. We want some reason to explain to us why we continue our path. If not, we will develop a slow descent to our own demise. We will not allow ourselves to believe in hope or in destiny, in a purpose. We don't want to accept the fact that we are just sacks of bacteria infested waste, polluting the airways. Good or bad, who the fuck cares anymore?

I think to live in true animal nature I should probably drive back and slap Shuega right across her face! She deserves it, tit for tat. No empathy, no special circumstances aside. She didn't have any empathy for me. Why should I be the bigger person? Why should I let things go? Making excuses for others behavior is supposedly frowned upon when self-empowering so why am I making an excuse for her behavior? Am I going to get a special reward for being the bigger person? Umm Nope. If wanting to save someone is so bad, why would I want to save her from being slapped back?

Society has no problem accepting that God would be the driving force behind me kissing this girl on the head, but has a problem with me slapping her head in the name of God? Kissing normal, slapping delusional. Yet, people were willing to kill their own children in the name of God. Why would God ask such a thing? To see if people were going to follow.

If people tried to follow such a thing now, they would be demonized in society as delusional mentally sick devil worshippers. You would be placed in a mental institution. Your only chance of escape being to wait for someone of equal mentality to be placed in a position of power to release you. Let's face it, society has some strong protocols with the hiring process for that nowadays. So, which is it? Are you a true follower of God, or are you a convenience follower? Worshiping when it suits you for a societal standing or a mask for what you want others to believe. That is in its very essence a sin itself.

There are so many levels for us to fall prey to. Constant lies, constant. Theories, beliefs, manifestation, as above and below. In reality, no one knows, but the last crushing blow to this earthly realm is to be let down by the one fucking thing you believed in. To realize it was all an illusion. To realize that labels aside, mental illness, delusional, whatever people want to describe it as. Let's face it, losing your faith is the final blow to a human. It is the most desperate despair in an immeasurable amount. Why are there so many people that seem to want to recruit others to their beliefs? Why can't people cling to their own perspectives and beliefs? Why do people have to align with societal beliefs, to make you feel safer? I will tell you what my mother always told me, the world doesn't revolve around you.

Just the knowledge that you have done unto others as you want done to you. Just the knowledge that you have had endless opportunities to enact revenge on someone, or to destroy them and you didn't because you wouldn't want it done to you. Why? Because of Karma? Is this the peddled delusion now? Karma? God and the devil? Yin and Yang, harmonious balance? Spiritual gurus, Preachers, trying to sell the depressed and depraved, the abused and the traumatized a new lease on life. A reason for hope. They say to live by God is to spread hope. If a society believes to be Good is to believe in God, why do these people repeatedly do everything on a daily basis to live in the bad?

A preacher of a big church that does little to give back to the community. I have witnessed this. Not to say that some don't give back, the little ones always do what they can. I have witnessed people being so brainwashed by trying to move up this "so-called" ladder to God's love in society. These people will fight for positions within a church to have "Godlier" standing in their community. They will fight over who gets the chance to drive the preacher around, because he is so Godly that he nor any of his family can drive themselves. He is so Godly that when they drop him off at his 900,000-dollar home, they have to help walk him to his front door. These very people fighting for the position to kiss the ass of this unholy, evil hack are the same people fucking the churches secretary on her desk. Quickly though, so his wife that he abuses doesn't see.

Church, tax free separation from state. No taxes are made to be paid into the country or society, but they want to make you believe they are trying to help the community on a whole. Is this because churches already believe society to be evil? The only thing I ever saw this church with a bookstore and a famous coffee chain inside of it do, where to send the children that attended out on a street corner.

I say this because in the 100 degrees plus sun, they had these little children stand on a busy intersection and give out water to pass-ersby. Shame on you. Children who you have made believe are help-ing in the name of God, and bottles of water. What was the cost of that water? Two hours of your coffee sales from the day? Way to give back to the community. Now drive this man back to his over-priced home in the air conditioning quickly. You wouldn't want him dropping from heat exhaustion, that's what the kids are for.

Brainwashing of the masses. It would seem in that sense that good people are called to do bad things.

Some people are called to preach his word. Yet the preacher is only valid in the church? The man with a sign in the grocery store parking lot isn't up to standards, so, he is mentally ill? Why because he rebuked societal standards? People with their close-minded blind beliefs are so funny to me. They walk around all week oblivious to their own shortcomings, but for some reason believe church on Sunday will redeem them.

A group of free and deep thinkers, highly rebuked within society. People want to blindly berate and belittle, even scoff at this group of people. Why? Because of the name? These people have taken a bold stance and have surfaced with their beliefs. They are just trying to grab the attention of the die-hard closed minded. Understand just because you were raised one way, doesn't mean you get to pass judgment on to others.

They are just trying to bring about the understanding of cultural and religious dominance. One religion seemed to dominate this country, when this country wasn't founded on that principle. Born out of religious freedom and democracy. Have they created some extreme over the top displays? Yes, they have and so have some Christians. Are they hard working good people? Yes, from everything I can see. They just oppose organized religion and the dominance of forcing people to look at things one way.

They believe in the power of self, just like a good majority of people. They live by a code that a massive amount of society would all agree with morally and they help by doing great things within their communities. Take the time to look at this group before passing judgment on something you have never taken the time to try to understand.

Would it have helped their beliefs and cause to hide behind a less frightening name within society? Yes, because I could guarantee if they called themselves "The church of roses." People would agree with their cause and be there with them every day. However, they didn't believe in hiding behind deception. Just this has to make people question the validity of a lot of what has been taught. Satanists, they have been scapegoated and projected on by the Christian religion, within society and with the media.

I will tell you what I was taught. There are good and bad in every race. There are good and bad in every religion. We as individuals must all walk our own paths back to God.

Every religion and belief are held with a central God of worship and a way to achieve this acceptance and enlightenment. Some religions seem to rebuke enlightenment and find themselves blindly enjoying a veil of unknowing. Satanists seem to want people to know of enlightenment. If it wasn't for Eve eating from the tree of knowledge and being tempted by the devil/snake, how would she know anything? Would she still be living in la la land under the direct control of a God? A God that didn't want her veil lifted. Did God want her to stay ignorant and naive to her surroundings? Like Gary's wife?

They are trying to get people to question why a God of this sort would want people to be mindless and naive to the knowledge that was around them? Is having knowledge and understanding a bad thing? Is this evil? If knowledge is a bad thing, then why do we have schools, libraries and learning centers? It would already seem that society as we know it, is laden with what the devil wants then, correct? These things were also always presented in the light of good for society.

Satanists code of ethics, empathy. Eve eating the apple from the forbidden tree of knowledge. Was she cursed with caring, nurturing, childbearing, and empathy? Was that her punishment for disobeying? Do all women carry this "curse" for Eve's choice?

Other beliefs existed centuries before Christianity. The first noted culture to be able to write. Sumerian. Women held positions of equality, apart from witnessing crimes in court. They had all the same rights as a man other than that. Do people today understand that other beliefs were of a knowing and feeling? These beliefs did not require many written words and instructions. The beliefs then were of an internal knowledge. Prior beliefs were wiped out by force and to force people to acknowledge another belief. A belief that aligned with what men in power believed. Any other knowing of God was persecuted and deemed evil. Witchcraft, the occult. Seemingly making the rules up as they go.

Women that spoke up were of evil or of a witch descent. Did the bible set up women to be in the wrong constantly? Gospel of Thomas, Nag Hammadi. Some derogatory language was used to describe women in the one statement that circulates. It did, however, offer women a chance to be restored to oneness by denouncing traditional roles of wives and mothers and living essentially as men. If supposedly women are not equal to a man or even worthy of life, as some customary beliefs would have us believe, then why is it scientifically proven today that all mammal embryos start life out as female? Another ethics code of Satanists, belief in proven science.

Does this keep a war raging? Were these many, many inferior women tortured and killed for stating their knowledge? Does this keep us distracted and divided? Archaic religious beliefs of disgruntled men with mommy issues? Is this the deep root of feminism, fighting the man with the brain of a hurt little boy? Fighting the very system and structure on which this world is seemingly based. Or is the root of feminism based in the belief that a pink fuzzy vagina hat and screaming about one man is going to change anything? Is anger being aimed in the correct direction?

Has society been set upon the premise of this belief? If so, why? The Romans were of great violence and greed. Yet Paul the apostle, during Roman rule, stated many moral beliefs that were selected for the bible. Selected I am sure by religious heads of male stature. He claimed to know of God's belief in obeying government structure. 13. Telling people to abide by the control of the government and its structure, because God has commanded it this way. *"Every person is to be in subjection to the governing authorities. For there is no authority except from God and those which exist are established by God. Therefore, whoever resists authority has opposed the ordinance of God."*

I mean was this said to keep peace. Was this stated so as not to look like an enemy of the state? I mean how many authorities existed back then and were established by God? I am sure there were nowhere near as many as there are today. Yet I didn't see any new prophecies declaring God's O.K. on their establishments.

Give to God what is God's and to Caesar what is Caesars. The words of Jesus when concerning taxes. Who's the damn Caesar today, because somehow our taxes due have been multiplied to many Caesars in massive plurality. If Jesus did prophesize this, then why do the very establishments that are built to "honor" God, not pay taxes like stated in the bible? Did God just stop talking to people after these time eras? I mean he must have spoken to people at one time, the bible is written in these contexts.

If the bible is a collection of prophecies and stories handed down from other people, wouldn't that be a form of what the legal world today would consider hearsay? Hearsay cannot be used in courts; it is not considered reliable. It however, was a good basis for the collection of the bible? Separation of church and state, understandable. Placing your hand on the bible within the very courts that have established the definition of hearsay; Contradictory.

.

How did hearsay occur if there is an understanding the bible was not added to for 400-500 years? Who was still alive five hundred years later to have the knowledge carried down for a supposed five hundred years? Was it a prophet taking direct knowledge instilled into them from God? Possibly a mentally ill religious head of grandeur? How much did religion influence politics and vice versa? Maybe someone with the great need to control a situation or a mass of unruly people? How about the possibility of duress under someone else's control? My 1155 is back.

What if there is one God of the Universe? What if he wants us all to live by the code of being good people and doing everything in our efforts to help others while we are here? What if religions and beliefs aside, we all just need to believe in the goodness of humanity and lifting it up, to make it home to him? Forgiveness of others' wrong deeds against us and leaving people better than we found them? Some of us can see through society and what has been taught and some of us can't. The sleeping.

Are the asleep doomed to stay asleep, to stay here? To continue fighting amongst themselves with the webs of distractions? If they are, do they stay here in hell? Does that mean that the people with no knowledge beyond themselves will be doomed to roam the earth zombified and ultimately align and fight with Satan? Why would the bible want people to stay asleep, so they can ultimately align with Satan? Maybe the ones gifted with knowledge are the ones God has anointed to do his work? Maybe the asleep will be the ones raptured and the ones with knowledge will have to stay and fight with Satan.

Unphased and unwavering to the beholden and their strategies are calloused. Do unto others as you would have done to you. People that cannot follow this most basic concept are not to be toyed with. Look within your life. Look within what most consider their lives. Look within your profession. Are you treating the people the way you would want to be treated in the same circumstance? If not, then fix yourself. People that cannot honor something as simple as that don't belong in a world full of knowledge and are doomed to keep foreshadowing their own lost fate. Staying in a state of ignorance and greed. How much of yourself do you keep giving? How much of your soul must you pour into others?

What if many of us were raised with the notion that God is all good? God is all love and peace. Everything will go well for us all if we abide in God's law and man's law. Oblivious only to the surface? When trauma happens and ultimately it will, does this cause one to reject God and all the teachings? Does one assume due to trauma caused they are now cursed by God? Does this cause someone to begin to live for what they believe accepts them? The other side? Does trauma cause one to just give up and follow the other side? The dark? Or do we have to maneuver the dark to find the light?

What if we are raised to fear God? Make no mistakes. Avoid all sins, even the thoughts of sin would make us bad people. Always watching, always judging. Would this cause someone to reject God? Would this cause someone to give up and believe they are evil, because they cannot avoid sinning, even in the smallest amounts? Would this cause people to understand those teachings are a control tactic based in fear and shame? Would this cause one to liken this to the magic of Santa Clause? Does it cause one to understand control is one of most evil addictions on the planet?

Do we learn with each trauma to get closer to God? Do we run to him for protection and refuge from our storms, our traumas? Each trauma will occur and with everyone you lean on God for, the lessons will ascend you higher. Do we stay complacent with what a society labels us to keep us stuck here or do we allow God to pull us higher and closer? Do we allow God to pull us above the veil of the world? Do we get to ascend? Maybe the knowledge of ascension is how they depict the rapture? Maybe God wants people of knowledge after all?

Understand that we are on earth so nothing will go completely well. We are on a soul journey. The devil is here, and God will test us. The two forces dueling it out for our souls will divide us. It is all in your perspective. The whole good and bad. Do we Illuminate for masses and allow the grab of the ones that want to evolve? Leaving the others behind because they want to stay? Victims of their own downfalls, asleep to the collective masses. Are the ones with knowledge and empathy of evil, or are they good?

Satanists believe in being empathetic. Eve ate the apple that cast us here. Was birthing, nurturing and empathy the curses women must bear? Was that a punishment? Why would God ``punish" all female forms to reproduce? Why would he punish female squirrels for something Eve did? Where does the confusion end? Do they want to stay? Or do we stay?

One's mind evolution above animalistic nature is a choice when it all comes down to it. One's choice to look outside themselves to give others hope or a reason. Their choice to direct others down a path of hope or to show appreciation or some resemblance of love. Ultimately this is someone spreading light. Walking in the light. Is there a chosen 144,000? Are there any light workers? How about spiritual guides, ancestors or whatever ideal we hitch a glimmer of idealistic hope to.

We are aware of a spiritual war, yet how many are willing to fight societal standards so the true light can shine? How many are willing to lose everything in the process of following God, and still show thanks for the tent they have over their head? Believing what is convenient for you is one thing, but following through is another. You must consciously believe God to be a delusion, otherwise you wouldn't label another's directions from God as a delusion. We don't all get the same assignment.

Resurrection
XX

The crashing reality that your mind can have such an effect on you, that you will carry on your life believing you are in a solid reality, when you are not. Invention of and buying into the belief of something better with angels and a God? Coping Mechanism? Society would name it psychosis and say trauma will cause this. How do you self-preserve when you're in a delusion? Which need was stronger? Your own survival or other's survival? How do we live in psychosis for thirteen years? How do we slip in further? Are we that desperate to escape our own realities that we will entertain delusion? Fuck I never even did any drugs! Why? Why did I avoid drugs all these years? Don't need them messing with my head, I like to stay clear headed, so I can make rational decisions.

Mitchell's sobriety lasted beyond my expectations of three months. I was so proud of him. He put so much work into his healing. He would listen to information on BPD and was taking steps to try and understand his disorder. Not how it affected other people, but how it affected him. He still had no knowledge of how any of his prior behaviors would affect others or the amount of damage he had caused to us. He still had the same overall heir of expectancy for my utter forgiveness for anything he did.

Mitchell would loosely blanket apologize but never in detail. He just expected that saying sorry would reset me. Good as new. Expecting me to be talkative and happy now. He could never explain why he was sorry. He just knew it was customary to say so. I would often say, sorry only means something if you change the behavior that caused it in the first place. He would become annoyed with this and insist he couldn't do anything good enough for me. Much like a child hitting a dog and then being mad at the dog when it doesn't want to play anymore. He had no concept of rebuilding trust within people because Mitchell himself didn't learn trust growing up from people.

He was extremely upset with me for not portraying a bubbly nature with his steps and was insulted that I continued to foolishly write. He couldn't figure out why I didn't center my everyday life around him to the degree I had before. He was trying so hard, so I guess to him I needed to verbally display my happiness with this.

I would tread on the thoughts of verbally expressing I was proud, because of his mixed reactions. Anytime I would tell him I was proud of him before; he would berate me and tell me I didn't mean it. A deep psychological entrenchment from his own upbringing. Now he seemed a little more open to the praise and acknowledgements I would give. Mitchell, however, was still pretty much pushing away any love that he desperately felt he wanted and needed.

After the three months mark, I began to almost talk myself into giving him a chance by observing him further. I couldn't let my guard down still, but I could engage a little longer and speak to him about future plans. He talked a lot about his business, and the way he wanted everything to be. I allowed him to take the lead. He was so excited, and I knew if he proceeded on through the rest of the summer sober, that I would help him to legitimately open his business.

Mitchell received a call on his birthday from his mother. They had not spoken since right before his last meth cycle. She finally stated she was proud of him and all his accomplishments. She tried to take credit for his achievements by stating all of this happened because she had him arrested.

It was three days later Mitchell came to me extremely anxiously and did not understand why he had such a compulsion to use again. "I haven't thought about it until just now, now I am craving it so bad." I tried to explain to him that he was not strong enough emotionally to be speaking with his parents just yet. They reinforce his self-sabotage cycle. It was three days later when he caved and began using it again. Of course, this was blamed on me.

God shield me from what is about to take place. Protect me from wanting to protect him, an empty well, a pit of despair. A fiery inferno of deceit and lies, let your wrath onto the deserving be known. He never believed. Instead, he has attacked me with his unwillingness to listen and to learn. He has made fun of my kindness. I can't carry him anymore. He is too heavy now and I can feel how you have allowed me to step away. I asked for a clear sign, I asked for many, and this is the clearest by far.

He made his decision to stay sick, he doesn't want better and who am I to keep trying to help him see? He made his choice with his own free will. My job is done here. I cannot interfere with free will. I don't need him to see me for who I was just yet, that ride on karma will see and find him soon enough. I can't use myself as a bargaining chip anymore when he sees me like the others. Lift his veil when we are through.

I was blessed this week three times with the sightings of pink flamingos. Once at a clothing store on a shirt, as I stood with my children. The next when we all went to the zoo that Mitchell had promised to attend with us but didn't, and the third. The night I pulled into my mother's driveway after my long trip back. There at the end of her driveway, flapping in the wind, was a summer welcome banner with a pink flamingo. I looked at the clock; I had pulled in at 11:22.

God did grace me with a moment of clarity between Mitchell and me. He allowed me enough energy to pick up his phone call a few days later. Mitchell called me and admitted that he knew he reneged on a deal he had with God. He knew he was about to get Karma. He was scared and he knew why I had to leave. I admitted that I had very little control over that decision, and it felt as though I was almost taken out of the situation mindlessly.

When our phone call ended, I dropped on both of my knees. I sobbed as I prayed to God to have mercy on Mitchell and his soul. I had prayed to God to protect me from wanting to protect him during this time, but God never answered that prayer. Had God been allowing Mitchell yet another chance with me? Mitchell prayed and promised he would give up meth if I came back to him that night. Did God hold me there with my swollen face to observe?

I can look back now in wonder and slight clarity. I can remember standing in my window 13 years ago. Tears in my eyes, begging God to please help me be happy. I was concerned I would never find happiness. It was less than six months later when I was afflicted with the strong feelings of Mitchell and knowing he was the one. Love at first sight across a field, had not even seen his face. Only felt his energy. I have been on this ride ever since.

Did God use Mitchell as my tribulation period? Was he the devil I had to fight and win? Was Mitchell the obstacle that God used to test my strength? Was God trying to see if I was strong in my desire to be happy? Was Mitchell my test? Or was God using me to get Mitchell back on his path? Was God ultimately going to be able to reward me after 13 years? Thirteen years, was this a curse or a promise fulfilled?

Five months of sitting in Maine, in peace and quiet away from Mitchell. I suppose to society a good majority of people would label this dynamic as a toxic trauma bond. I can assure you that it is not. They say partners of people with mental disorders need to take time for themselves to recharge. God allows me this time always.

This round of Maine time I sat relaxing and just seeing a whole different set of numbers. Every day, in every combination. Several times a day. Questioning my very sanity and why so many numbers. They kept me distracted from Mitchell though while we lived our lives once again, apart.

I know why I was sent back to Maine now. It was a test. Not a test for me this time, but a test for all the others. It allowed me the time I needed to see the people that truly were going to help me in my time of need. The people that truly had my back, while God worked mysteriously behind mine.

My return to Mitchell was vastly different this time. God sent me back with an entirely different energy. He was still just as anxious and conceited, dominant, and lost. The apartment was filthy. Droplets of blood and hand drawn symbols aligned the twelve-foot ceilings and walls. His self-loathing evident with the splays of blood delivered with every forceful plunge of the needle hitting his veins. Sheetrock dug out in an attempt to find me in hiding spots. Denial that his compass had left. Trying to fill that void with more drugs and mindless whores.

I always love it when people look at me and say. "He gets like this every time you leave him. He just can't take it; he loves you so much and he is on a mission to hurt himself when you leave. He feels so lost without you." Change in perspective. Mitchell is permanently like this, you just never notice it, because he demands so much of my energy to hold him together. He is a full-time job. Stop trying to exploit my empathy.

I once again grew weary as I prayed to God the strength to endure. Mitchell was still abusive and stammering with ignorance. Vindictive and spiteful. He raged as he professed arrogantly that he was glad that I lost people I loved, when he was locked up. He then stated he was the reason behind the losses because he dabbled in witchcraft and cast spells from behind bars. I looked up and fought back every emotion that welled in me at that moment. The numbers 717 still being thrown constantly my way. Corinthians 7:17, and don't be wishing you were someplace else or with someone else. Where you are right now is God's place for you.

Mitchell left and returned from his smoke break outside of the apartment when he began raging about a man outside walking a dog. I never saw the man as I remained indoors, but in Mitchell's mind the man was outside waiting to meet up with me. As Mitchell raged, he wasted no time shoving me into the bathroom wall and biting my face. The usual coping strategy for his overwhelming thought process. It was in this moment that I knew God had finally giving me the honors to call judgement. I smiled silently and gave it all back to God. This time I prayed that God would give Mitchell a glimpse into the clarity that God had instilled in me. I prayed for his soul and left the apartment.

It was three days later when Mitchell called me back. He was depressed and crusty lying in his own filth. I encouraged him to peel himself off the couch and I would help him clean his apartment. He needed me to talk him off the ledge as usual. I was always his voice of reasoning that he so much needed but never listened to. I figured I could help him kill two birds with one stone.

Clumsily cleaning the dishes, he apologized to me. I stood closely by as encouragement and reassurance. Mitchell hates to do the dishes. It was within moments under the same lights as the dog and I previously, Mitchell began to cry out. He ran feverishly around the apartment holding on to his head. The silent look of amazement with his mouth hung open wide. All he could keep saying was "Oh my God" "Oh my God."

He repeated the information he was receiving, and his eyes were so wide. He started to echo back his understanding of the Twin Flame Journey and just kept crying out. He was confused, overwhelmed, and just amazed. I had never spoken to Mitchell about Twin Flames. I had never spoken to Mitchell about my moment with the Most High, to this day Mitchell doesn't know any of my story. Mitchell and I never had what people would consider progressive conversations.

He kept apologizing to me profusely and begged me for an answer. "Is this why you are so quiet all the time?" Is this everything you know all the time?" I stated, "I don't know what he is telling you, but yes. I prefer the quiet to sort out all my thoughts most of the time." All I could do for the second time was stand silently pondering the significance of the three-day period of resurrection.

Through all the darkness we endured and through his old held on to belief of self-hatred. Through all his family dysfunction and his learned coping mechanisms. Through his massive drug addiction that plagued him for nearly twenty-five years. Through his homelessness, all his arrests and his prison years. Through the criminal and mentally ill labels society had projected onto him. All his gut-wrenching pleas and cries begging me to help him to get better. Begging me through all his pain and anguish. He never understood until then exactly how much I had always been there.

Mitchell was giving his purpose from God on this day, and I know because Mitchell stated so. He was full of confidence and contentment as he revealed to me that he was asked by God to provide for us. While 1222 flashed on the clock in the background. *Therefore I tell you, do not worry about your life, what you will eat, or about your body and what you will wear.* I knew in that moment God was aligning Mitchell with people that had the finances to help him provide for me while I wrote.

It was a few months later that I was once again coaxed by God with 717, to follow Mitchell. He had an offer of a different residence from a man he did carpentry work for. I didn't ask many questions; I just helped Mitchell pack his apartment up and followed.

It was a beautiful small home on a lake. So many windows, and so much natural light, I had to keep the blinds drawn while I finished writing most days.

I can't thank God enough for allowing this man to enter Mitchell's life. This man is a true gem. Intelligent, logical, stoic and of high value. A man that is traveled and worldly. Credible and professionally honored. He has been a hard worker his whole life. I can't thank him enough for sharing with me stories of Morrocco and how deeply touched he was by him. Just know God loves you and regardless of what form delivered, he knows in our lives when and what we need. Thank you for being an upstanding role model and restoring my faith in the people that work for the justice system. Oh yeah, he is one hell of a defense attorney too.

It was three weeks after moving to this new town before I learned of its true name. Before this I referred to it by its township. It was only a couple of short weeks later when I was honored with meeting his wife. One of the most authentic and genuine people I have ever been able to meet. Her ability to radiate warmth, sweetness and acceptance is unmatched by anyone I have ever met. I do not wonder for a moment what her husband sees in her. He regardless of any material achievement in his life, is a very lucky man.

Nestled quietly on a six-acre gorgeous estate, in a little town named Bethlehem, his wife truly deserves the material lifestyle that she has. I can't thank her enough for inviting me into her world and her garden. It was a pleasure of rest and retreat that I very much needed. I know that God placed you on my path so I could finish his book. It has been a privilege to make your acquaintance, Thank you and much love to you always Eve.

I am not going to sing gospel music. I am not going to go around grabbing people and trying to heal them. I am not going to make signs. I am not going to force those around me to pray to see if they accept him too. I am not going to force people to believe around me. I know how society sets this up. I know what people say and what they think. I have been there. The Jesus Freaks, the church people, the people that preach out about being anointed. I am not going to preach to the lost or the fallen about how they need to find a good church. Their light is too dim right now, they are lost. They don't want to hear about finding a good church. They don't understand spiritual war, they don't understand divine protection. They want their next fix, that's it.

They want their existence to mean something and to them it feels like it doesn't. I can't begin to explain how fucking much they are un-conditionally loved. I can't explain to them they have a purpose. I can't explain to them the depths they will have to sink to be redeemed. I am not going to lecture people on their life choices, for I am a sinner too. No one here is perfect. We are in his image, but not him. We all make questionable decisions in the eyes of another.

I am not going to be foolish enough to believe God will use me to physically heal people with my touch. God does work through us, but not with special babble or superpowers as society knows them. I am not going to be foolish enough to believe I can completely emo-tionally or mentally heal someone. No one has that power on this earth, other than self.

I am going to be foolish enough to believe I have the power to be a piece of the puzzle. A piece on some people's journeys. I have the power to help others find him along their way. I have been blessed with the ability to inspire people on their paths, after all what is our journey if it's not a path back to him?

In the darkest of your days, in your most desperate hours. In our complete and utter despair and disgust with our surroundings. In our absolute bottom moment while we contemplate even still going on here, I promise you, he doesn't hate you. He's not wishing for your demise. You haven't been an outcast or thrown away. You haven't been forgotten. He is testing your strength and your reserve. He will test. I know some strong motherfuckers too!

We won't know why; we will cry out asking with no answer from him. Some will doubt his existence and may even turn from him. Some of us will still have faith in his existence and carry on, never

ever being able to fathom even a miniscule fraction of why, but we will allow him to lead us through his essence, with faith and prayer.

Will you survive it? Will you forge on for him? Will you allow him to use you? In your absolute weakest of body and mind, will you continue? Does he get to reward you? Can he use you? Are you, his soldier? Or will you allow the distractions to eat you alive? He wants you home, and this will be the fucking hardest thing you ever do!

I am more than happy and willing just for fifteen seconds of his unconditional love to accept this and my assignments. All the trials, tribulations, dark, evil, I survived. I knew he had me and for the remainder of my days always will. The highest of all highs. A high like no one would believe if they haven't experienced it themselves. Indescribable. A high of knowing and acceptance that would make self-empowering success feel like a scratch on your ankle. Nothing compares to this on earth, this is divine and not of this place.

To bee or not to bee
XXI

Mitchell regardless of being touched with God's clarity and command, could never completely reconcile the process. He questioned Gods commands that day. He continued to use meth, rage, abuse, and threaten both of our lives. He would still be adamant about wanting to die and would mockingly make up stories of how he should force me to kill him for a nice ending to my stupid book. A stupid book that he demands I need to pay him for, because without him I would never have been able to write the fucking thing.

He would gleefully and mockingly express his gratitude to God for never falling in the marriage trap with me, because I was a lying thief and God knew it. God loved him more than me because God was protecting him from making the biggest mistake of his life. He would then insist I needed to express more gratitude, as he used Gods blessings to provide for everyone before me.

I watched from an outside perspective as Mitchell arrogantly flaunted and blessed everyone around him with kindness, time and gifts. While I and my basic needs went unmet. Putting anyone and everything before me. I also had to observe quietly as Mitchell received Karma every time he mistreated me. It was so obvious to him that he was being punished that he would beg me to take away the curse I had placed on him. I would chuckle, point up and say, "Don't look at me."

I had told Mitchell before that I could leave him without even leaving the room, but he never believed me. I watched quietly as The Most High removed all the gifts and blessings he had bestowed upon Mitchell to help provide for me. Mitchell had no choice but to start seeing the people in his life with full clarity. The fog was lifting in his world and once again the only person still sitting quietly in the room was me.

Understand, God makes things happen for you, not to you. Religious beliefs aside, Jesus was sent as an example for how we should live our lives. I am the way, the truth and the life. No one comes to the father except through me. Believe in Jesus's title and status, or not. You need to behave and understand as Jesus did, that is your way to God.

Be conscious of how you treat others. Be a light. Don't hide behind the label of helping. Actually help, by making yourselves better. People need to understand respect is given and kept as an individual, not because of a title you hold within society. Use your positions here to help those trying to help themselves. Remember we were all given different assignments along our journey.

Is God preparing his 144,000 now before he opens the silence of the seventh seal? Is God sending his light out now to wake others up? Can some of you feel a shift? Can you feel something happening? Symbolically bumblebees are sent as messengers from the spiritual realm. Do they help bridge the physical and spirit world? Symbolically, do they?

Have I been chosen to speak in a fluent language that some will understand? Was I chosen to take the deep psychological plunge of living with and understanding the truly disordered? Was I chosen to dive to depths unforeseen by many others? Was I chosen to ignore societal standards all to bring forth answers to simple questions? Ultimately, it's all about our choices as individuals to look outside of ourselves for the answers to questions. Questions that were designed for the entertainment of us ones that decided to evolve outside of animalistic nature.

Some things we are not allowed to reveal, I can ask these though. Should the criminal justice system take a closer look at family dynamics when dealing with younger "criminals?" Should it evolve to cutting all ties with family for a probationer or a parolee? Should it force its men to grow individually without the familiar comforts of enablement and toxicity? Is rehabilitation impossible for some? Are there so many flaws and corruption within this system that it essentially should be dismantled and rebuilt?

Does Lady Justice, born from ancient Roman times depict a blindfold? A blindfold to inequality amongst people? Or is she blindfolded to a lie and being mocked within the very system?

Did God hold me with one of the most damaged, manipulative men possible? Did God want me to be able to understand the depths and countless layers of manipulation, so I could see too? Women are sick and tired of having their empathy exploited. What we are expected to give for free is the same thing a man would charge for.

Do people fear the New World Order, is it a special group that means harm? Will they allow for the continuation of a couple more generations to surpass? Will they drop upon the unprepared complete annihilation of technology? Leaving us with only the ability to look upon the governing parties? Or is it the return of how it's supposed to be? The return of the old.

Did God promise heaven on earth? Did he promise to reign again someday? Was the curse of the woman, a curse? Or was it a blessing made into a curse because men feared it? Did men kill off what they feared using their physical superiority? Has the battle been forced to rage between man and woman? Did men view the snake as an evil that can be physically fought off? Was it a prowess of strength to fight off the evil lurking lie? Has it been a contest of whose gift has been better, instead of uniting our emotional and physical superiorities together? Were women blessed with emotional strength? Are we superior with this, a head start blessing. Embrace this always within yourselves.

Can we watch the world getting closer one step at a time? Can we see just simple acts of bravery and kindness bridging the gap? The pageant contestant with no makeup, inspiring women to be themselves. Remember girls, in most of the animal kingdom, it is the male species that must stand out and earn us, as the female species does the picking. We are the prize. God gifted Adam with Eve.

All the cancer survivors fighting and beating the odds to encourage others every day. The women athletes and the few women of our political structure that take no shit. We see you and we love you. Small steps of advancement and courage.

Don't shame us for what you have not been chosen for. Women are some fearless bad ass bitches, and we will play your game. We follow your lead, remember? As an equal as God intended. Others that do not understand give us space and support. We have been chosen to go in and help heal the severely damaged and neglected. The ones that were not raised properly because their mothers couldn't endure anymore. It is all part of the plan. Can you not comprehend? Know you haven't been chosen to do so. Women need the support of other women, not beratement and division.

Is the focus of the third eye in the middle of one's forehead so polluted and clogged now with societal expectations that we can consider it marked with these beliefs? Clogging our intuition, our spirituality, our insights? Is this gift of insight so marked and labeled by society now that everyone sees it as mental illness, evil and witchcraft? Have the old ways been almost annihilated and replaced? Was the right hand depicted as strength and reality? Could someone be marked within society with the rise and broad use of psychology? Could they be marked with the label of weak, dishonorable, or delusional?

Men don't try to portray us in a weaker image or a less than, because you are resisting the urge to grow up. We are very empathic, loving, nurturing creatures, we will forgive you. It's the blessing bestowed upon us from God. Us women have already been rewarded as the obedient. We are blessed with slaying the beast and rising from the ashes in complete transformation. We will forgive you. We will allow you to continue just so. We will be supportive from an equal standpoint, and we will encourage you every step of the way.

We will help you and be your strength in your absolute weakest. We will make do with what's provided, and we will multiply it. We will be your biggest cheerleader. We will raise the kids; we will keep the house clean. We will even keep the house at the temperature you prefer sometimes too.

We will give to you endlessly. We will be your refuge and your safe place to land. We will protect you from what we are able. We will sacrifice ourselves to great ends to allow you to live in comfort. It could be a parliament every night in your little castle as we treat you like our king. We will be your paradise. We expect the same treatment back. Through all the complexities there is simplicity, and you have to get there.

We could all have everything the way it needs to be, the way it was intended. No more distractions. Mental struggles of generations past and ones to come. Disorder, chaos, the world going awry. We have the power to make it all stop. 111 Uniting. Allow us to embrace our blessings and strengths from God. Allow us to guide you too, as females and women of earth. Allow us to be the support of some women that you can only dream of. Let us do that for you. All the gaslighting, mind games, the mind fucks of the world. Women can make it all go away in your world. You could have heaven on earth. No more teams, just equals playing to our strengths and weaknesses.

You can still have your own personality, while you regulate your hormone testosterone too. We will dismiss your displays of aggression, your cockiness, and your arrogance. We will forgive you for saying things you don't mean. We will giggle at you when you display acts of dominance among the other men around your territorial possession of us. We will know that it is your own regulation of your hormones and that both sexes go through it equally. We will even forgive you for always blaming our "unreasonable actions" on our hormones.

I kind of like to think of hot flashes as Gods way of giving us back all the energy that has been stolen from us throughout the years. We are equal to you in every way, just the opposite end of the spectrum. We are nurturers and we guide.

Tell us what we already know, we just want to hear you own up to the world's greatest mistake. Bow your head, thank us for choosing you even when in the presence of your own insecurities. Thank us for our loyalty. Thank us for the compassion we have shown and the cycles we have helped you break. Thank us for our guidance and riding your crazy roller coaster of distractions, and layers and layers of manipulation and deceit. Thank us for choosing you first and foremost.

Know that we made the choice to follow you with our God giving free will and forgive you, even in the presence of so much greater. Our God giving free will. Make it all go away now. Tell us all the things we already know. We do not need an apology; we already know what we have been blessed with. Women can communicate perfectly fine. We have no blocked throat chakra or a protruding Adam's apple in our way. Just line up now as you stand in the weight of its consequences and the ultimate reality. Look us in the eyes and say these simple tiny five little words. Allow yourselves to listen to a woman for once. Not listening to us is what got us in this mess in the first place. Count to three, breathe out and repeat after me. Adam ate the fucking apple!

Messenger Manifesto
XXII

Feminists, social justice warriors and pro or anti-abortion men. Women wanted to be seen equal to a man. We were sick of being looked at as less than. Men looked at us less because they believed themselves more valuable, because of the money they brought in. Money, the root of all evil. Women were a possession, that they controlled with money and physical strength. Women wanted to be seen equal to a man. We wanted recognition for the jobs we did.

Women since the beginning of time have counted their time spent in a much different way than men. Still volunteering our time because we possibly believe that our time is not worth anything. Our encouragement, love, and appreciation are just expected to be given for free. To be used up at their command. We encourage and elevate them with everything we have, and we are left on the wayside financially and physically drained of everything. Women are made to be viewed as the stupid naive ones for given love as our currency.

Men ask yourselves this. After you are done emotionally neglecting and abusing your woman. A woman that freely gave you her love and adoration. After you are done verbally abusing your woman. A woman that freely gave you her time and respect. After you are done physically abusing your woman. A woman that looked to you for protection and unity. After you are done financially abusing your woman. A woman that trusted you with her vulnerability of depending on you. After you have abused her so much that she is depleted and weak. Ask yourselves this. How much money will it take to buy back the love of that woman? I already know, do you? Yet, a woman's currency goes way undervalued in society.

Society. Most women are content in a position in life with a thank you and an appreciation of gratitude from our employer. Generations evolving, we still expect the same. A man however, they want their thank you in their pay checks. "Tell me how much you appreciate me with a raise." They instinctually know that they must provide, even if the wife/family dynamic has not come into play yet. Physically superior and emotionally superior. These are our strengths, that we need to unite.

Men that felt they could wait much later in life to start a family. They couldn't be bothered looking for anything serious and used a woman's essence at their own disposal. Leaving trails of women behind because they were not ready to commit. They focused on making themselves what they deemed to be the most desirable. Financial stability and a place in life where they could be happy enough. Happy and confident enough with themselves to pluck out a "cream of the crop" twenty years younger wife.

They appear upset now as they look back upon their options. Gorgeous young women that make just as much money as themselves. Women that no longer want children or a family life. They are living for themselves. Men don't be upset; they were just collectively following your lead. They are only aspiring to be an equal to you. Woman your own age dating younger men? Don't be upset, they are only following your lead. We as a collective are only holding a mirror back to you.

Men that require pre-nups before marriage. I understand. I understand that you are not secure enough regardless of your money to believe a woman would truly want you for you. I say ladies, sign them, but have a contract of your own. Most of us have no problem working. We can earn our keep and more. We are not interested in what they had, only what we are about to earn.

Personal assistant, therapist, nurse, and errand runner. Dishwasher, housekeeper, cook and inventory specialist. Nannies and hookers. We have various jobs within a relationship and in society these all pay. Depending on how much she loves you, will be what she charges per hour within the home. Your woman might love you so much that she does 40 hours a week for minimum wage per hour. She might love you so much that she will only charge you for sex at the rate of an ugly prostitute. I believe that is a negotiation between the couple.

Men want a woman to make him feel like a top priority. Much like men make their careers and the companies they work for a top priority. They expect their woman to be happy and content because they provide and pay some or all the household bills. Would a man be just as happy to get up every day and go to work for a company that paid all its bills. Sure, the company he works for is expected to pay their bills or the company and its future fails to exist.

What if the company paid great, but then begins to struggle? What if the company promises to pay double your original earnings, but requires you to temporarily work at a reduced rate? Just temporarily to keep the company afloat? Does the man stay with the instability of not knowing the fate of the company, or does he look elsewhere? After all he needs money to live. Under the same societal expectations for women, a truly devoted and loyal man would stay and sacrifice to see the company through its hard times.

What if you men believed in the company you worked for so much that you knew potentially someday it would be worth something. You believe in it so much that you stay and work at that company for ten years with reduced pay. Not a drop of that promised money comes your way for the job you do, because the company needs to pay its bills. Your sacrifices will pay off someday though if you are grateful now and keep up the teammate mentality.

Would you keep working there, would you stick it out? It's been ten years with reduced pay. Eventually most men would decide they need to move on. It hasn't come through with its promise yet and chances are it's only staying afloat because of you.

You men will move on, to a new company that can deliver on what it says. Working at the new company that compensates you for what you do. This choice would probably make you feel more valuable. What if the old company begins turning a profit after all the hours you gave reduced to help establish it? Does that excuse them for paying you the retro money that over the past ten years still owes you? Are you just going to walk away from that money you earned with your hard work and sacrifices? Or do you expect it to pay you?

What if the company looks at you and says "what work you left. You decided not to hang in there with us any longer, so that is your problem, not ours. Have a good day.' What about if the old company that owes you money says, "Why are you asking us, you work at a new company now, let them pay you." Or my ultimate favorite. The old company says to you "You wanted to leave and thought you could be independent and stand on your own. You want to be independent, so go ahead. Why would you need our money?

Most men would become infuriated and want their money that was owed. What happens if the boss of the company is a lot bigger and stronger than you? What is your recourse now? Oh, I know, you can go to court. The judge then will decide how little of that money you are actually owed.

Men don't be complaining about alimony. You are not providing for her. You are being allowed graciously to pay back retro money that is owed. She believed in the promises you made. She believed in your potential. She believed in hanging on for that someday that you promised, while keeping you afloat. Now pay her what is hers.

Pro-noun people. Are you consciously aware that you have been directed to help in the fight against inequality? Accomplished by your subconscious belief that you will eliminate this factor, by removing the importance of our existing gender names. I have been asked to redirect you now.

Trans women. I am going to tell you the same thing that I would tell Rich if he was still here. Welcome to our side. Come on over. We as women are very accepting of you. We understand that a good majority of you chose us. You have chosen our side because we are empathetic, caring and nurturing. You can talk about your problems with us, and you feel heard. You feel seen, you feel accepted and validated. An element you more than likely didn't receive from men.

Come on over, but if you truly want to be a woman, we have a few rules for you. First off, do not hit on men of straight origin. You as a born man, should know how the male ego works. It's no no. Do not irritate them. If they choose, they will chase you. Second, men are visual creatures. You should already know this too. Do not come over to our side if you only have the ability to mimic us skin deep. Real women do not have six hours a day to apply makeup and push up bras. Teenagers with no responsibilities do.

Thirdly, if you truly admire us enough to join us then you should already know. Competing against us is very contradictory. It is disrespectful and us woman don't enjoy disrespect very well. Lastly, real women bear the burden of compassion, nurturing, and empathy. We bear emotional strength. Put your male ego away. This is not about you and what you want anymore. It is about everyone else. Remember we wear a lot of hats every day.

Welcome. Now there is no time for makeup and put your hair in a bun. Kick your heels off and get ready to take care of everyone else but yourself, while you run.

Feminism has taken an extreme hard left. Although the movement was very much needed and appreciated to a depth that no words could ever express. They are still winning while we run extra-long and exhausted trying to attack a patriarchal society from the wrong direction.

I do not know of one woman on earth that rushes out of bed in the morning getting her children ready for daycare. Rushing to gather up everything needed for the day. Children crying because they don't want to go. Getting them dressed and trying to nicely explain to them that you will be back later that night to get them. Getting their children safely in the car and ready to go for the day, while cramping and bleeding half to death. Half on the verge of tears because they are making a choice between their children and competing with a man.

We are now expected to choose. Society accepts this and men expect women to work and pay half the bills now too. Remarking to us passive aggressively that "we wanted to be equal." We are already equal. We have proven that we can do it all, while dealing with things a man will never understand or be able to endure. We wear many hats, and I think us women fully understand that.

As grown women, we are here to guide our children and release them into a world as a collective whole. We are here to be their voice for a short time in their lives, one in which they will carry forever. Sometimes we may not even know why we say or prohibit some of the things we do with them. We just instinctively know it's for their own good. We listen to our own inner voices to help guide our children. Mothers do essentially have the biggest job on this planet. To put it simply, as a collective, the weight of the world and generations to come does rest on our shoulders. I do believe 99% of mothers do not know this beforehand.

What truly is the definition of mother and father? Definition of mother in dictionary. A woman in relation to her child or children. Verb the action it represents. Bring up a child with care and affection. Father, the verb, to cause a pregnancy resulting in the birth of a child. I see nowhere in these definitions even close to what is expected. Which one needs to pay financially to fit into a man's world. Appears anyone can be a mother if they provide care and nurture, while fathers can only be fathers if they impregnate. Do we assume the men that step up to the plate to help care and nurture are really mothers? Really broad and indiscriminate definitions; I am confused.

The nannies and daycare workers that we employ are they now our children's mothers? Why is our definition not equal to a man? Why are mothers not people that let their eggs get fertilized? That would be equal to the definition of father. We have a job description in its very definition. Why are we still expected societally to do a job with no pay?

Nothing fills my heart with more love than envisioning my daughters being able to rock my grandchildren to sleep. To comfort them when they are sick. To spend quality time with them and allow them to have a secure attachment bond. Knowing that my daughters could leave a bad relationship at any time and remain independent with their confidence intact. Not having to beg because they chose to do their jobs as mothers. Additionally knowing the man, they loved and had children with could rest easier and not feel like he isn't doing enough financially.

Oppression, for decades and decades. Abuse, not being seen as equal. To be seen as equal to a man? Want to compete with them to get their attention? Stay for the kids because we need protection financially. Condescension and abuse, control. Not being seen for the creatures that we are. Made to feel less than always. We couldn't leave! The ones that could leave the abuse were forced to make a gut-wrenching heart-stopping choice between hanging on to their last shred of sanity or staying for their children and losing their sanity.

Downplayed, shamed for having children that we can't afford. State help, benefits for being low income. Food stamps, begging for a handout. Yet they have taken away our right to choose? We are expected to have children and stressfully follow suit by paying someone else to raise them.

Rise in sociopaths, confused mixed up children. Anxious-Avoidant attachment styles, homicidal and suicidal. Traditionally the women stayed home providing emotional needs and safety, cleanliness and order for their children and men. Society has made that impossible now. However, with all of us working now they have managed to be able to expend billions in daycare program vouchers, snap benefits, and low-income health insurance. Any program possible to make a mother feel like she is at its mercy. To keep her in the mentality of believing she is less than and begging for handouts.

Does living in poverty make us angry? Does it put us in fight mode like a man? Provide and protect, that is their job. Women we receive. We receive the men that we feel deserve to have a legacy. What kind of men should still exist in generations to come? We are gatekeepers for future generations.

There are three levels of men and only one deserves to excel. We often burn ourselves out, raising them to this level. More often than not, it becomes the job of many women to raise one man.

Level one, this is the lowest rung. The man that works a job to help you financially. He isn't concerned with being the head of the house. He isn't concerned with obligations and feels it is alright to just contribute slightly financially. He will take jobs that make less than his previous. He will roll in after his shift and just sit down. He needs to relax now and play his video games. He will let you pay most of the bills and do all the housework. When you address this with him, he will play dumb and act like he wants to help more. This is a man that is still looking for a mommy. He wants you to take care of him. Send him back home until his mother finishes her job.

Level two, The Roommate. This is a man that expects a woman to earn and pay half of the bills. He expects that she still does most of the housework and gets upset when she doesn't give him sex. He expects you to do half his job but expects you to do all of what he perceives to be yours in full. I suggest that you have your own room with this type, ladies. Make your own meals, clean up your own mess and keep looking for level three.

Don't be fooled ladies. Level one and two often appear very sweet and friendly. They are often the "good guy" type. They are the ones that cannot understand why women would pass them up for the "bad boy" type. They still have a lot of growing up to do.

Level three, a desirable man. Does this make him perfect? No, none of us are. This makes him worth your investment. He will pay most or all the bills. Not because he wants to control, but because he wants you to be as stress free as possible. He understands a woman with less stress will be more inviting for him. He wants you to be comfortable to do as you please within the home. He will not put expectations on you to do his job. In the absence of working outside of the home, he will have expectations for you in it. He is investing in you too.

We don't receive unbalanced, ego driven, superficial, entitled perverts in their feminine energy. Why do women have to give up their everything? Expected to stay and endure these abuses for money? If not, we must work ourselves to death and our children suffer. Give these men five years to advance their careers, to step up to the plate. No more having to keep yourself attached to a man for money while we sit oppressed. Allow them to advance themselves, to become better providers.

The men that do not step up to the plate as a family man will then pay. They will pay for half of the mother's and child's hospital/birth bill. The after-school care, health insurance, gas stipends, car repair bills and the children's clothes as child support. The ones that do not can then be jailed. Why do we have to beg? Why do we have to endure all the stress? Just so we can be viewed in society as a struggling, now undesirable, no good for nothing baby maker. Yet, be expected to have children and live in poverty. That still sounds like male entitlement to me. Hold them accountable for the title they preach. What was that number for man again in the bible? Oh yes, now I remember, 6. Hebrew 6, works of man. Three dimensions. Mind, body and soul. 666.

We will give them a head start in good faith. Supportive or not of your choice to have a child with this woman that child is here. Regardless of, you will take part in raising the next generation on your end. It is time for every one of you to man the hell up. Provider and protector? Remember your role the next time you pick up Susy Skank from the bar. While you're pulling her hair and balls deep from behind. Would you trust her with your children? No? Would you buy her a house? No? Then here's a solution for you, get your dick out.

No more feeling like second rate citizens and unequal to a man. Men and women are not designed the same way. A man will never know what we go through and will only be able to feign empathy. No more being made to feel like we are begging for handouts from taxpayers. We want to earn our keep as taxpayers just like everyone else.

We want the ability to choose whether we stay in an abusive or dead-end relationship or not. We want the ability to provide safety and the least amount of chaos for our children. We want the authority to assert what is right for our children. We want the ability to keep them as safe as possible. We should have the ability to allow our children to form healthy attachments in stability. It has been far too long in history that women have been oppressed, and we want to be able to have the right to choose.

Why has society set up the birth of most children to cause a poverty mind set or to make the birth of a child feel like a burden financially? Forcing women to have children, men to provide financially and resentment and drama. If a woman stays with you now, then you will know it is for love. Why does society keep perpetuating poverty? Through all the complexities and distractions, there truly is simplicity.

Any good mother knows the excruciating anguish that comes from deciding. If it's not an important part of the world, why do we pay for nannies or daycare to start with? It should be free. However, according to federal consensus, the average pay for a nanny, is 700+ a week. This is not to take care of the parents or the household, only the children and their needs. Why are women feeling like they must get a job at a daycare, just to spend time with their own children?

Program expenditures, still all these generations later. See what happens when we are not allowed to do our jobs? See what you have caused? Keep disrespecting us, keep downplaying us! We are about to meet you on the only level you understand. Our time is worth just as much as yours.

Government subsidies backing at billions on average per state for one program. Hand out to beg. The same source of money that pays for these women to feel like second rate begging recipient's is the same source that allows these men to not have to step up to be a man. Funny to me. Allowance of not only taxpayer source but allowance of a new view on this glorious miraculous job and position in life that only women hold.

Women should be able to feel the same confidence of a man and know she can leave the abuse. Why are women not being paid and having taxes taking out until their children go to school? It apparently is an appealing benefit from employers. Paid maternity leave. Why if a business recognizes this, not our own government? We lose money on our time spent away from the workforce, and some women don't even earn enough quarters to draw disability if needed. Why is this still accepted in society? Made to feel like they are begging for a handout.

Why are women expected to do one of the most complex jobs on earth for free? Why are we expected societally to raise our children to blend in and work hard for a societal structure? Contend with schools, doctors, social workers, neighbors and comply with all the rules that society expects from us, for free?

I am not trying to undermine governmental structure, it is needed and commanded by God. I am simply asking why? Why is society making everything so hard? Why do you have to be 21 to purchase alcohol, marijuana, or cigarettes? Yet not to go to war, watch porn or have a sex change?

The government can still have population control by putting a cap on the number of children we get paid to stay home with. The good men that use that beautiful time in a woman's life to encourage and inspire her, will be thankful for the financial help. Every new mother can have another older woman advocate that is responsible for checking on the mother and child periodically. No child would slip through the "cracks." An advocate who will also offer support to a mother that may be cut off from everyone else. A feeling of kinship and community. When children enter school then the teachers have a watchful eye and can advocate. Everyone wins.

Why is the gap in time we take out for our children being used by some men to make us feel like we are not contributing? That what we do is worthless. Emotional, verbal, and physical abuse on top of all the stress that comes with children can quickly take a woman down, sometimes for life.

Our mothers inspire us to be the people we are today. They either excel or trip to the finish line. For all the women that have come before us, for all the abuse they endured. Half the island calls her grandma, yet she sits on disability caused from emotional abuse, severe neglect and control. Although raising her own children, being the neighborhood mom and actively babysitting her grandchildren and most of the island. She feels like she has contributed nothing notable in life. Forcing herself to stay with a man that emotionally abandoned her and cheated because she can't afford to live otherwise. Oblivious to the fact that she has caused the thought process behind quite possibly the next movement for women.

Men you will get to choose the fate of your legacies. Do right by your woman and your children or don't. You will either be paying for your child's college or their bail money. It will still be all up to you to be the leader. Us women will follow.

I have been asked to make people aware of the dark and the light. I have been assigned. If you are a part of the collective receiving numbers, you are being called to wake up and do your part. You are being asked to rise now and take part in the next advancement. Do it for the generations before you that are too tired now. Do it for your ancestors, do it for your children and generations to come. Most importantly now, do it for the biggest thank you to your own mothers. You have no idea what they have endured. Oh look, a baby bumblebee just landed on my hand.

As I look to the highest, the most high; he has asked that we bow our heads. Bow our heads for him the same way he bows to look upon us every day. Talk to him. Hear God as he sits high above the world in complete ascension. Help him from having to look down upon us while shaking his head in disbelief. Join him to conclude our daily prayer with only one thing left to say.

Ahh Men.

Let me meditate and be one with nature. The most high will tell me what I need to do. I still choose to live as though I am living for the proverbial God. After numerous yoga and Pilates sessions, meditation, chakra cleansing and hours of mountain sitting alone in a light silk robe. After fasting, reflection on my life and mounds of self-awareness. After psychology and self-growth, helping others achieve and instilling hope. After countless hours of giving to others and sacrificing my own basic needs. After the emergence of trauma and suffering; crying and praying. Learning history before Christianity and giving up all control and all outcomes to God.

I have emerged from the long walk through the tunnel with the Most High. I have been instilled with new hope and novel words of wisdom. "Do unto others as you would have done to you. Give to the needy. Use your empathy to put yourself in others' shoes.

The Most High had finally spoken out my purpose, "Put yourself in their shoes, realize they did unto you and gave unto you what they were taught. The extortion of human hope, and money remain unbalanced and who in the hell are these two God and Devil guys? Now go forth my child. Some people like to keep their milk warm in a blanket and I used Shuega to turn your other cheek.